Bloom's Modern Critical Views

African American
  Poets:
  Wheatley–Tolson
African American
  Poets:
  Hayden–Dove
Edward Albee
Dante Alighieri
Isabel Allende
American and
  Canadian Women
  Poets,
  1930–present
American Women
  Poets, 1650–1950
Hans Christian
  Andersen
Maya Angelou
Asian-American
  Writers
Margaret Atwood
Jane Austen
Paul Auster
James Baldwin
Honoré de Balzac
Samuel Beckett
The Bible
William Blake
Jorge Luis Borges
Ray Bradbury
The Brontës
Gwendolyn Brooks
Elizabeth Barrett
  Browning
Robert Browning
Italo Calvino
Albert Camus
Truman Capote
Lewis Carroll
Miguel de Cervantes
Geoffrey Chaucer

Anton Chekhov
G.K. Chesterton
Kate Chopin
Agatha Christie
Samuel Taylor
  Coleridge
Joseph Conrad
Contemporary Poets
Julio Cortázar
Stephen Crane
Daniel Defoe
Don DeLillo
Charles Dickens
Emily Dickinson
E.L. Doctorow
John Donne and the
  17th-Century Poets
Fyodor Dostoevsky
W.E.B. DuBois
George Eliot
T.S. Eliot
Ralph Ellison
Ralph Waldo Emerson
William Faulkner
F. Scott Fitzgerald
Sigmund Freud
Robert Frost
William Gaddis
Johann Wolfgang
  von Goethe
George Gordon,
  Lord Byron
Graham Greene
Thomas Hardy
Nathaniel Hawthorne
Robert Hayden
Ernest Hemingway
Hermann Hesse
Hispanic-American
  Writers
Homer

Langston Hughes
Zora Neale Hurston
Aldous Huxley
Henrik Ibsen
John Irving
Henry James
James Joyce
Franz Kafka
John Keats
Jamaica Kincaid
Stephen King
Rudyard Kipling
Milan Kundera
Tony Kushner
Ursula K. Le Guin
Doris Lessing
C.S. Lewis
Sinclair Lewis
Norman Mailer
Bernard Malamud
David Mamet
Christopher Marlowe
Gabriel García
  Márquez
Cormac McCarthy
Carson McCullers
Herman Melville
Arthur Miller
John Milton
Molière
Toni Morrison
Native-American
  Writers
Joyce Carol Oates
Flannery O'Connor
George Orwell
Octavio Paz
Sylvia Plath
Edgar Allan Poe
Katherine Anne
  Porter

Bloom's Modern Critical Views

Marcel Proust
Thomas Pynchon
Philip Roth
Salman Rushdie
J. D. Salinger
José Saramago
Jean-Paul Sartre
William Shakespeare
William Shakespeare's
    Romances
George Bernard Shaw
Mary Wollstonecraft
    Shelley
Alexander Solzhenitsyn

John Steinbeck
Jonathan Swift
Amy Tan
Alfred, Lord Tennyson
Henry David Thoreau
J.R.R. Tolkien
Leo Tolstoy
Ivan Turgenev
Mark Twain
John Updike
Kurt Vonnegut
Derek Walcott
Alice Walker
Robert Penn Warren

H.G. Wells
Eudora Welty
Edith Wharton
Walt Whitman
Oscar Wilde
Tennessee Williams
Tom Wolfe
Virginia Woolf
William Wordsworth
Jay Wright
Richard Wright
William Butler Yeats
Émile Zola

Bloom's Modern Critical Views

RALPH WALDO EMERSON
Updated Edition

Edited and with an introduction by
Harold Bloom
Sterling Professor of the Humanities
Yale University

CHELSEA HOUSE
PUBLISHERS
An imprint of Infobase Publishing

Bloom's Modern Critical Views: Ralph Waldo Emerson, Updated Edition

Copyright ©2007 by Infobase Publishing

Introduction ©2007 by Harold Bloom

Chelsea House
An imprint of Infobase Publishing
132 West 31st Street
New York, NY 10001

Library of Congress Cataloging-in-Publication Data

Ralph Waldo Emerson / Harold Bloom, editor.
p. cm—(Bloom's modern critical views)
Includes bibliographical references and index.
ISBN 0-7910-9316-6
1. Emerson, Ralph Waldo, 1803–1882—Criticism and interpretation.
I. Bloom, Harold.
PS1638.R28 2006
814'.2—dc22

Contributing Editor: Jesse Zuba
Cover designed by Takeshi Takahashi
Cover photo © The New York Public Library

Printed in the United States of America
Bang EJB 10 9 8 7 6 5 4 3 2 1

This book is printed on acid-free paper.

Contents

Editor's Note

My introduction celebrates Emerson's American version of power as belonging always to transition, as such.

Stephen E. Whicher, forerunner of the spirit of our current stances towards Emerson, emphasizes the Sage of Concord's extraordinary independence, after which I argue that an American Gnosis was at the Emersonian center, and so made of the essayist himself the Central Man he prophesied.

Emerson's greatest essay, "Experience," is lovingly expounded by Barbara L. Packer, after which Julie Ellison illuminates the intricate figurations that constitute Emersonian rhetorical art.

Mark Edmundson fuses Freud with Emerson so as to analyze the American prophet's "methods of self-recreation through crisis," while David Bromwich performs a brilliant reading of Emerson's "Channing Ode."

Sharon Cameron incisively demonstrates a certain coldness in Emerson's reactions to suffering, whether his own or of others, while George Kateb subtly probes the social aspects of Emersonian Self-Reliance.

The philosopher Stanley Cavell confronts the grand death-march of "Fate" in *The Conduct of Life*, after which I ruefully conclude this volume by brooding upon Emerson's continual relevance in our Evening Land, where he had presided over what might be called the Death of Europe in America.

HAROLD BLOOM

Introduction

Emerson is an experiential critic and essayist, and not a Transcendental philosopher. This obvious truth always needs restating, perhaps now more than ever, when literary criticism is so overinfluenced by contemporary French heirs of the German tradition of Idealist or Transcendental philosophy. Emerson is the mind of our climate, the principal source of the American difference in poetry, criticism, and pragmatic post-philosophy. That is a less obvious truth, and it also needs restating, now and always. Emerson, by no means the greatest American writer, perhaps more an interior orator than a writer, is the inescapable theorist of all subsequent American writing. From his moment to ours, American authors either are in his tradition, or else in a counter-tradition originating in opposition to him. This continues even in a time when he is not much read, such as the period from 1945 to 1965 or so. During the last twenty years, Emerson has returned, burying his undertakers. "The essays of Emerson," T.S. Eliot remarked, "are already an encumbrance," one of those judicial observations that governed the literary academy during the Age of Eliot, but that now have faded into an antique charm.

Other judicial critics, including Yvor Winters and Allen Tate, sensibly blamed Emerson for everything they disliked in American literature and even to some extent in American life. Our most distinguished living poet,

Robert Penn Warren, culminated the counter-traditional polemic of Eliot and Tate in his lively sequence, "Homage to Emerson, on Night-Flight to New York." Reading Emerson's essays in the "pressurized gloom" of the airliner, Warren sees the glowing page declare: "There is / No sin. Not even error." Only at a transcendental altitude can Warren's heart be abstract enough to accept the Sage of Concord, "for / At 38,000 feet Emerson / Is dead right." At ground level, Emerson "had forgiven God everything" because "Emerson thought that significance shines through everything."

Sin, error, time, history, a God external to the self, the visiting of the crimes of the fathers upon the sons: these are the topoi of the literary cosmos of Eliot and his Southern followers, and these were precisely of no interest whatsoever to Ralph Waldo Emerson. Of Emerson I am moved to say what Borges said of Oscar Wilde: he was always right. But he himself always says it better:

> That is always best which gives me to myself. The sublime is excited in me by the great stoical doctrine, obey thyself. That which shows God in me, fortifies me. That which shows God out of me, makes me a wart and wen. There is no longer a necessary reason for my being.

One might say that the Bible, Shakespeare, and Freud show us as caught in a psychic conflict, in which we need to be everything in ourselves while we go on fearing that we are nothing in ourselves. Emerson dismisses the fear, and insists upon the necessity of the single self achieving a total autonomy, of becoming a cosmos without first ingesting either nature or other selves. He wishes to give us to ourselves, although these days supposedly he preaches to the converted, since it is the fashion to assert that we live in a culture of narcissism, of which our smiling President is the indubitable epitome. Emerson, in this time of Reagan, should be cited upon the limitations of all American politics whatsoever:

> We might as wisely reprove the east wind, or the frost, as a political party, whose members, for the most part, could give no account of their position, but stand for the defence of those interests in which they find themselves.... A party is perpetually corrupted by personality. Whilst we absolve the association from dishonesty, we cannot extend the same charity to their leaders. They reap the rewards of the docility and zeal of the masses which they direct.... Of the two great parties, which, at this hour, almost share the nation between them, I should say, that, one has

the best cause, and the other contains the best men. The philosopher, the poet, or the religious man, will, of course, wish to cast his vote with the democrat, for free trade, for wide suffrage, for the abolition of legal cruelties in the penal code, and for facilitating in every manner the access of the young and the poor to the sources of wealth and power. But he can rarely accept the persons whom the so-called popular party propose to him as representatives of these liberalities.

Emerson writes of the Democrats and of the Whigs (precursors of our modern Republicans) in the early 1840's, when he still believes that Daniel Webster (foremost of "the best men") will never come to advocate the worst cause of the slaveholders. Though his politics have been categorized as "transcendental anarchism," Emerson was at once a believer in pure power and a prophet of the moral law, an apparent self-contradiction that provoked Yvor Winters in an earlier time, and President Giamatti of Yale more recently. Yet this wise inconsistency led Emerson to welcome Whitman in poetry for the same reasons he had hailed Daniel Webster in politics, until Webster's Seventh of March speech in 1850 moved Emerson to the most violent rhetoric of his life. John Jay Chapman, in a great essay on Emerson, remarked that, in his polemic against Webster, Emerson "is savage, destructive, personal, bent on death." Certainly no other American politician has been so memorably denounced in public as Webster was by Emerson:

> Mr. Webster, perhaps, is only following the laws of his blood and constitution. I suppose his pledges were not quite natural to him. He is a man who lives by his memory; a man of the past, not a man of faith and of hope. All the drops of his blood have eyes that look downward, and his finely developed understanding only works truly and with all its force when it stands for animal good; that is, for property.

All the drops of his blood have eyes that look downward; that bitter figuration has outlived every phrase Webster himself ventured. Many modern historians defend Webster for his part in the compromise of 1850, by which California was admitted as a free state while the North pledged to honor the Fugitive Slave Law. This defense maintains that Webster helped preserve the Union for another decade, while strengthening the ideology of Union that culminated in Lincoln. But Emerson, who had given Webster every chance, was driven out of his study and into moral prophecy by Webster's support of the Fugitive Slave Law:

We are glad at last to get a clear case, one on which no shadow of doubt can hang. This is not meddling with other people's affairs: this is hindering other people from meddling with us. This is not going crusading into Virginia and Georgia after slaves, who it is alleged, are very comfortable where they are:—that amiable argument falls to the ground: but this is befriending in our own State, on our own farms, a man who has taken the risk of being shot or burned alive, or cast into the sea, or starved to death, or suffocated in a wooden box, to get away from his driver: and this man who has run the gauntlet of a thousand miles for his freedom, the statute says, you men of Massachusetts shall hunt, and catch, and send back again to the dog-hutch he fled from. And this filthy enactment was made in the nineteenth century, by people who could read and write. I will not obey it, by God.

As late as 1843, Emerson's love of Webster as incarnate Power had prevailed: "He is no saint, but the wild olive wood, ungrafted yet by grace." After Webster's defense of the Fugitive Slave Law, even Emerson's decorum was abandoned: "The word *liberty* in the mouth of Mr. Webster sounds like the word *love* in the mouth of a courtezan." I suspect that Emerson's deep fury, so uncharacteristic of him, resulted partly from the violation of his own cheerfully amoral dialectics of power. The extraordinary essay on "Power" in *The Conduct of Life* appears at first to worship mere force or drive as such, but the Emersonian cunning always locates power in the place of crossing over, in the moment of transition:

> In history, the great moment is, when the savage is just ceasing to be a savage, with all his hairy Pelasgic strength directed on his opening sense of beauty:—and you have Pericles and Phidias,— not yet passed over into the Corinthian civility. Everything good in nature and the world is in that moment of transition, when the swarthy juices still flow plentifully from nature, but their astringency or acridity is got out by ethics and humanity.

A decade or so before, in perhaps his central essay, "Self-Reliance," Emerson had formulated the same dialectic of power, but with even more exuberance:

> Life only avails, not the having lived. Power ceases in the instant of repose; it resides in the moment of transition from a past to a new state, in the shooting of the gulf, in the darting to an aim.

This one fact the world hates, that the soul *becomes*; for that for ever degrades the past, turns all riches to poverty, all reputation to a shame, confounds the saint with the rogue, shoves Jesus and Judas equally aside. Why, then, do we prate of self-reliance? Inasmuch as the soul is present, there will be power not confident but agent. To talk of reliance is a poor external way of speaking. Speak rather of that which relies, because it works and is.

Magnificent, but surely even the Webster of 1850 retained his Pelasgic strength, surely even that Webster works and is? Emerson's cool answer would have been that Webster had failed the crossing. I think Emerson remains *the* American theoretician of power—be it political, literary, spiritual, economic—because he took the risk of exalting transition for its own sake. Admittedly, I am happier when the consequence is Whitman's "Crossing Brooklyn Ferry" than when the Emersonian product is the first Henry Ford, but Emerson is canny enough to prophesy both disciples. There is a great chill at the center of his cosmos, which remains ours, both the chill and the cosmos:

> But Nature is no sentimentalist,—does not cosset or pamper us. We must see that the world is rough and surly, and will not mind drowning a man or a woman; but swallows your ship like a grain of dust. The cold, inconsiderate of persons, tingles your blood, benumbs your feet, freezes a man like an apple.

This is from the sublime essay "Fate," which leads off *The Conduct of Life*, and culminates in the outrageous question: "Why should we fear to be crushed by savage elements, we who are made up of the same elements?" Elsewhere in "Fate," Emerson observes: "The way of Providence is a little rude," while in "Power" he restates the law of *Compensation* as "nothing is got for nothing." Emerson too is no sentimentalist, and it is something of a puzzle how he ever got to be regarded as anything other than a rather frightening theoretician of life or of letters. But then, his personality also remains a puzzle. He was the true American charismatic, and founded the actual American religion, which is Protestant without being Christian. Was the man one with the essayist, or was only the wisdom uncanny in our inescapable sage?

II

A biography of Emerson is necessarily somewhat redundant at best, because Emerson, like Montaigne, is almost always his own subject, though hardly in

Montaigne's own mode. Emerson would not have said: "I am myself the matter of my book," yet Emerson on "History" is more Emerson than history. Though he is almost never overtly autobiographical, his best lesson nevertheless is that all true subjectivity is a difficult achievement, while supposed objectivity is merely the failure of having become an amalgam of other selves and their opinions. Though he is in the oral tradition, his true genre was no more the lecture than it had been the sermon, and certainly not the essay, though that is his only formal achievement, besides a double handful of strong poems. His journals are his authentic work, and seem to me poorly represented by all available selections. Perhaps the journals simply ought not to be condensed, because Emerson's reader needs to be immersed in their flow and ebb, their own experience of the influx of insight followed by the perpetual falling back into skepticism. They move endlessly between a possible ecstasy and a probable shrewdness, while knowing always that neither daemonic intensity nor worldly irony by itself can constitute wisdom.

The essential Emerson begins to emerge in the journals in the autumn of 1830, when he was twenty-seven, with his first entry on Self-Reliance, in which he refuses to be "a secondary man" imitating any other being. A year later (October 27, 1831) we hear the birth of Emerson's *reader's Sublime*, the notion that what moves us in the eloquence, written or oral, of another must be what is oldest in oneself, which is not part of the Creation, and indeed is God in oneself:

> Were you ever instructed by a wise and eloquent man? Remember then, were not the words that made your blood run cold, that brought the blood to your cheeks, that made you tremble or delighted you,—did they not sound to you as old as yourself? Was it not truth that you knew before, or do you ever expect to be moved from the pulpit or from man by anything but plain truth? Never. It is God in you that responds to God without, or affirms his own words trembling on the lips of another.

On October 28, 1832, Emerson's resignation from the Unitarian ministry was accepted (very reluctantly) by the Second Church, Boston. The supposed issue was the proper way of celebrating the Lord's Supper, but the underlying issue, at least for Emerson himself, was celebrating the self as God. Stephen Whicher in his superb *Emerson: An Organic Anthology* (still the best one-volume Emerson) gathered together the relevant notebook texts of October 1832. We find Emerson, sustained by daemonic influx, asserting: "It is light. You don't get a candle to see the sun rise," where clearly Jesus is the candle and Emerson is the sunrise (prophetic, like so much else in early Emerson, of Nietzsche's *Zarathustra*). The most outrageous instance of an inrush of God in Emerson is the notorious and still much derided "transparent eyeball" passage in *Nature* (1836), which is based upon a journal entry of March 19, 1835. But I give the final text from *Nature*:

> Crossing a bare common, in snow puddles, at twilight, under a clouded sky, without having in my thoughts any occurrence of special good fortune, I have enjoyed a perfect exhilaration. I am glad to the brink of fear.... There I feel that nothing can befall me in life,—no disgrace, no calamity, (leaving me my eyes,) which nature cannot repair. Standing on the bare ground,—my head bathed by the blithe air, and uplifted into infinite space,—all mean egotism vanishes. I become a transparent eyeball; I am nothing; I see all; the currents of the Universal Being circulate through me; I am part or particle of God.

Nature, in this passage as in the title of the little book, *Nature*, is rather perversely the wrong word, since Emerson does not mean "nature" in any accepted sense whatsoever. He means Man, and not a natural man or fallen Adam, but original man or unfallen Adam, which is to say America, in the transcendental sense, just as Blake's Albion is the unfallen form of Man. Emerson's primal Man, to whom Emerson is joined in this epiphany, is all eye, seeing earliest, precisely as though no European, and no ancient Greek or Hebrew, had seen before him. There is a personal pathos as well, which Emerson's contemporary readers could not have known. Emerson feared blindness more than death, although his family was tubercular and frequently died young. But there had been an episode of hysterical blindness during his college years, and its memory, however repressed, hovers throughout his work. Freud's difficult "frontier concept" of the bodily ego, which is formed partly by introjective fantasies, suggests that thinking can be associated with any of the senses or areas of the body. Emerson's fantastic introjection of the transparent eyeball as bodily ego seems to make thinking and seeing the same activity, one that culminated in self-deification.

Emerson's power as a kind of interior orator stems from this self-deification. Nothing is got for nothing, and perhaps the largest pragmatic consequence of being "part or particle of God" is that your need for other people necessarily is somewhat diminished. The transparent eyeball passage itself goes on to manifest an estrangement from the immediacy of other selves:

The name of the nearest friend sounds then foreign and accidental: to be brothers, to be acquaintances, master or servant, is then a trifle and a disturbance.

This passage must have hurt Emerson himself, hardly a person for whom "to be brothers" ever was "a trifle and a disturbance." The early death of his brother Charles, just four months before *Nature* was published in 1836, was one of his three terrible losses, the others being the death of Ellen Tucker, his first wife, in 1831, after little more than a year of marriage, and the death of his first-born child, Waldo, in January 1842, when the boy was only five years old. Emerson psychically was preternaturally strong, but it is difficult to interpret the famous passage in his great essay "Experience," where he writes of Waldo's death:

An innavigable sea washes with silent waves between us and the things we aim at and converse with. Grief too will make us idealists. In the death of my son, now more than two years ago, I seem to have lost a beautiful estate—no more. I cannot get it nearer to me. If tomorrow I should be informed of the bankruptcy of my principal debtors, the loss of my property would be a great inconvenience to me, perhaps, for many years; but it would leave me as it found me,—neither better nor worse. So is it with this calamity; it does not touch me; something which I fancied was a part of me, which could not be torn away without tearing me nor enlarged without enriching me, falls off from me and leaves no scar.

Perhaps Emerson should have written an essay entitled "The Economic Problem of Grief," but perhaps most of his essays carry that as a hidden subtitle. The enigma of grief in Emerson, after all, may be the secret cause of his strength, of his refusal to mourn for the past. Self-reliance, the American religion he founded, converts solitude into a firm stance against history, including personal history. That there is no history, only biography, is the Emersonian insistence, which may be why a valid biography of Emerson appears to be impossible. John McAleer's biography sets out shrewdly to evade the Emersonian entrapment, which is that Emerson knows only biography, a knowledge that makes personal history redundant. What then is the biographer of Emerson to do?

Such worthy practitioners of the mode as Ralph Rusk and Gay Wilson Allen worked mightily to shape the facts into a life, but are evaded by Emerson. Where someone lives so massively from within, he cannot be caught by chroniclers of events, public and private. McAleer instead molds his facts as a series of encounters between Emerson and all his friends and associates. Unfortunately, Emerson's encounters with others—whether his brothers, wives, children, or Transcendental and other literary colleagues, are little more revelatory of his inner life than are his encounters with events, whether it be the death of Waldo or the Civil War. All McAleer's patience, skill and learning cannot overcome the sage's genius for solitude. A biography of Emerson becomes as baffling as a biography of Nietzsche, though the two lives have nothing in common, except of course for ideas. Nietzsche acknowledged Emerson, with affection and enthusiasm, but he probably did not realize how fully Emerson had anticipated him, particularly in unsettling the status of the self while proclaiming simultaneously a greater overself to come.

III

The critic of Emerson is little better off than the biographer, since Emerson, again like Nietzsche and remarkably also akin to Freud, anticipates his critics and does their work for them. Emerson resembles his own hero, Montaigne, in that you cannot combat him without being contaminated by him. T.S. Eliot, ruefully contemplating Pascal's hopeless agon with Montaigne, observed that fighting Montaigne was like throwing a hand grenade into a fog. Emerson, because he appropriated America, is more like a climate than an atmosphere, however misty. Attempting to write the order of the variable winds in the Emersonian climate is a hopeless task, and the best critics of Emerson, from John Jay Chapman and O.W. Firkins through Stephen Whicher to Barbara Packer and Richard Poirier, wisely decline to list his ideas of order. You track him best, as writer and as person, by learning the principle proclaimed everywhere in him: that which you can get from another is never instruction, but always provocation.

But what is provocation, in the life of the spirit? Emerson insisted that he called you forth only to your self, and not to any cause whatsoever. The will to power, in Emerson as afterwards in Nietzsche, is reactive rather than active, receptive rather than rapacious, which is to say that it is a will to interpretation. Emerson teaches interpretation, but not in any of the European modes fashionable either in his day or in our own, modes currently touching their nadir in a younger rabblement celebrating itself as having repudiated the very idea of an individual reader or an individual critic. Group criticism, like group sex, is not a new idea, but seems to revive whenever a sense of resentment dominates the aspiring clerisy. With resentment comes guilt, as though societal oppressions are caused by how we read, and so we get those academic covens akin to what Emerson, in his 1838 journal, called "philanthropic meetings and holy hurrahs," for which read now "Marxist literary groups" and "Lacanian theory circles":

> As far as I notice what passes in philanthropic meetings and holy hurrahs there is very little depth of interest. The speakers warm each other's skin and lubricate each other's tongue, and the words flow and the superlatives thicken and the lips quiver and the eyes moisten, and an observer new to such scenes would say, Here was true fire; the assembly were all ready to be martyred, and the effect of such a spirit on the community would be irresistible; but they separate and go to the shop, to a dance, to bed, and an hour afterwards they care so little for the matter that on slightest temptation each one would disclaim the meeting.

Emerson, according to President Giamatti of Yale, "was as sweet as barbed wire," a judgment recently achieved independently by John Updike. Yes, and doubtless Emerson gave our politics its particular view of power, as Giamatti laments, but a country deserves its sages, and we deserve Emerson. He has the peculiar dialectical gift of being precursor for both the perpetual New Left of student non-students and the perpetual New Right of preacher non-preachers. The American Religion of Self-Reliance is a superb *literary* religion, but its political, economic and social consequences, whether manifested Left or Right, have now helped place us in a country where literary satire of politics is impossible, since the real thing is far more outrageous than even a satirist of genius could invent. Nathanael West presumably was parodying Calvin Coolidge in *A Cool Million*'s Shagpoke Whipple, but is this Shagpoke Whipple or President Reagan speaking?

> America is the land of opportunity. She takes care of the honest and industrious and never fails them as long as they are both. This is not a matter of opinion, it is one of faith. On the day that Americans stop believing it, on that day will America be lost.

Emerson unfortunately believed in Necessity, including "the offence of superiority in persons," and he was capable of writing passages that can help to justify Reagan's large share of the Yuppie vote, as here in "Self-Reliance":

> Then again, do not tell me, as a good man did today, of my obligation to put all poor men in good situations. Are they my poor? I tell thee, thou foolish philanthropist, that I grudge the

dollar, the dime, the cent I give to such men as do not belong to me and to whom I do not belong. There is a class of persons to whom by all spiritual affinity I am bought and sold; for them I will go to prison if need be; but your miscellaneous popular charities; the education at college of fools; the building of meeting-houses to the vain end to which many now stand; alms to sots; and the thousand-fold Relief Societies;—though I confess with shame I sometimes succumb and give the dollar, it is a wicked dollar, which by and by I shall have the manhood to withhold.

True, Emerson meant by his "class of persons" men such as Henry Thoreau and Jones Very and the Reverend William Ellery Channing, which is not exactly Shagpoke Whipple, Ronald Reagan, and the Reverend Jerry Falwell; but Self-Reliance translated out of the inner life and into the marketplace is difficult to distinguish from our current religion of selfishness, as set forth so sublimely in the recent grand epiphany at Dallas. Shrewd Yankee that he was, Emerson would have shrugged off his various and dubious paternities. His spiritual elitism could only be misunderstood, but he did not care much about being misread or misused. Though he has been so oddly called "the philosopher of democracy" by so many who wished to claim him for the Left, the political Emerson remains best expressed in one famous and remarkable sentence by John Jay Chapman: "If a soul be taken and crushed by democracy till it utter a cry, that cry will be Emerson."

IV

I return with some relief to Emerson as literary prophet, where Emerson's effect, *pace* Yvor Winters, seems to me again dialectical but in the end both benign and inevitable. Emerson's influence, from his day until ours, has helped to account for what I would call the American difference in literature, not only in our poetry and criticism, but even in our novels and stories— ironic since Emerson was at best uneasy about novels. What is truly surprising about this influence is its depth, extent, and persistence, despite many concealments and even more evasions. Emerson does a lot more to explain most American writers than any of our writers; even Whitman or Thoreau or Dickinson or Hawthorne or Melville serve to explain *him*. The important question to ask is not "How?" but "Why?" Scholarship keeps showing the "how" (though there is a great deal more to be shown), but it ought to be a function of criticism to get at that scarcely explored "why."

Emerson was controversial in his own earlier years, and then became all but universally accepted (except, of course, in the South) during his later years. This ascendancy faded during the Age of Literary Modernism (*circa* 1915–1945) and virtually vanished, as I remarked earlier, in the heyday of academic New Criticism or Age of Eliot (*circa* 1945–1965). Despite the humanistic protests of President Giamatti, and the churchwardenly mewings of John Updike, the last two decades have witnessed an Emerson revival, and I prophesy that he, rather than Marx or Heidegger, will be the guiding spirit of our imaginative literature and our criticism for some time to come. In that prophecy, "Emerson" stands for not only the theoretical stance and wisdom of the historical Ralph Waldo, but for Nietzsche, Walter Pater and Oscar Wilde, and much of Freud as well, since Emerson's elitist vision of the higher individual is so consonant with theirs. Individualism, whatever damages its American ruggedness continues to inflict on our politics and social economy, is more than ever the only hope for our imaginative lives. Emerson, who knew that the only literary and critical method was oneself, is again a necessary resource in a time beginning to weary of Gallic scientism in what are still called the Humanities.

Lewis Mumford, in *The Golden Day* (1926), still is the best guide as to why Emerson was and is the central influence upon American letters: "With most of the resources of the past at his command, Emerson achieved nakedness." Wisely seeing that Emerson was a Darwinian before Darwin, a Freudian before Freud, because he possessed "a complete vision," Mumford was able to make the classic formulation as to Emerson's strength: "The past for Emerson was neither a prescription nor a burden: it was rather an esthetic experience." As a poem already written, the past was not a force for Emerson; it had lost power, because power for him resided only at the crossing, at the actual moment of transition.

The dangers of this repression of the past's force are evident enough, in American life as in its literature. In our political economy, we get the force of secondary repetition; Reagan as Coolidge out-Shagpoking Nathanael West's Whipple. We receive also the rhythm of ebb and flow that makes all our greater writers into crisis-poets. Each of them echoes, however involuntarily, Emerson's formula for discontinuity in his weird, irrealistic essay "Circles":

> Our moods do not believe in each other. Today I am full of thoughts and can write what I please. I see no reason why I should not have the same thought, the same power of expression, tomorrow. What I write, whilst I write it, seems the most natural thing in the world; but yesterday I saw a dreary vacuity in this direction in which now I see so much; and a month hence, I doubt not, I shall wonder who he was that wrote so many

continuous pages. Alas for this infirm faith, this will not strenuous, this vast ebb of a vast flow! I am God in nature; I am a weed by the wall.

From God to weed and then back again; it is the cycle of Whitman from "Song of Myself" to "As I Ebb'd with the Ocean of Life," and of Emerson's and Whitman's descendants ever since. Place everything upon the nakedness of the American self, and you open every imaginative possibility from self-deification to absolute nihilism. But Emerson knew this, and saw no alternative for us if we were to avoid the predicament of arriving too late in the cultural history of the West. Nothing is got for nothing; Emerson is not less correct now than he was 170 years ago. On November 21, 1834, he wrote in his journal: "When we have lost our God of tradition and ceased from our God of rhetoric then may God fire the heart with his presence." Our God of tradition, then and now, is as dead as Emerson and Nietzsche declared him to be. He belongs, in life, to the political clerics and the clerical politicians and, in letters, to the secondary men and women. Our God of rhetoric belongs to the academies, where he is called by the name of the Gallic Demiurge, Language. That leaves the American imagination free as always to open itself to the third God of Emerson's prayer.

STEPHEN E. WHICHER

The Question of Means

To bring to the test of experience his vague but powerful ambition to be a doer was the chief service performed for Emerson by the wave of social reform that arose in the late thirties and early forties in New England. The reformers called on him to perform exactly the kind of action he recognized a duty and claimed a potential capacity to perform—and when confronted with the actuality of his ambition, he discovered that it was something which he had no aptitude or wish to do, and which threatened the very liberation to which his faith had opened the way. As a consequence, the whole atmosphere of his faith underwent a pervasive change, as he adjusted his beliefs to protect the old values in the new situation. Not that the issue of reform alone caused this change. His original faith had been attuned to a millennialism which time and experience alone inevitably did much to weaken. In point of fact, we can see other contributing circumstances which increased the instability of his initial hopes, until the question of action forced on him by the reform movement precipitated their revision.

The kind of action Emerson understood best was that of the preacher. His proper role in society, he felt, was that inspired communication of truth which he called eloquence. '... it is the end of eloquence,' he held, 'in a half-hour's discourse,—perhaps by a few sentences,—to persuade a multitude of persons to renounce their opinions, and change the course of life.' This

ambition was particularly strong in the early 1830's, while he still hoped
sometime to replace his old church with a 'little chapel of the truth.' Then
he imagined, 'The high prize of eloquence may be mine, the joy of uttering
what no other can utter, and what all must receive'; and at moments he felt
'budding the powers of a Persuasion that by and by will be irresistible.' Here
was a mode of greatness which he could aspire to with some color of
plausibility. 'If I could persuade men to listen to their interior convictions, if
I could express, embody their interior convictions, that were indeed life. It
were to cease being a figure, and to act the action of a man.'

There is some evidence that the Divinity School *Address* in 1838 was
involved emotionally more than he knew with this personal sense of mission.
It had perhaps the deepest roots in his thoughts of any of his lectures, being
an exposition of the spiritual religion for the sake of which he had abandoned
the pulpit. The substance of the address was explicit in the journals in 1833,
and already by 1835 he had formed an intention to 'write & print a discourse
upon Spiritual & Traditional Religion....' The address came as close to the
irresistible truth he felt called on to announce to his generation as any of his
utterances. Had he not written, 'When anyone comes who speaks with better
insight into moral nature, he will be the new gospel; miracle or not, inspired
or uninspired, he will be the Christ ...'?

He was correspondingly affected by its hostile reception. Though
outwardly unruffled and even amused, inwardly he was definitely perturbed,
as the repeated self-defenses in his journals show. The reception of his
address was the sharpest hint yet given him from the actual that its
limitations were not to be lightly ignored. Inherently a contradiction of fact,
the faith in his potential mastery was constantly exposed to the erosion of
experience, which daily reminded him that the mountains he had declared to
be moving were still in place. The reception of the *Address* was an angular
intrusion of fact into the smooth world of his thoughts, which, while rousing
him to an unprecedented vigor of defiance, helped to undermine in the long
run his capacity to identify the ideal and the real.

His sharpest immediate response was a renewed defiance of society. In
the solitude of his study he rose in the insulted majesty of the Soul and
prophesied against his critics.

> ... The world lies in night of sin. It hears not the cock crowing: it
> sees not the grey streak in the East. At the first entering ray of
> light, society is shaken with fear and anger from side to side. Who
> opened that shutter? they cry, Wo to him! They belie it, they call
> it darkness that comes in, affirming that they were in light before.
> Before the man who has spoken to them the dread word, they

tremble and flee.... The wild horse has heard the whisper of the tamer: the maniac has caught the glance of the keeper. They try to forget the memory of the speaker, to put him down into the same obscure place he occupied in their minds before he spake to them.... But vain, vain, all vain. It was but the first mutter of the distant storm they heard,—it was the first cry of the Revolution,—it was the touch, the palpitation that goes before the earthquake. Even now society is shaken because a thought or two have been thrown into the midst.... It now works only in a handful.... But the doom of State Street, and Wall Street, of London, and France, of the whole world, is advertised by those thoughts; is in the procession of the Soul which comes after those few thoughts.

The passage is a magnificent eruption of the apocalyptic fire that smoldered in the heart of this son of the Puritans.

Yet he was stirred to this peak of aggressiveness partly by a certain shock to his confidence, as its whole context in the journals suggests. Some years later, he allegorically and ironically reviewed the affair in his poem 'Uriel,' for which the passage just quoted may well have been the germ. The stress in the poem falls on the two points I wish to bring out: the revolutionary nature of Uriel's utterance, and the lapse of Uriel himself that followed it.

The address itself was calculated to give no offense, on grounds of vocabulary at least, to a Unitarian audience. To compensate for the audacity of his purpose, perhaps, he instinctively emphasized the regularity and morality of the inner life with which he would replace external forms. That freedom, and not just a higher law, was the intent of the spiritual religion advocated in the Divinity School *Address* is made clear in 'Uriel.' There Uriel is not the discoverer of a new principle of order, but is subversive of all order.

> One, with low tones that decide,
>
> . . . .
>
> Gave his sentiment divine
> Against the being of a line.
> 'Line in nature is not found;
> Unit and universe are round;
> In vain produced, all rays return;
> Evil will bless, and ice will burn.'

True, the tone of the poem is ironical. Uriel is the deadly child in the house who does not know better than to speak the truth in company. The old war gods are right: such a menace must be removed at once. Emerson ironically accepts the respectable definition of good and evil and deliberately leaves out of account the higher order which in fact he had advocated to replace the false conventions of his society. But in so doing he reveals what his address glossed over, his sharp consciousness that his gospel was disruptive of the actual social order. Uriel is the enemy of all worldly authority, and one can read between the lines that he delights in the confusion his treason caused.

His lapse, in turn, is no repentance. The self-knowledge that withers him is a knowledge of his impotence. Perhaps he is not ready to speak, perhaps he is 'grown too bright,' but certainly his society cannot bear to hear him; his hour is not ripe. He stands outside his conventional society in the freedom and the solitude of outer space. The most he can do is to shake its security with occasional hints of his cherub scorn. The poem thus involuntarily conveys the depth of Emerson's antipathy to the community he challenged. Uriel's truth is allied to the inanimate forces of nature, and its utterance, while it shakes society, transforms him also into something fey and inhuman. In this poem, as elsewhere in his writings, we touch the chilling core of Emerson's idealism and sense the presence there of something with which no community is possible.

In a life lived so entirely in the mind as his, every serious engagement with the outer world had long-continued repercussions, as he gradually assimilated the implications of the brute event into the tissue of his thought. His break with his Boston church was such a key event, and so to a lesser extent was the *Address*. It forced him to see that society did not *want* to renounce their opinions for the truth. In *The American Scholar* Emerson had described a new Moses; 'Uriel' is the ironical allegory of such a Moses whose people preferred the desert. After this time Emerson's image of the hero-scholar, leading mankind to the promised land, steadily gave way to that of the solitary observer, unregarded and unregarding of the multitude, quietly faithful to his inspired glimpses of worlds not realized.

> Let theist, atheist, pantheist,
> Define and wrangle how they list,
> Fierce conserves, fierce destroyer,—
> But thou, joy-giver and enjoyer,
> Unknowing war, unknowing crime,
> Gentle Saadi, mind thy rhyme ....

*   *   *

The process thus assisted by the affair of the Divinity School *Address* was carried on and brought to a conclusion by the wave of reforming excitement that swept over certain elements in New England at the end of the fourth and the beginning of the fifth decade of the nineteenth century. As a phenomenon, Emerson welcomed and encouraged it. When impelled to ask, 'Is the ideal society always to be only a dream, a song, a luxury of thought, and never a step taken to realize the vision for living and indigent men without misgivings within and wildest ridicule abroad?' he could point to the reformer: 'I, for my part, am very well pleased to see the variety and velocity of the movements that all over our broad land, in spots and corners, agitate society. War, slavery, alcohol, animal food, domestic hired service, colleges, creeds, and now at last money, also, have their spirited and unweariable assailants, and must pass out of use or must learn a law.'

He acquired for a time a 'habitual feeling that the whole of our social structure—State, School, Religion, Marriage, Trade, Science—has been cut off from its root in the soul, and has only a superficial life, a "name to live."' Reform became his name for whatever would allow him 'to restore for myself these fruits to their stock, or to accept no church, school, state, or society which did not found itself in my own nature.... I should like to put all my practices back on their first thoughts, and do nothing for which I had not the whole world for my reason.'

Yet the gap between dream and fact remained. He never undertook the leap of faith and avoided the heroic life in practice. In his discussion of reform, we can perceive an underlying consciousness, increasing with time, that the whole enterprise is essentially romance. Thus, side by side with his deep sympathy with reform as a general idea, we find a progressive disillusionment with all actual reforms. Typical of his feeling toward concrete schemes of reform is his refusal to join the Brook Farm community.

This refusal is superficially surprising, because the root idea of that transcendental asylum was the most attractive of all reforms to Emerson, the one he called the Doctrine of the Farm: the scholar should not live by thought alone but should put himself into primary relations with the soil and nature by performing his part in the manual labor of the world. This sensible suggestion that the sedentary intellectual should spend some of his time outdoors and take adequate exercise meant much more to Emerson. Most of all, it seemed to him a means of approaching that *entirety* in his own life and his outer relations which was his deepest desire. The doctrine expressed an ideal of self-sufficiency through simplicity. A man should scale his needs down to the point where he could meet them by his own exertions. Such an ideal, of course, could never be completely realized, but steps could be taken to draw closer to it, each one of which would free one that much more from living for show and bring one that much closer to the holy and mysterious recesses of life. *Walden* is the logical outcome of this way of thinking, and Thoreau's 'Simplify, simplify' its slogan. But this was also an aim of Brook Farm—to simplify life and restore its primary relations with the soil. *Walden* and Brook Farm are alternative means for attaining the end that Emerson formulated for both when he wrote, 'The power which is at once spring and regulator in all efforts of reform is the conviction that there is an infinite worthiness in man, which will appear at the call of worth, and that all particular reforms are the removing of some impediment.'

But if the aim of reform for Emerson was independence, we can understand why he decided not join the Brook Farmers, even though their aim was similar; for 'At the name of a society all my repulsions play, all my quills rise & sharpen.' 'I do not wish to remove from my present prison to a prison a little larger,' he wrote. 'I wish to break all prisons.' Ripley's project seemed a pretty circuitous route to the few, simple conditions he required. 'I have not yet conquered my own house. It irks and repents me. Shall I raise the siege of this hencoop, and march baffled away to a pretended siege of Babylon?' The only reform that mattered to him, after all, was moral and personal.

His objection to Brook Farm, he found, applied to all cooperative schemes of reform; they were all external. 'The Reformers affirm the inward life, but they do not trust it, but use outward and vulgar means.' They were partial in their aims, exhausting their efforts on some contemptible village or dog-hutch; they banded themselves together in associations or philanthropic societies, relying on numbers instead of themselves. In coming closer to such reform he did not hear the call of worth, but found himself 'jostled, crowded, cramped, halved, quartered, or on all sides diminished of his proportion'; and he swung back, with some violence, to the sanctuary of the heart. 'I cannot find language of sufficient energy to convey my sense of the sacredness of private integrity.'

He thus found forced on him an open repudiation of his supposed obligation to act. True, 'These reforms are ... our own light, and sight, and conscience; they only name the relation which subsists between us and the vicious institutions which they go to rectify.' Yet no one of them but was partial and superficial. Plainly then, such manipular attempts to realize the world of thought were premature. 'Many eager persons successively make an experiment in this way, and make themselves ridiculous.... Worse, I observe that in the history of mankind there is never a solitary example of success,— taking their own tests of success.' Then perforce he must consent to inaction. Henry Nash Smith points out that when, in his lecture on 'The Times,' Emerson divides the movement party into the actors and the students, and rejects the former for the latter, he is formally repudiating the ideal of great action.

Yet the students are reformers too. Impressed, like the actors, with 'the contrast of the dwarfish Actual with the exorbitant Idea,' they see also that all practical effort to reduce this contrast is inadequate and are thus thrown back on beholding. 'It is not that men do not wish to act; they pine to be employed, but are paralyzed by the uncertainty what they should do.' One would suppose that such passive futility would earn Emerson's disapproval equally with the busy futility of the actors, and certainly he does not approve the students unreservedly. They do not show the natural firmness of a man, but a certain imbecility that is the result of their insoluble perplexities. Sicklied o'er with the pale cast of thought, their life is deprived of its natural spontaneity and joy and is oppressed with ennui and melancholy.

Yet Emerson values the students above the actors: 'Of the two, I own I like the speculators best.' The reason is, 'Their unbelief arises out of a greater Belief....' Their aim and wish is to give up entirely to the spiritual principle, and therefore they abstain from low methods of changing society, realizing that all higher modes of living and action must proceed from a prior renovation of the actor. 'Their fault is that they have stopped at the intellectual perception; that their will is not yet inspired from the Fountain of Love.' 'But whose fault is this?' Emerson asks. At least they understand what and where is the spring of all power. The student is sustained, however, like the actor, by a sense of his potential greatness and of an imminent revolution in society. He will keep in training, trim his lamp and wait. 'A patience which is grand; a brave and cold neglect of the offices which prudence exacts, so it be done in a deep upper piety; a consent to solitude and inaction which proceed out of an unwillingness to violate character, is the century which makes the gem.'

Emerson returned to the students and characterized them at greater length in his lecture 'The Transcendentalist,' fourth in the same series on *The Times*. This lecture by the fact of its title, has acquired a factitious authority, as though it were a definitive statement of what Emerson and his movement-party friends were about. It does indeed tell us much about its creator and about his times, but it must be read against some such background as I have tried to sketch in to be fully understood. In this case, he is clearly describing a *second choice*. Since the ideal of the scholar, who does live in the soul and lead men like a hero, has increasingly come to seem unrealizable, Emerson describes instead the closest practical substitute—a scholar on the waiting list, so to speak. He repeatedly makes it clear that his highest praise is reserved, as before, for strong spirits, for heroes. The transcendentalist is only the negative half of a man; he is an empty cup, but at least the cup is ready for filling.

The lack of spontaneity in the character of the transcendentalist soon disaffected Emerson with him also. Somehow his faith in greatness had led him into a blind alley. 'If we suddenly plant our foot and say,—I will neither eat nor drink nor wear nor touch any food or fabric which I do not know to be innocent, or deal with any person whose whole manner of life is not clear and rational, we shall stand still.' It is reasonable to rebel against one bad custom, as did the reformers, but the effort to uproot all custom from our life can end only in emptying it of everything except the paralyzing custom of saying No.

At this point we are ready to pay attention to the case of the Conservative, to whom Emerson devoted a lecture in the same series that included 'The Transcendentalist.' Though included, perhaps, as Burke seems to have been included in the series on *Biography*, for proper variety, he is portrayed with considerable sympathy. The conservative is one who respects facts—as Emerson was learning to do. His fault is that he has no faith; he also is a half-man. Yet his partial statement is within its limits indisputable and is something the reformer ignores at his peril.

> That which is best about conservatism ... is the Inevitable.... Here is the fact which men call Fate, and fate in dread degrees, fate behind fate, not to be disposed of by the consideration that the Conscience commands this or that, but necessitating the question whether the faculties of man will play him true in resisting the facts of universal experience? ... We have all a certain intellection or presentiment of reform existing in the mind, which does not yet descend into the character, and those who throw themselves blindly on this lose themselves. Whatever they attempt in that direction, fails, and reacts suicidally on the actor himself. This is the penalty of having transcended nature. For the existing world is not a dream, and cannot with impunity be treated as a dream; neither is it a disease; but it is the ground on which you stand, it is the mother of whom you were born. Reform converses with possibilities, perchance with impossibilities; but here is sacred fact.

Though Emerson in the end still affirms his allegiance to the movement party, he treats the reformer in this lecture as a half-man, too. Each is an example of the exaggerating propensities of man, who cannot be a whole, but seizes on a half-truth and pursues it beyond all proportion. In the person of his conservative, a forerunner of his skeptic (see Chapter 6), Emerson takes a long step away from his earlier commitment to the movement party, toward a greater disengagement and a more balanced recognition of the permanent part played in life by both idea and fact. Other lectures of this pivotal course reflect the same step to a lesser degree.

Emerson's answer to a heroic declaration of Alcott's, some five years later, shortly after the latter, with his English friends Lane and Wright, and their 'twelve manuscript volumes of J. P. Greaves, and his head in a plaster cast,' had failed with their scheme for a 'Concordium' at Fruitlands, was by then his answer to every transcendental reformer, including the one in himself. 'Alcott thought he could find as good a ground for quarrel in the state tax as Socrates did in the edict of the judges. Then I say, Be consistent.... Say boldly, "There is a sword sharp enough to cut sheer between flesh and spirit, and I will use it, and not any longer belong to this double-faced, equivocating, mixed, Jesuitical universe."

'... Your objection, then, to the State of Massachusetts is deceptive. Your true quarrel is with the state of Man.' Very neat, very well put, we can agree; but we may put to Emerson his own later question to Webster, *How came he there*? What else had the transcendentalist ever objected to than the state of Man? A new scepticism controls this comment on Alcott's anarchistic objection to the State which might well have disconcerted that good man, who had only to turn to Emerson's recently printed essay on 'Politics' to find objections to the states of Man and Massachusetts very similar to his own. But that essay was based on a lecture given in 1837, with additions from another of 1840, and since then Emerson had been visited by many second thoughts.

Emerson's farewell to action is finally as explicit as his earlier rejection of society, and for much the same reasons: his freedom was threatened. 'Do not ask me to your philanthropies, charities, and duties, as you term them;— mere circumstances, flakes of the snow-cloud, leaves of the trees;—I sit at home with the cause, grim or glad. I think I may never do anything that you shall call a deed again.' The conclusion of the essay 'Spiritual Laws,' in particular, is a rapid barrage of arguments against the name of action, most of them dating from the same year as the passage just quoted. '... why should we be cowed by the name of Action? 'T is a trick of the senses,—no more. We know that the ancestor of every action is a thought.' '... real action,' this essay argues, 'is in silent moments,' in the silent thought that revises our entire manner of life. He stated what he was getting at most plainly in 1845. 'The near-sighted people have much to say about action. But ... It is by no means action which is the essential point, but some middle quality indifferent both to poet and to actor, and which we call Reality.'

He had already in at least one passage come to the same point from the opposite direction in *The American Scholar*, when disillusioned with the partiality of thought, as he is in 'Spiritual Laws' with that of action. '... when thoughts are no longer apprehended,' he then argued, '... [the scholar] has always the resource to *live*.... This is a total act. Thinking is a partial act.... Time shall teach him that the scholar loses no hour which the man lives.'

Against this background we can understand his increasing admiration for what he called Character. This 'elemental force,'—'a certain solidity of merit, ... which is so essentially and manifestly virtue, that it is taken for granted that the right ... step will be taken by it'—a combination of probity and practical competence in cooperation with, rather than in defiance of, the order of society—which in *The American Scholar* Emerson had found higher than intellect, became more and more his practical ideal, as his hope of a life of discovery and performance died out. His realization of the futility of reform correspondingly increased his valuation of this 'reserved force, which acts directly by presence and without means,' until, in his second series of essays, he went so far as to look to it for a 'victory to the senses' that would eclipse the 'great defeat' of Christ on the cross! But this attractive idea of action by magnetism does not solve his problem; it only lays bare the heart of it: How is such private quality bred?

Beneath the question of action lay a deeper problem, that of man's compound nature. This was the question that most seriously concerned the transcendentalists, beside which society's criticism of their inaction was superficial. '.... the two lives, of the understanding and of the soul, which we lead, really show very little relation to each other; ... one prevails now, all buzz and din; and the other prevails then, all infinitude and paradise.' 'The object of the man,' he wrote elsewhere, 'the aim of these moments [of silent thought], is to make daylight shine through him, to suffer the law to traverse his whole being without obstruction.... Now he is not homogeneous, but heterogeneous, and the ray does not traverse....' Even if we drop the question of action, and seek only 'Reality,' the problem still remains, How is such wholeness to be won and kept? Is there any ground for hope 'that the moments will characterize the days'?

* * *

The means to this wholeness was what Emerson called Culture, a topic to which he devoted a lecture series in 1837–38. 'His own Culture,—the unfolding of his nature, is the chief end of man,' he told his audience. 'A divine impulse at the core of his being, impels him to this. The only motive at all commensurate with his force, is the ambition to discover by *exercising* his latent power....' The single man, ideally the master of the world, is actually its pupil. No little part of Emerson's journals and other writings, particularly around this time, amount to an extended inventory of the educational facilities open to him.

Culture is a term that one associates more with his later thought than with the years of transcendental protest. He devoted an essay to it in *The Conduct of Life*; a Phi Beta Kappa address in 1867 at Harvard treated 'The Progress of Culture'; his essay on Goethe in *Representative Men* also discussed it. In these cases it signified chiefly all the influences that went to refine and redeem the raw egoism of the natural man. In the 1830's, however, when he had just picked up this 'Germanic term,' it meant rather the means that would release the wild nature of a man and redeem him from custom and tradition. 'Culture, in the high sense, does not consist in polishing or varnishing, but in so presenting the attractions of nature that the slumbering attributes of man may burst their iron sleep and rush, full-grown, into day.' It was a method of conversion, and its goal the kind of supernatural primitivism celebrated in the Divinity School *Address*, the awakening of the Soul. 'To coax and woo the strong Instinct to bestir itself and work its miracle is the end of all wise endeavor.'

By rights, Emerson felt, man should enter at a bound into his proper nature, annihilating his lower life by one blow of moral revolution. The bent spring, released, should snap upright by its own strength. But what were the means of release? The soul has various faculties, particularly the reason and the will; through which is its redemption to be achieved? Emerson did not know and at different times conceded primacy to each. The question to which he devoted much of his thought, especially in the decade or so after 1833, was that of the means of both moral and intellectual culture—the purification of the heart and the inspiration of the mind.

At the outset, he appears to have hoped for much from a course of ascetic self-discipline. Natural goodness was to be bred by a stern, high, stoical self-denial. 'I believe that virtue purges the eye, that the abstinent, meek, benevolent, industrious man is in a better state for the fine influences of the great universe to act upon him than the cold, idle, eating disputant.' So the paragraph in *Nature* containing the revelation that man is himself the creator in the finite concludes, 'This view, which admonishes me where the sources of wisdom and power lie, and points to virtue as to

> The golden key
> Which opes the palace of eternity,

carries upon its face the highest certificate of truth, because it animates me to create my own world through the purification of my soul.' The same preparatory asceticism is expounded in his address 'Literary Ethics,' where for discipline he recommends to the scholar solitude, labor, modesty and charity. '... we have need of a more rigorous scholastic rule; such an asceticism, I mean, as only the hardihood and devotion of the scholar himself can enforce.... Silence, seclusion, austerity, may pierce deep into the grandeur and secret of our being, and so diving, bring up out of secular darkness the sublimities of the moral constitution.' 'If [the scholar] have this twofold goodness,—the drill and the inspiration,—then he has health....'

As it turned out, however, the drill and the inspiration had little relation to each other; health remained an unpredictable miracle. For this reason the theme of preparatory asceticism in time virtually dropped out of his thought; it simply did not work. The ethical life he knew was necessarily divided between moments of inspiration, and long intermediary times in which all his obedience to duty brought little visible fruit.

Duty he obeyed, nevertheless—for this was a primary obligation, whatever his state of grace. 'If we cannot at once rise to the sanctities of obedience and faith,' he wrote, 'let us at least resist our temptations....' 'It is very hard to know what to do if you have great desires for benefitting mankind; but a very plain thing is your duty.' In the anomalous life of delay and waiting to which he was generally condemned, adrift in time and mortality, the one sea-anchor was the old elementary moral code he had learned in childhood. 'Play out the game,' he wrote his friends in later life. 'If the Gods have blundered, we will not.' 'We are thrown back on rectitude forever and ever, only rectitude,—to mend one; that is all we can do.'

Intellectual culture looked more promising. Here, he found, 'The means of culture is the related nature of man.' The same outside world from which culture was to wean the soul was also in all its parts a means to culture. '(Man) is so strangely related to every thing that he can go nowhere without meeting objects which solicit his senses, and yield him new meanings.' 'Let none wrong the truth,' he reminded himself, 'by too stiffly standing on the cold and proud doctrine of self-sufficiency.' '... nothing but God is self-dependent. Man is powerful only by the multitude of his affinities.' Since the NOT ME is, in the phrase from *The American Scholar*, a 'shadow of the soul, or *other me*,' man may confidently turn to it to find the means to awaken the 'me of me.'

The simplest way to distinguish between Emerson's rebellion against the outside world and his reliance on it for culture is to point out that in the former case he was thinking primarily of organized society, and in the latter primarily of nature. There is no question that nature could on occasion prompt the strong instinct to work its miracle. Several moments of sacred exhilaration are recorded in *Nature*, of which the 'transparent eyeball' passage is the most famous. Emerson's moments of gladness in nature, however, like Wordsworth's, diminished in number and intensity as he grew older. He soon came to see, also, that '... it is certain that the power to produce this delight does not reside in nature, but in man, or in a harmony of both.' Nature was at most 'a differential thermometer detecting the presence or absence of the divine spirit in man.' The illusion which he cherished in 1836 of a possible divine rapture to grow out of his wild poetic delight in nature had vanished by 1844. 'That bread which we ask of Nature is that she should entrance us, but amidst her beautiful or her grandest pictures I cannot escape the *second thought*....'

But in the earlier period he entertained a more specific hope from nature which appears in the chapter of *Nature* on 'Language.' Nature was not merely a tonic to the spirit; she was significant of herself and spoke to the intelligence. Newly severed from the authority of the Bible, this reminiscent Puritan sought to read a new gospel from nature, God's perpetual revelation. 'Nature is a language, and every new fact that we learn is a new word; but rightly seen, taken all together, it is not merely a language, but the language put together into a most significant and universal book. I wish to learn the language, not that I may learn a new set of nouns and verbs, but that I may read the great book which is written in that tongue.'

For a brief while Emerson was attracted to Emanuel Swedenborg and his followers as interpreters of the language of nature. The influence of the Swedenborgians on his thought started with his reading of Sampson Reed's *The Growth of the Mind* in 1826 and reached its high point about ten years later. *Nature* contains numerous Swedenborgian echoes, more by a good margin than any subsequent writing of Emerson's. After that time he became increasingly conscious of Swedenborg's limitations—there is a distinct cooling off apparent between the paragraph on Swedenborg in *The American Scholar* and the essay on Swedenborg in *Representative Men*—at the same time that the New Church men in New England began publicly to repudiate him and the transcendentalism he represented.

What drew him was clearly the doctrine of correspondence. Swedenborg developed this as a method of interpreting Scripture, but it was easily susceptible of a poetic extension, and that by warrant of the master: 'The whole natural world corresponds to the spiritual world, and not merely the natural world in general, but also every particular of it; and as a consequence every thing in the natural world that springs from the spiritual world is called a correspondent.... The animals of the earth correspond in general to affection, mild and useful animals to good affections, fierce and useless ones to evil affections. In particular, cattle and their young correspond to the affections of the natural mind, sheep and lambs to the affections of the spiritual mind; while birds correspond, according to their species, to the intellectual things of the natural mind or the spiritual mind,' etc., etc. Emerson easily took the short step from this notion of a fixed natural symbolism to the conclusion that nature is not only a language but a book, that spiritual truths may be read directly from nature, by a purged mind, without the intervention of any other revelation. Hence, 'All things ... preach to us.'

However congenial the thought of a mute gospel in nature to his truth-hungry mind, he quickly exhausted the Swedenborgians. Already in 1835 he was writing to Elizabeth Peabody, 'I sympathize with what you say of your aversion at being confined to Swedenborg's associations....' The literalism of Swedenborg became one of his main points of criticism in *Representative Men*. 'The slippery Proteus is not so easily caught. In nature, each individual symbol plays innumerable parts, as each particle of matter circulates in turn through every system.... Nature avenges herself speedily on the hard pedantry that would chain her waves. She is no literalist.' He soon dropped the notion that the meanings of natural objects could ever be fixed and written down. Yet a general sense that somewhere, beneath the surfaces of nature, lurked some great final meaning, if he could only get at it, continued to tease his reflections on nature. 'The love of Nature,—what is that but the presentiment of intelligence of it? Nature preparing to become a language to us.'

A more far-reaching attack on the meaning of nature was through natural science. Emerson shared the lively interest in the findings of science of his time, particularly in the emerging studies of geology and biology, but his spirit was hardly scientific. He read the ordinary fare available to the general reader of the day: J. F. W. Herschel, Cuvier, Humboldt, Playfair and later Lyell on geology, Kirby and Spence's *Entomology* and other such texts, various volumes in popular collections such as the *Library of Useful Knowledge*, *The American Library of Useful Knowledge*, Lardner's *The Cabinet Cyclopaedia*, several of the Bridgewater treatises, not to speak of browsings in the *Transactions of the Royal Society* and other periodical literature. Scientists like Galileo, Newton, Laplace, Lamarck, Linnaeus, Davy, Euler were high in his extensive list of great names.

What did he read this literature for? In the somewhat desultory years just after his return from Europe, when he did much such reading and lectured several times to groups of amateur students of science like himself, he more than once asked himself that question and finally confessed that he did not entirely know. '... all the reasons seem to me to fall far short of my faith upon the subject. Therefore, boldly press the cause as its own evidence; say that you love Nature, and would know her mysteries, and that you believe in your power by patient contemplation and docile experiment to learn them.' He read what the scientists had to say because he hoped to find in them some clue to nature's meanings.

Much of the writing on science that came to his hand was more or less apologetic in character, the Bridgewater treatises being an extreme example, anxious to protect science against the charge of atheism and encouraging a habit of sifting the scientific facts for evidences of divine contrivance. In this semipious atmosphere it was easy for Emerson to treat science, as he did, as a kind of embryonic revelation. His key thought on science was what he called, prompted by Coleridge, the 'humanity of science.' Nature was the 'externization' of something deep in man's consciousness; therefore man had somewhere within him the means of understanding all the phenomena of nature. True science was then as much a matter of extracting from oneself the Idea of the phenomena one knew as of collecting facts to be understood; find the true principles of unity in things, and the more or less of mere facts becomes unimportant. Since Goethe's scientific accomplishment, genetic and anti-Newtonian student of nature as he was, consisted largely in just such a disclosure of unifying ideas, he became something like Emerson's ideal scientist, one 'always watching for the glimmering of that pure, plastic Idea.'

Accordingly, Emerson was on the whole unsympathetic with the patient experimentation on which scientific achievement is based and prescribed instead a moral and spiritual reformation in the scientist. Scientists will never understand nature, he wrote in *Nature*, using Swedenborgian language, until they approach her in the fire of holiest affections, and not simply with the intellect. It was the duty of the naturalist, he wrote in an early lecture, to study in faith and in love; or, as he put it in 1840, 'science always goes abreast with the just elevation of the man....'

With this view of science, it would appear that there was small hope of culture, in Emerson's sense, in the study of science, since the elevation culture was intended to bring about was necessary to make true science possible. And in point of fact he did not look to science much to coax and woo the great instinct; rather 'the greatest office of natural science [is] ... to explain man to himself,' to help him to understand if not to heal his divided nature. The scientist, like the true orator, should be one 'who could reconcile your moral character and your natural history, who could explain your misfortunes, your fevers, your debts, your temperament, your habits of thought, your tastes, and in every explanation not sever you from the Whole, but unite you to it....' In the rare moments of union with the Whole such questionings dropped away. Generally, however, as he put it, 'I have this latent omniscience coexistent with omnignorance.' Knowledge of the One did not explain the Many; 'The Idea according to which the Universe is made is wholly wanting to us....' For this reason, we may suppose, the idea of evolution, throwing nature into the perspective of a new unifying idea, was able to catch his imagination in his later life. He accepted it uncritically as a conspicuous confirmation of his hope that science might 'uncover the living ligaments ... which attach the dull men and things we converse with, to the splendor of the First Cause....'

The Idea of nature Emerson desired, needless to say, was not forthcoming; the inspiration he sought from nature's influence was evanescent and illusory. Man could not immerse himself in the unconsciousness of nature, nor could he conquer her through consciousness, by achieving her explanation. He imaged his frustration in a series of mythological parallels. Nature was the Sphinx, asking her riddle of each passerby. She was Proteus, whose meanings changed as often as she was studied. Her lover was Tantalus, bated by an apparent wealth of meaning that withdrew as often as he tried to seize it. Nature was an enchanted circle, which he was forbidden to enter. Like some creature of old romance, the 'universal dame' repeated her old challenge:

> Who telleth one of my meanings
>   Is master of all I am.

But he knew that a hero with stronger magic than a mere sauntering poet could command would be needed to lift her spell. Nature served as a perpetual mute invitation to man to assume his rightful lordship but had no power to teach him to accept it. As he summed it up in a lecture, 'The co-presence of the living Soul is essential to all teaching.'

But this same fatal flaw held true of all the means of culture. In his lecture on 'The School,' for example, he spoke of persons and books as two of man's teachers. But these, which may be taken to sum up between them the cultural influences of man, as opposed to nature, had the same unpredictability. Emerson read books for scarcely any other reason than to provide himself with a stimulus to inspiration, 'for the lustres,' as he said, and was often successful. Yet books were, after all, but black marks on paper. They could live only with the life of the reader. 'As the proverb says, "He that would bring home the wealth of the Indies, must carry out the wealth of the Indies." ... When the mind is braced by labor and invention, the page of whatever book we read becomes luminous with manifold allusion.' Again, the soul illumines the book, not the book the soul.

Persons, the conversation of contemporaries, were a still more uncertain means. Emerson summed up the situation when he wrote in 'Friendship,' 'I do then with my friends as I do with my books.' Exactly—and as was true of books, a response to friends required 'the uprise of nature in us to the same degree it is in them.' All came back in the end to instinct, the primary teacher. 'Persons I labor at, and grope after, and experiment upon, make continual effort at sympathy, which sometimes is found and sometimes is missed; but I tire at last, and the fruit they bring to my intellect or affections is oft small and poor. But a thought has its own proper motion which it communicates to me, not borrows of me, and on its Pegasus back I override and overlook the world.'

The whole matter of the means of culture is summed up in one sentence in his journals: 'A day is a rich abyss of means, yet mute and void.' The poem Emerson wrote thirteen years later on this theme, 'Days,' testifies to his lasting regret at not achieving his morning wishes, but in its implied self-reproach is not representative of his by then settled acquiescence in the irremediable waywardness of the divine uprush of soul through which alone they could become reality.

Yet we would mistake his mood if we supposed that he ever finally despaired of culture. A day was a rich abyss of means. The daily anticipation, often rewarded, that the whole solid world might roll aside like a mist and show the living soul underneath, was ground for an ever-renewed hope, not despair. If we find that the days pass by and we are still the same, yet we can believe that the years teach much which the days never knew. As a ship advances by a succession of tacks, 'so in life our profession, our amusements, our errors even, give us with much parade, or with our own blushes, a little solid wisdom.' The upper world is always there, like the air we breathe, even when we are not aroused to awareness of it. How can it fail to affect us? 'Every moment instructs, and every object; for wisdom is infused into every form. It has been poured into us as blood; it convulsed us as pain; it slid into us as pleasure; it enveloped us in dull, melancholy days, or in days of cheerful labor; we did not guess its essence until after a long time.'

NOTE

A bibliography on Brook Farm appears in Lawrence S. Hall, *Hawthorne: Critic of Society* (New Haven, 1944), pp. 191–93. On reform, see Gilbert V. Seldes, *The Stammering Century* (New York, 1928), and Alice Felt Tyler, *Freedom's Ferment* (Minneapolis, 1944), not overlooking her bibliography. For the Swedenborgian background, see the numerous articles by Clarence P. Hotson, as listed in Walter Fuller Taylor, *A History of American*

Letters (New York, 1936), p. 512.; also Marguerite B. Block, *The New Church in the New World* (New York, 1932). I have also had the advantage of reading an unpublished paper on Emerson and science by H. D. Piper.

HAROLD BLOOM

Emerson:
The American Religion

I start from a warning of Lichtenberg's:

> As soon as a man begins to see everything, he generally expresses
> himself obscurely—begins to speak with the tongues of angels.

But Lichtenberg also wrote, "The itch of a great prince gave us long
sleeves." The lengthened shadow of our American culture is Emerson's, and
Emerson indeed saw everything in everything, and spoke with the tongue of
a daemon. His truest achievement was to invent the American religion, and
my reverie intends a spiraling out from his center in order to track the
circumferences of that religion in a broad selection of those who emanated
out from him, directly and evasively, celebratory of or in negation to his
Gnosis. Starting from Emerson we came to where we are, and from that
impasse, which he prophesied, we will go by a path that most likely he
marked out also. The mind of Emerson is the mind of America, for worse
and for glory, and the central concern of that mind was the American
religion, which most memorably was named "self-reliance."

Of this religion, I begin by noting that it is *self*-reliance as opposed to
God-reliance, though Emerson thought the two were the same. I will
emphasize this proper interpretation by calling the doctrine "self-reliance,"

From *Agon: Towards a Theory of Revisionism*. © 1982 by Oxford University Press.

in distinction from Emerson's essay *Self-Reliance*. "Reliance" is not of the essence, but the Emersonian *self* is: "To talk of reliance is a poor external way of speaking. Speak rather of that which relies because it works and is." What "works and is" is the stranger god, or even alien god, within. Within? Deeper than the *psyche* is the *pneuma*, the spark, the uncreated self, distinct from the soul that God (or Demiurge) created. *Self*-reliance, in Emerson as in Meister Eckhart or in Valentinus the Gnostic, is the religion that celebrates and reveres what in the self is before the Creation, a whatness which from the perspective of religious orthodoxy can only be the primal Abyss.

In September 1866, when he was sixty-three, and burned out by his prophetic exultation during the Civil War, Emerson brooded in his journals on the return of the primal Abyss, which he had named Necessity, and which his descendant Stevens was to hail as "fatal Ananke the common god." Earlier in 1866, pondering Hegel, Emerson had set down, with a certain irony, his awareness of the European vision of the end of speculation:

> Hegel seems to say, Look, I have sat long gazing at the all but imperceptible transitions of thought to thought, until I have seen with eyes the true boundary.... I know that all observation will justify me, and to the future metaphysician I say, that he may measure the power of his perception by the degree of his accord with mine. This is the twilight of the gods, predicted in the Scandinavian mythology.

A few months later, this irony at another's apocalyptic egocentricity was transcended by a post-apocalyptic or Gnostic realization:

> There may be two or three or four steps, according to the genius of each, but for every seeing soul there are two absorbing facts,—*I and the Abyss*.

This grand outflaring of negative theology is a major text, however gnomic, of *the* American religion, Emersonianism, which this book aspires to identify, to describe, to celebrate, to join. I am not happy with the accounts of Emersonianism available to me. Of the religions native to the United States, Emersonianism or *our literary religion* remains the most diffuse and diffused, yet the only faith of spiritual significance, still of prophetic force for our future. An excursus upon the religions starting in America is necessary before I quest into the wavering interiors of the American religion proper. Sydney Ahlstrom in his definitive *A Religious History of the American People* (1972) recognizes "that Emerson is in fact the theologian of something we may almost term 'the American religion.'" Who were or could have been Emerson's rivals? Of religious geniuses our evening-land has been strangely unproductive, when our place in Western history is fully considered. We have had one great systematic theologian, in Jonathan Edwards, and something close to a second such figure in Horace Bushnell. But we have only the one seer, Emerson, and the essentially literary traditions that he fostered.

The founders of American heresies that have endured are quite plentiful, yet our major historians of American religion—Ahlstrom, W. W. Sweet, H. R. Niebuhr, M. E. Marty, S. E. Mead, C. E. Olmstead, among others—tend to agree that only a handful are of central importance. These would include Ellen Harmon White of the Seventh Day Adventists, Joseph Smith of the Mormons, Alexander Campbell of the Disciples of Christ, Mary Baker Eddy of Christian Science, and Charles Taze Russell of Jehovah's Witnesses. To read any or all of these is a difficult experience, for the founder's texts lack the power that the doctrines clearly are able to manifest. There is, thankfully, no Emersonian church, yet there are certain currents of Harmonial American religion that dubiously assert their descent from the visionary of *Nature* and the *Essays*. Aside from Mrs. Eddy, who seized on poor Bronson Alcott for an endorsement after the subtle Emerson had evaded her, the "health and harmony" Positive Thinkers notably include Ralph Waldo Trine, author of *In Tune with the Infinite* (1897), and his spiritual descendants Harry Emerson Fosdick and Norman Vincent Peale. We can add to this pseudo-Emersonian jumble the various Aquarian theosophies that continue to proliferate in America a decade after the sixties ebbed out. I cite all these sects and schisms because all of them have failed the true Emersonian test for the American religion, which I will state as my own dogma: *it cannot become the American religion until it first is canonized as American literature.* Though this explicit dogma is mine, it was the genius of Emerson implicitly to have established such a principle among us.

2

What in the nineteenth and twentieth centuries is religious writing? What can it be? Which of these passages, setting their polemics aside, is better described as religious writing?

People say to me, that it is but a dream to suppose that Christianity should regain the organic power in human society which once it possessed. I cannot help that; I never said it could. I am not a politician; I am proposing no measures, but exposing a fallacy, and resisting a pretence. Let Benthamism reign, if men dare no aspirations; but do not tell them to be romantic, and then solace them with glory; do not attempt by philosophy what was once done by religion. The ascendancy of Faith may be impracticable, but the reign of Knowledge is incomprehensible....

... He that has done nothing has known nothing. Vain is it to sit scheming and plausibly discoursing: up and be doing! If thy knowledge be real, put it forth from thee: grapple with real Nature; try thy theories there, and see how they hold out. Do one thing, for the first time in thy life do a thing; a new light will rise to thee on the doing of all things whatsoever....

I have taken these passages randomly enough; they lay near by. The distinguished first extract is both truly religious and wonderfully written, but the second is religious writing. Newman, in the first, from *The Tamworth Reading Room* (1841), knows both the truth and his own mind, and the relation between the two. Carlyle, in the second, from *Corn-Law Rhymes* (1832), knows only his own knowing, and sets that above both Newman's contraries, religion and philosophy. *Corn-Law Rhymes* became a precursor text for Emerson because he could recognize what had to be religious writing for the nineteenth century, and to that recognition, which alone would not have sufficed, Emerson added the American difference, which Carlyle could not ever understand. Subtle as this difference is, another intertextual juxtaposition can help reveal it:

"But it is with man's Soul as it was with Nature: the beginning of Creation is—Light. Till the eye have vision, the whole members are in bonds. Divine moment, when over the tempest-tossed Soul, as once over the wild-weltering Chaos, it is spoken: Let there be Light! Ever to the greatest that has felt such moment, is it not miraculous and God-announcing; even as, under simpler figures, to the simplest and least. The mad primeval Discord is hushed; the rudely-jumbled conflicting elements bind themselves into separate Firmaments: deep silent rock-foundations are built beneath; and the skyey vault with its everlasting Luminaries above: instead of a dark wasteful Chaos, we have a blooming, fertile, heaven-encompassed World."

"Nature is not fixed but fluid, Spirit alters, molds, makes it. The immobility or bruteness of nature is the absence of spirit; to pure spirit it is fluid, it is volatile, it is obedient. Every spirit builds itself a house, and beyond its house a world, and beyond its world a heaven. Know then that the world exists for you. For you is the phenomenon perfect. What we are, that only can we see.... Build therefore your own world. As fast as you conform your life to the pure idea in your mind, that will unfold its great proportions.... The kingdom of man over nature, which cometh not with observation,—a dominion such as now is beyond his dream of God,—he shall enter without more wonder than the blind man feels who is gradually, restored to perfect sight."

This juxtaposition is central, because the passages are. The first rhapsode is Carlyle's Teufelsdröckh uttering his Everlasting Yea in *Sartor Resartus*; the second is Emerson's Orphic poet chanting the conclusion of *Nature*. Carlyle's seeing soul triumphs over the Abyss, until he can say to himself: "Be no longer a Chaos, but a World, or even Worldkin. Produce! Produce!" The Abyss is bondage, the production is freedom, somehow still "in God's name!" Emerson, despite his supposed discipleship to Carlyle in *Nature*, has his seeing soul proclaim a world so metamorphic and beyond natural metamorphosis that its status is radically *prior* to that of the existent universe. For the earth is only part of the blind man's "dream of God." Carlyle's imagination remains orthodox, and rejects Chaos. Emerson's seeing, beyond observation, is more theosophical than Germanic Transcendental. The freedom to imagine "the pure idea in your mind" is the heretical absolute freedom of the Gnostic who identified his mind's purest idea with the original Abyss. American freedom, in the context of Emerson's American religion, indeed might be called "Abyss-radiance."

I return to the question of what, in the nineteenth century, makes writing *religious*. Having set Carlyle in the midst, between Newman and Emerson, I cite next the step in religious writing beyond even Emerson:

... we have an interval, and then our place knows us no more. Some spend this interval in listlessness, some in high passions, the wisest, at least among "the children of this world," in art and song. For our one chance lies in expanding that interval, in getting as many pulsations as possible into the given time....

Pater, concluding *The Renaissance*, plays audaciously against Luke 16:8, where "the children of this world are in their generation wiser than the children of light." Literalizing the Gospel's irony, Pater insinuates that in his generation the children of this world are the only children of light. Light expands our fiction of duration, our interval or place in art, by a concealed allusion to the Blakean trope that also fascinated Yeats; the pulsation of an artery in which the poet's work is done. Pater sinuously murmurs his credo, which elsewhere in *The Renaissance* is truly intimated to be "a strange rival religion" opposed to warring orthodoxies, fit for "those who are neither for Jehovah nor for His enemies."

To name Emerson and Pater as truly "religious writers" is to call into question very nearly everything that phrase usually implies. More interestingly, this naming also questions that mode of displacement M. H. Abrams analyzes in his strong study *Natural Supernaturalism*: "not ... the deletion and replacement of religious ideas but rather the assimilation and reinterpretation of religious ideas." I believe that the following remarks of Abrams touch their limit precisely where Carlyle and Emerson part, on the American difference, and also where Carlyle and Ruskin part from Pater and what comes after. The story Abrams tells has been questioned by Hillis Miller, from a Nietzschean linguistic or Deconstructive perspective, so that Miller dissents from Abrams exactly where Nietzsche himself chose to attack Carlyle (which I cite below). But there is a more ancient perspective to turn against Abrams's patterns-of-displacement, an argument as to whether poetry did not inform religion before religion ever instructed poetry. And beyond this argument, there is the Gnostic critique of creation-theories both Hebraic and Platonic, a critique that relies always upon the awesome trope of the primal Abyss.

Abrams states his "displacement" thesis in a rhetoric of continuity:

> Much of what distinguishes writers I call "Romantic" derives from the fact that they undertook, whatever their religious creed or lack of creed, to save traditional concepts, schemes, and values which had been based on the relation of the Creator to his creature and creation, but to reformulate them within the prevailing two-term system of subject and object, ego and non-ego, the human mind or consciousness and its transactions with nature. Despite their displacement from a supernatural to a natural frame of reference, however, the ancient problems, terminology, and ways of thinking about human nature and history survived, as the implicit distinctions and categories through which even radically secular writers saw themselves and their world....

Such "displacement" is a rather benign process, as though the incarnation of the Poetic Character and the Incarnation proper could be assimilated to one another, or the former serve as the reinterpretation of the latter. But what if poetry as such is always a counter-theology, or Gentile Mythus, as Vico believed? Abrams, not unlike Matthew Arnold, reads religion as abiding in poetry, as though the poem were a saving remnant. But perhaps the saving remnant of *poetry* is the only force of what we call theology? And what can theology be except what Geoffrey Hartman anxiously terms it: "a vast, intricate domain of psychopoetic events," another litany of evasions? Poems are the original lies-against-time, as the Gnostics understood when they turned their dialectics to revisionary interpretations not only of the Bible and Plato, but of Homer as well. Gnosticism was the inaugural and most powerful of Deconstructions because it undid all genealogies, scrambled all hierarchies, allegorized every microcosm/macrocosm relation, and rejected every representation of divinity as non-referential.

Carlyle, though he gave Abrams both the scheme of displacement find the title-phrase of "natural supernaturalism," seems to me less and less self-deceived as he progressed onwards in life and work, which I think accounts for his always growing fury. Here I follow Nietzsche, in the twelfth "Skirmish" of *Twilight of the Idols* where he leaves us not much of the supposedly exemplary life of Carlyle:

> ... this unconscious and involuntary farce, this heroic-moralistic interpretation of dyspeptic states. Carlyle: a man of strong words and attitudes, a rhetor from *need*, constantly lured by the craving for a strong faith and the feeling of his incapacity for it (in this respect, a typical romantic!). The craving for a strong faith is no proof of a strong faith, but quite the contrary. If one has such a faith, then one can afford the beautiful luxury of skepticism; one is sure enough, firm enough, has ties enough for that. Carlyle drugs something in himself with the fortissimo of his veneration of men of strong faith and with his rage against the less simple minded: he *requires* noise. A constant passionate dishonesty against himself—that is his *proprium*; in this respect he is and remains interesting. Of course, in England he is admired precisely for his honesty. Well, that is English; and in view of the fact that the English are the people of consummate cant, it is even as it should be, and not only comprehensible. At bottom, Carlyle is an English atheist who makes it a point of honor not to be one.

It seems merely just to observe, following Nietzsche's formidable wit, that Carlyle contrived to be a religious writer without being a religious man.

His clear sense of the signs and characteristics of the times taught him that the authentic nineteenth-century writer had to be religious *qua* writer. The burden, as Carlyle knew, was not so much godlessness as belatedness, which compels a turn to Carlyle (and Emerson) on history.

3

Carlyle, with grim cheerfulness, tells us that history is an unreadable text, indeed a "complex manuscript, covered over with formless inextricably-entangled unknown characters,—nay, which is a Palimpsest, and bad once prophetic writing, still dimly legible there...." We can see emerging in this dark observation the basis for *The French Revolution*, and even for *Past and Present*. But that was Carlyle *On History* in 1830, just before the advent of Diogenes Teufelsdröckh, the author of *On History Again* in 1833, where the unreadable is read as Autobiography repressed by all Mankind: "a like unconscious talent of remembering and of forgetting again does the work here." The great instance of this hyperbolic or Sublime repression is surely Goethe, whose superb self-confidence breathes fiercely in his couplet cited by Carlyle as the first epigraph to *Sartor Resartus*:

> Mein Vermächtnis, wie herrlich weft und breit!
> Die Zeit ist mein Vermächtnis, mein Acker ist die Zeit.

Goethe's splendid, wide and broad inheritance is time itself, the seed-field that has the glory of having grown Goethe! But then, Goethe had no precursors in his own language, or none at least that could make him anxious. Carlyle trumpets his German inheritance: Goethe, Schiller, Fichte, Novalis, Kant, Schelling. His English inheritance was more troublesome to him, and the vehemence of his portrait of Coleridge reveals an unresolved relationship. This unacknowledged debt to Coleridge, with its too-conscious swerve away from Coleridge and into decisiveness and overt courage, pain accepted and work deified, may be the hidden basis for the paradoxes of Carlyle on time, at once resented with a Gnostic passion and worshipped as the seed-bed of a Goethean greatness made possible for the self. It is a liberation to know the American difference again when the reader turns from Carlyle's two essays on history to History, placed first of the *Essays* (1841) of Emerson:

> This human mind wrote history, and this must read it. The Sphinx must solve her own riddle. If the whole of history is in one man, it is all to be explained from individual experience....

... Property also holds of the soul, covers great spiritual facts, and instinctively we at first hold to it with swords and laws and wide and complex combinations. The obscure consciousness of this fact is the light of all our day, the claim of claims; the plea for education, for justice, for charity; the foundation of friendship and love and of the heroism and grandeur which belong to acts of self-reliance. It is remarkable that involuntarily we always read as superior beings.. ..

... The student is to read history actively and not passively; to esteem his own life the text, and books the commentary....

So much then for Carlyle on history; so much indeed for history. The text is not interpretable? But there is no text! There is only your own life, and the Wordsworthian light of all our day turns out to be: self-reliance. Emerson, in describing an 1847 quarrel with Carlyle in London, gave a vivid sense of his enforcing the American difference, somewhat at the expense of a friendship that was never the same again:

Carlyle ... had grown impatient of opposition, especially when talking of Cromwell. I differed from him ... in his estimate of Cromwell's character, and he rose like a great Norse giant from his chair—and, drawing a line with his finger, across the table, said, with terrible fierceness: "Then, sir, there is a line of separation between you and me as wide as that, and as deep as the pit."

Hardly a hyperbole, the reader will reflect, when he reads what two years later Carlyle printed as *The Nigger Question*. This remarkable performance doubtless was aimed against "Christian Philanthropy" and related hypocrisies, but the abominable greatness of the tract stems from its undeniable madness. The astonished reader discovers not fascism, but a terrible sexual hysteria rising up from poor Carlyle, as the repressed returns in the extraordinary trope of black pumpkin-eating:

... far over the sea, we have a few black persons rendered extremely "free" indeed.... Sitting yonder with their beautiful muzzles up to the ears in pumpkins, imbibing sweet pulps and juices; the grinder and incisor teeth ready for ever new work, and the pumpkins cheap as grass in those rich climates: while the sugar-crops rot round them uncut, because labour cannot be hired, so cheap are the pumpkins....

... and beautiful Blacks sitting there up to the ears in pumpkins, and doleful Whites sitting here without potatoes to eat....

... The fortunate Black man, very swiftly does he settle *his* account with supply and demand:—not so swiftly the less fortunate white man of those tropical locations. A bad case, his, just now. He himself cannot work; and his black neighbor, rich in pumpkin, is in no haste to help him. Sunk to the ears in pumpkin, imbibing saccharine juices, and much at his ease in the Creation, he can listen to the less fortunate white man's "demand" and take his own time in supplying it....

... An idle White gentleman is not pleasant to me: though I confess the real work for him is not easy to find, in these our epochs; and perhaps he is seeking, poor soul, and may find at last. But what say you to an idle Black gentleman, with his rum-bottle in his hand (for a little additional pumpkin you can have red-herrings and rum, in Demerara),—rum-bottle in his hand, no breeches on his body, pumpkin at discretion....

... Before the West Indies could grow a pumpkin for any Negro, how much European heroism had to spend itself in obscure battle; to sink, in mortal agony, before the jungles, the putrescences and waste savageries could become arable, and the Devils be in some measure chained there!

... A bit of the great Protector's own life lies there; beneath those pumpkins lies a bit of the life that was Oliver Cromwell's....

I have cited only a few passages out of this veritable procession of pumpkins, culminating in the vision of Carlyle's greatest hero pushing up the pumpkins so that unbreeched Blacks might exercise their potent teeth. Mere racism does not yield so pungent a phantasmagoria, and indeed I cannot credit it to Carlyle's likely impotence either. This pumpkin litany is Carlyle's demi-Gnosticism at its worst, for here time is no fair seed-bed but rather devouring time, Kronos chewing us up as so many pumpkins, the time of "Getting Under Way" in *Sartor Resartus*:

... Me, however, as a Son of Time, unhappier than some others, was Time threatening to eat quite prematurely; for, strike as I might, there was no good Running, so obstructed was the path, so gyved were the feet....

Emerson, in truth, did not abide in his own heroic stance towards Time and History. The great declaration of his early intensity comes in the 1838

Journals: "A great man escapes out of the kingdom of time; he puts time under his feet." But the next decade featured ebb rather than influx of the Newness. What matter? The American, difference, however ill prepared to combat experience, had been stated, if not established. To come to that stating is to arrive fresh at Emerson's *Nature*, where the *clinamen* from Carlyle, and from Coleridge, is superbly turned.

4

Deconstructing any discourse by Ralph Waldo Emerson would be a hopeless enterprise, extravagantly demonstrating why Continental modes of interpretation are unlikely to add any lustres to the most American of writers. Where there are classic canons of construction, protrusions from the text can tempt an unravelling, but in a text like *Nature* (1836) all is protrusion. Emerson's first book is a blandly dissociative apocalypse, in which everything is a cheerful error, indeed a misreading, starting with the title, which says "Nature" but means "Man." The original epigraph, from Plotinus by way of the Cambridge Platonist Cudworth, itself deconstructs the title:

> Nature is but an image or imitation of wisdom, the last thing
> of the soul; nature being a thing which doth only do, but not
> know.

The attentive reader, puzzling a way now through Emerson's manifesto, will find it to be more the American Romantic equivalent to Blake's *The Marriage of Heaven and Hell* than to Coleridge's *Aids to Reflection* (which however it frequently echoes). At the Christological age of thirty-three (as was Blake in the *Marriage*), Emerson rises in the spirit to proclaim his own independent majority, but unlike Blake Emerson cheerfully and confidently proclaims his nation's annunciation also. Unfortunately, Emerson's vision precedes his style, and only scattered passages in *Nature* achieve the eloquence that became incessant from about a year later on almost to the end, prevailing long after the sage had much mind remaining. I will move here through the little book's centers of vision, abandoning the rest of it to time's revenges.

Prospects, and not retrospectives, is the Emersonian motto, as we can see by contrasting the title of the last chapter, "Prospects," to the opening sentences of the Introduction:

> Our age is retrospective. It builds the sepulchres of the fathers.
> It writes biographies, histories, and criticism. The foregoing

generations beheld God and nature face to face; we, through their eyes. Why should we not also enjoy an original relation to the universe?

The "fathers" are not British High Romantics, Boston Unitarians, New England Calvinist founders, but rather an enabling fiction, as Emerson well knows. They are Vico's giants, magic primitives, who invented all Gentile mythologies, all poetries of earth. Emerson joins them in the crucial trope of his first chapter, which remains the most notorious in his work:

> Crossing a bare common, in snow puddles, at twilight, under a clouded sky, without having in my thoughts any occurrence of special good fortune, I have enjoyed a perfect exhilaration. I am glad to the brink of fear. In the woods, too, a man casts off his years, as the snake his slough, and at what period soever of life is always a child.... There I feel that nothing can befall me in life,— no disgrace, no calamity (leaving me my eyes), which nature cannot repair. Standing on the bare ground,—my head bathed by the blithe air and uplifted into infinite space,—all mean egotism vanishes. I become a transparent eyeball; I am nothing; I see all; the currents of the Universal Being circulate through me; I am part or parcel of God....

This is not a "Spiritual Newbirth, or Baphometic Fire-baptism," akin to those of Carlyle's Teufelsdröckh or Melville's Ahab, because Emerson's freedom rises out of the ordinary, and not out of crisis. But, despite a ruggedly commonplace genesis, there is little that is ordinary in the deliberately outrageous "I become a transparent eyeball." Kenneth Burke associates Emerson's imagery of transparence with the *crossing* or *bridging* action that is transcendence, and he finds the perfect paradigm for such figuration in the Virgilian underworld. The unburied dead, confronted by Charon's refusal to ferry them across Stygia, imploringly "stretched forth their hands through love of the farther shore." Emersonian transparency is such a stretching, a Sublime crossing of the gulf of solipsism, but *not* into a communion with others. As Emerson remarks: "The name of the nearest friend sounds then foreign and accidental: to be brothers, to be acquaintances, master or servant, is then a trifle and a disturbance." The farther shore has no persons upon it, because Emerson's farther shore or beyond is no part of nature, and has no room therefore for created beings. A second-century Gnostic would have understood Emerson's "I am nothing; I see all" as the mode of negation through which the knower again could stand in the Abyss, the place of original fullness, *before* the Creation.

A transparent eyeball is the emblem of the Primal Abyss regarding itself. What can an Abyss behold in an Abyss?

The answer, in our fallen or demiurgical perspective, can be dialectical, the endless ironic interplay of presence and absence, fullness and emptiness; in Gnostic vocabulary, Pleroma and Kenoma. But the Emerson of *Nature* was not yet willing to settle for such a deconstruction. Not upon an elevation, but taking his stance upon the bare American ground, Emerson demands Victory, to his senses as to his soul. The perfect exhilaration of a perpetual youth which comes to him is akin to what Hart Crane was to term an improved infancy. Against Wordsworth, Coleridge, Carlyle, the seer Emerson celebrates the American difference of *discontinuity*. "I am nothing" is a triumph of the Negative Way; "I see all" because I am that I am, discontinuously present not wherever but whenever I will to be present. "I am part or parcel of God," yet the god is not Jehovah but Orpheus, and Emerson momentarily is not merely the Orphic poet but the American Orpheus himself.

Poetic Orphism is a mixed and vexed matter, beyond disentanglement, and it is at the center of Emerson, even in the rhetorically immature *Nature*. I will digress upon it, and then rejoin *Nature* at its Orphic vortices.

5

The historian of Greek religion M. P. Nilsson shrewdly remarked that "Orphicism is a book religion, the first example of the kind in the history of Greek religion." Whatever it *may* have been historically, perhaps as early as the sixth century B.C.E., Orphism became the natural religion of Western poetry. Empedocles, an Emersonian favorite, shares Orphic characteristics with such various texts as certain Platonic myths, some odes of Pindar and fragments of poems recovered from South Italian Greek grave-sites. But later texts, mostly Neoplatonic, became the principal source for Emerson, who did not doubt their authenticity. W. K. C. Guthrie surmises a historical Orphism, devoted to Apollo, partly turned against Dionysos, and centered on a "belief in the latent divinity and immortality of the human soul" and on a necessity for constant purity; partly achieved through *ekstasis*.

Between the Hellenistic Neoplatonists and the seventeenth-century Cambridge variety, of whom Cudworth mattered most to Emerson, there had intervened the Florentine Renaissance mythologies, particularly Ficino's, which Christianized Orpheus. The baptized Orpheus lingers on in Thomas Taylor, whose cloudy account may have been Emerson's most direct source for Orphism. But from *Nature* on, Emerson's Orpheus is simply Primal Man; who preceded the Creation, and very little occult lore actually gets into Emerson's quite autobiographical projection of himself as American Orpheus. His final Orphic reference, in the 1849 Journals, has about it the authority of a self-tested truth though its burden is extravagant, even for Emerson:

> ... Orpheus is no fable: you have only to sing, and the rocks will crystallize; sing, and the plant will organize; sing, and the animal will be born.

If Orpheus is fact in Emerson's life and work, this must be fact when seen in the light of an idea. The idea is the Central or Universal Man, the American More-than-Christ who is *to come*, the poet prefigured by Emerson himself as voice in the wilderness. In some sense he arrived as Walt Whitman, and some seventy years later as Hart Crane, but that is to run ahead of the story. In Emerson's mythopoeic and metamorphic conception, Central or Orphic Man is hardly to be distinguished from an Orphic view of language, and so breaks apart and is restituted just as language ebbs and flows:

> ... In what I call the cyclus of Orphic words, which I find in Bacon, in Cudworth, in Plutarch, in Plato, in that which the New Church would indicate when it speaks of the truths possessed by the primeval church broken up into fragments and floating hither and thither in the corrupt church, I perceive myself addressed thoroughly. They do teach the intellect and cause a gush of emotion; which we call the moral sublime; they pervade also the moral nature. Now the Universal Man when he comes, must so speak. He must recognize by addressing the whole nature.

Bacon's Orpheus was a Baconian philosopher-natural scientist; Cudworth's a Neoplatonic Christian; Plutarch's and Plato's, an image of spiritual purification. It is sly of Emerson to bring in the not very Orphic Swedenborgians of the New Church, but he really means his Central Man to be universal. The *sparagmos* of Orpheus is a prime emblem for the American; religion, whose motto I once ventured as: *Everything that can be broken should be broken.* Emerson's all-but-everything can be given in a brief, grim list:

February 8, 1831: death of his first wife, Ellen;
May 9, 1836: death of his brother, Charles;
January 27, 1842: death of his first son, Waldo.

These Orphic losses should have shattered the American Orpheus, for all his life long these were the three persons he loved best. As losses they mark the three phases in the strengthening of his self-reliant American religion, an Orphism that would place him beyond further loss, at the high price of coming to worship the goddess Ananke, dread but sublime Necessity. But that worship came late to Emerson. He deferred it by a metamorphic doctrine of Orpheus, best stated in his essay *History*:

> The power of music, the power of poetry, to unfit and as it were clap wings to solid nature, interprets the riddle of Orpheus....

This sentence is strangely flanked in the essay, though since Emerson's unit of discourse tends more to be the sentence than the paragraph, the strangeness is mitigated. Still, the preceding sentence is both occult and puzzling:

> Man is the broken giant, and in all his weakness both his body and his mind are invigorated by habits of conversation with nature.

The Orphic riddle is the dialectic of strength and weakness *in Orpheus himself*. Is he god or man? St. Augustine placed Orpheus at the head of poets called theologians, and then added: "But these theologians were not worshipped as gods, though in some fashion the kingdom of the godless is wont to set Orpheus as head over the rites of the underworld." This is admirably clear, but not sufficient to unriddle Orpheus. Jane Harrison surmised that an actual man, Orpheus, came belatedly to the worship of Dionysus and modified those rites, perhaps partly civilizing them. Guthrie assimilated Orpheus to Apollo, while allowing the Dionysiac side also. E. R. Dodds, most convincingly for my purposes, associates Orpheus with Empedocles and ultimately with Thracian traditions of shamanism. Describing Empedocles (and Orpheus), Dodds might be writing of Emerson, granting only some temporal differences

> ... Empedocles represents not a new but a very old type of personality, the shaman who combines the still undifferentiated functions of magician and naturalist, poet and philosopher, preacher, healer, and public counsellor. After him these functions fell apart; philosophers henceforth were to be neither poets nor magicians.... It was not a question of "synthesising" these wide domains of practical and theoretical knowledge; in their quality as

Men of God they practised with confidence in all of them; the
"synthesis" was personal, not logical.

Emerson's Orpheus and Empedocles, like those of Dodds, were
mythical shamans, and perhaps Emerson as founder of the American
religion is best thought of as another mythical shaman. His Orphism was
a metamorphic religion of power whose prime purpose was divination, in
what can be called the Vichian sense of god-making. But why Orphism,
when other shamanisms were available? The native strain in Emerson
rejected any received religion. I am unable to accept a distinguished
tradition in scholarship that goes from Perry Miller to Sacvan Bercovitch,
and that finds Emerson to have been the heir, however involuntary, of the
line that goes from the Mathers to Jonathan Edwards. But I distrust also
the received scholarship that sees Emerson as the American disciple of
Wordsworth, Coleridge and Carlyle, and thus indirectly a weak
descendant of German High Transcendentalism, of Fichte and Schelling.
And to fill out my litany of rejections, I cannot find Emerson to be another
Perennial Philosophy Neoplatonist, mixing some Swedenborgianism into
the froth of Cudworth and Thomas Taylor. Since *Nature* is the text to
which I will return, I cite as commentary Stephen Whicher's *Freedom and
Fate*, still the best book on Emerson after a quarter-century:

> ... The lesson he would drive home is man's entire
> independence. The aim of this strain in his thought is not
> virtue, but freedom and mastery. It is radically anarchic,
> overthrowing all the authority of the past, all compromise or
> cooperation with others, in the name of the Power present and
> agent in the soul.
>
> Yet his true goal was not really a Stoic self-mastery, nor
> Christian holiness, but rather something more secular and harder
> to define—a quality he sometimes called *entirety*, or *self-union*....
>
> This self-sufficient unity or wholeness, transforming his
> relations with the world about him, is, as I read him, the central
> objective of the egoistic or transcendental Emerson, the prophet
> of Man created in the 1830's by his discovery of his own proper
> nature. This was what he meant by "sovereignty," or "majesty,"
> or the striking phrase, several times repeated, "the erect
> position." ...

"This strain in his thought" I would identify as what, starting from
Emerson, became the Native Strain in our literature. But why call Orphism

a religion of "freedom and mastery," anarchic in overthrowing all the past and all contemporary otherness? The choice is Emerson's, as the final chapter of *Nature* shows, so that the question becomes: Why did Emerson identify his Primal, Central or Universal Man with Orpheus?

Hart Crane, Emerson's descendant through Whitman, provokes the same question at the formal close of *The Bridge*:

> Now while thy petals spend the suns about us, hold
> (O Thou whose radiance doth inherit me)
> Atlantis,—hold thy floating singer late!
>
> So to thine Everpresence, beyond time,
> Like spears ensanguined of one tolling star
> That bleeds infinity—the orphic strings,
> Sidereal phalanxes, leap and converge:
> —One Song, one Bridge of Fire!

The belated floating singer is still the metamorphic Orpheus of Ovid

> ... The poet's limbs were scattered in different places, but the waters of the Hebrus received his head and lyre. Wonderful to relate, as they floated down in midstream, the lyre uttered a plaintive melody and the lifeless tongue made a piteous murmur, while the river banks lamented in reply....

But beyond time, upon the transcendental bridge of fire that is his poem, Crane as American Orpheus vaults the problematics of loss even as Brooklyn Bridge vaultingly becomes the Orphic lyre bending, away from America as lost Atlantis, to whatever Crane can surmise beyond earth. If Coleridge could salute *The Prelude* as "an Orphic song indeed," then the American Crane could render the same salute to *The Bridge*. Emerson's Orphic songs, first in *Nature* and later in his essay *The Poet*, are Crane's ultimate paradigm, as he may not have known. To answer the question: Why an American Orpheus? I turn back now to *Nature*.

6

Between "Nature" proper, the little book's first chapter, with its epiphany of the transparent eyeball, and the final chapter "Prospects," with its two rhapsodies of the Orphic poet, intervene six rather inadequate chapters, all of which kindle at their close. I give here only these kindlings:

A man is fed, not that he may be fed, but that he may work.

But beauty in nature is not ultimate.

That which was unconscious truth, becomes, when interpreted and defined as an object, a part of the domain of knowledge—a new weapon in the magazine of power.

... the human form, of which all other organizations appear to be degradations....

... the soul holds itself off from a too trivial and microscopic study of the universal tablet. It respects the end too much to immerse itself in the means....

The world proceeds from the same spirit as the body of man. It is a remoter and inferior incarnation of God, a projection of God in the unconscious....

Perhaps Emerson might have kindled these kernels of his vision into something finer than the six chapters they crown. Their design is clear and impressive. Man's work moves beyond natural beauty through a power-making act of knowledge, which identifies the human form, beyond merely natural evidence, as the incarnation of God, an incarnation not yet elevated to full consciousness. That elevation is the enterprise of the Orphic poet, in the chapter "Prospects."

"... Man is the dwarf of himself. Once he was permeated and dissolved by spirit. He filled nature with his overflowing currents. Out from him sprang the sun and moon; from man the sun, from woman the moon. The laws of his mind, the periods of his actions externized themselves into day and night, into the year and the seasons. But, having made for himself this huge shell, his waters retired; he no longer fills the veins and veinlets; he is shrunk to a drop. He sees that the structure still fits him, but fits him colossaly. Say, rather, once it fitted him, now it corresponds to him from far and on high. He adores timidly his own work. Now is man the follower of the sun, and woman the follower of the moon. Yet sometimes he starts in his slumber, and wonders at himself and his house, and muses strangely at the resemblance betwixt him and it. He perceives that if his law is still paramount, if still he have elemental power, if his word is sterling yet in nature, it is not conscious power, it is not inferior but superior to his will. It is instinct." Thus my Orphic poet sang.

This "instinct" scarcely can be biological; like the Freudian drives of Eros and Thanatos it can only be mythological. Orphic, Gnostic or even Neoplatonic, it appears now in American colors and tropes. Call the Primal Man American, or even America (as Blake called him Albion, or Shelley, more misleadingly, Prometheus). America was a larger form than nature, filling nature with his emanative excess. Not Jehovah Elohim nor a Demiurge made the cosmos and time, but America, who thereupon shrunk to a drop. When this dwarf, once giant, starts in his sleep, then "gleams of a better light" come into experiential darkness. Very American is Emerson's catalog of those gleams of Reason:

> ... Such examples are, the traditions of miracles in the earliest antiquity of all nations; the history of Jesus Christ; the achievements of a principle, as in religious and political revolutions, and in the abolition of the slave-trade; the miracles of enthusiasm, as those reported of Swedenborg, Hohenlohe, and the Shakers; many obscure and yet contested facts, now arranged under the name of Animal Magnetism; prayer; eloquence; self-healing; and the wisdom of children.

A contemporary Carlyle might react to this list by querying: "But why has be left out flying saucers?" I myself would point to "eloquence" as the crucial item, fully equal and indeed superior in Emerson's view to "the history of Jesus Christ" or "prayer." Eloquence is the true Emersonian instance "of Reason's momentary grasp of the scepter; the exertions of a power which exists not in time or space, but an instantaneous in-streaming causing power." Eloquence is Influx, and Influx is a mode of divination, in the Vichian or double sense of god-making and of prophecy. Emerson, peculiarly American, definitive of what it is to be American, *uses* divination so as to transform all of nature into a transparent eyeball:

> ... The ruin or the blank, that we see when we look at nature, is in our own eye. The axis of vision is not coincident with the axis of things, and so they appear not transparent but opaque. The reason why the world lacks unity, and lies broken and in heaps, is because man is disunited with himself....

The American swerve here is from Milton, when in his invocation to Book III of *Paradise Lost* he lamented that to his literal blindness nature appeared a universal blank. But, more subtly, Emerson revises Coleridge's previous swerve from Milton's lament, in the despairing cry of *Dejection: An Ode*, where Coleridge sees literally but not figuratively: "And still I gaze— and with how blank an eye." The American transumption of Emerson's revisionary optics comes late, with the tragic self-recognition of the aged Wallace Stevens in *The Auroras of Autumn*, when Stevens walks the Emersonian-Whitmanian shores of America unable to convert his movements into a freshly American figuration, a new variation upon the tradition: "The man who is walking turns blankly on the sand."

What would it mean if the axis of vision and of things were to coincide? What would a transparent world be, or yield? Wordsworth's *Tintern Abbey* spoke of seeing into the life of things, while Blake urged a seeing *through* rather than *with* the eye. Is Emerson as much reliant upon trope as these British forerunners were, or do his optics prod us towards a pragmatic difference? I suggest the latter, because Emerson as American seer is always the shrewd Yankee, interested in what he called "commodity," and because we ought never to forget that if he fathered Whitman and Thoreau and Frost and (despite that son's evasions) Stevens, his pragmatic strain ensued in William James, Peirce and even John Dewey.

The optics of transparency disturb only the aspect of this text that marks it as a fiction of duration, while the topological residuum of the text remains untroubled. Most tropes, as Emerson knew, have only a spatial rather than a temporal dimension, metaphor proper and synecdoche and metonymy among them. Irony and transumption or metalepsis, which Emerson called the comic trick of language and Nietzsche the Eternal Recurrence, are the temporal as well as spatial modes. The Emersonian transparency or transcendence does not oppose itself to presence or spatial immanence, but to the burden of time and of historical continuity. As the quintessential American, Emerson did not need to transcend *space*, which for him as for Whitman, Melville and Charles Olson was the central fact about America. Transparency is therefore an agon with time, and not with space, and opacity thus can be re-defined, in Emersonian terms, as being fixed in time, being trapped in continuity. What Nietzsche called the will's revenge against time's "it was" Emerson more cheerfully sees as a transparency.

Pragmatically this did not mean, for Emerson, seeing things or people as though they were ectoplasm. It meant not seeing the fact except as an epiphany, as a manifestation of the God within the self-reliant seer:

... We make fables to hide the baldness of the fact and conform it, as we say, to the higher law of the mind. But when the fact is seen under the light of an idea, the gaudy fable fades and shrivels....

Why should Orpheus be incarnated again in America? Because he is the authentic prophet-god of discontinuity, of the breaking of tradition, and of re-inscribing tradition as a perpetual breaking, mending and then breaking again. The Orphic seer says of and to time: *It must be broken*. Even so, Emerson's own Orphic poet ends *Nature* by chanting a marvelous breaking:

> Nature is not fixed but fluid. Spirit alters, molds, makes it. The immobility or bruteness of nature is the absence of spirit; to pure spirit it is fluid, it is volatile, it is obedient. Every spirit builds itself a house, and beyond its house a world, and beyond its world a heaven. Know then that the world exists for you. For you is the phenomenon perfect. What we are, that only can we see. All that Adam had, all that Caesar could, you have and can do. Adam called his house, Rome; you perhaps call yours, a cobbler's trade; a hundred acres of ploughed land; or a scholar's garret. Yet line for line and point for point your dominion is as great as theirs, though without fine names. Build therefore your own world....

The metaphoric-mobile, fluid, volatile is precisely the Orphic stigma. I discussed this passage in section a, above, in terms of Abyss-radiance, but return to it now to venture a more radical interpretation. Pure spirit, or influx, is a remedial force not akin to what moved over the Abyss in merely demiurgical Creation, but rather itself the breath of the truly Primal Abyss. "Build therefore your own world" cannot mean that you are to emulate demiurgical creativity by stealing your material from the origin. Every man his own Demiurge hardly can be the motto for the Emersonian freedom. If seeing ranks above having, for Emerson, then knowing stands beyond seeing:

> The kingdom of man over nature, which cometh not with observation,—a dominion such as now is beyond his dream of God,—he shall enter without more wonder than the blind man feels who is gradually restored to perfect sight.

The crucial words are "now" and "gradually." If the dream of God were to be an Orphic and Gnostic dream of one's own occult self, then the reliance or religion would come now, and with great wonder. Emerson's curiously serene faith, as he closes *Nature*, is that gradually we will be restored to the perfect sight of our truly knowing self.

7

Emerson's theology of being an American, his vision of self-reliance, has nothing much in common with historical Gnosticism. In Gnosticism, this world is hell, and both man's body and man's soul are the work of the Demiurge who made this world. Only the *pneuma* or spark within the Gnostic elect is no part of the false and evil Creation. Emerson's monism, his hope for the American new Adam, and his Wordsworthian love of nature all mark him as a religious prophet whose God, however internalized, is very distinct from the alien God or Primal Abyss of Gnosticism.

I speak therefore not of Emerson's Gnosticism but of his Gnosis, of his way of knowing, which has nothing in common with philosophic epistemology. Though William James, Peirce and Dewey, and in another mode, Nietzsche, all are a part of Emerson's progeny, Emerson is not a philosopher, nor even a speculator with a philosophic theology. And though he stemmed from the mainstream Protestant tradition in America, Emerson is not a Christian, nor even a non-Christian theist in a philosophic sense. But I am not going to continue this litany of what our central man is not. Rather I will move directly to an account of Emerson's Gnosis, of that which he was and is, founder of *the* American religion, fountain of our literary and spiritual elite.

I will begin and end with my own favorite Emersonian sentence, from the first paragraph of the essay *Self-Reliance*:

> In every work of genius we recognize our own rejected thoughts; they come back to us with a certain alienated majesty.

Emerson says "rejected" where we might use the word "repressed," and his Gnosis begins with the reader's Sublime, a Freudian Negation in which thought comes back but we are still in flight from the emotional recognition that there is no author but ourselves. A strong reading indeed is the only text, the only revenge against time's "it was" that can endure. Self-estrangement produces the uncanniness of "majesty," and yet we do "recognize our own." Emerson's Gnosis rejects all history, including literary history, and dismisses all historians, including literary historians who want to tell the reader that what he recognizes in Emerson is Emerson's own thought rather than the reader's own Sublime.

A discourse upon Emerson's Gnosis, to be Emersonian rather than literary historical, itself must be Gnosis, or part of a Gnosis. It must speak of a knowing in which the knower himself is known, a reading in which he is read. It will not speak of epistemology, not even deconstructively of the epistemology of tropes, because it will read Emerson's tropes as figures of will, and not figures of knowledge, as images of voice and not images of writing.

"Why then do we prate of self-reliance?" is Emerson's rhetorical question, halfway through that essay. Falling back, with him, upon power as agent and upon a rich internal "way of speaking," I repeat his injunction: "Speak rather of that which relies because it works and is." "Works" as an Emersonian verb has Carlyle's tang to it. Prate not of happiness, but work, for the night cometh. But Emerson's *clinamen* away from Europe, away even from Coleridge and Carlyle, is to be heard in "that which relies because it works and is." In the American swerve, tradition is denied its last particle of authority, and the voice that is great within us rises up:

> Life only avails, not the having lived. Power ceases in the instant
> of repose; it resides in the moment of transition from a past to a new
> state, in the shooting of the gulf, in the darting of an aim....

There is no power in what already has been accomplished, and Emerson has not come to celebrate a new state, a gulf crossed, an aim hit. Power is an affair of crossings, of thresholds or transitional moments, evasions, substitutions, mental dilemmas resolved only by arbitrary acts of will. Power is in the traversing of the black holes of rhetoric, where the interpreter reads his own freedom to read. Or, we are read only by voicing, by the images for power we find that free us from the *already said*, from being one of the secondary men, traces of traces of traces.

I am suggesting that what a Gnosis of rhetoric, like Emerson's, prophetically wars against is every philosophy of rhetoric, and so now against the irony of irony and the randomness of all textuality. The Emersonian self, "that which relies because it works and is," is voice and not text, which is why it must splinter and destroy its own texts, subverting even the paragraph through the autonomy of sentences, the aggressivity of aphorisms. The sudden uncanniness of voice is Emerson's prime image for vocation, for the call that his Gnosis answers, as here in *Spiritual Laws*:

> Each man has his own vocation. The talent is the call....
> ... It is the vice of our public speaking that it has not
> abandonment. Somewhere, not only every orator but every man

should let out the length of all the reins; should find or make a frank and hearty expression of what force and meaning is in him....

Of this Emersonian spark or *pneuma*, this Gnostic true or antithetical self, as opposed to *psyche* or soul, we can observe that as an aggressive image of voice it will resist successfully all deconstruction. For this image is not a fiction *produced by* the original breaking-apart of the vessels of language but rather itself *tropes for* that primal breaking-apart. Emerson's image of voice is precisely a prophetic transumption of his son Nietzsche's image of truth as an army of figures of speech on the march, a march for which Heidegger gives us "language" or Derrida "writing" as a trope. The march keeps breaking up as voice keeps flowing in again, not as the image of presence but of Gnostic aboriginal absence, as here again in *Spiritual Laws* where the *thrownness* of all Gnosis returns in a forward falling:

> ... When the fruit is ripe, it falls. When the fruit is despatched, the leaf falls. The circuit of the waters is a mere falling. The walking of man and all animals is a falling forward. All our manual labor and works of strength, as prying, splitting, digging, rowing and so forth, are done by dint of continual falling, and the globe, earth, moon, comet, sun, star, fall forever and ever.
>
> ... Place yourself in the middle of the stream of power and wisdom which flows into you as life, place yourself in the full centre of that flood, then you are without effort impelled to truth, to right, and a perfect contentment....

I gloss these Emersonian passages by the formula: every fall is a *fall forward*, neither fortunate nor unfortunate, but *forward*, without effort, impelled to the American truth, which is that the stream of power and wisdom flowing in as life is eloquence. Emerson *is* the fountain of our will because he understood that, in America, in the evening-land, eloquence *had* to be enough. The image of voice is the image of influx, of the Newness, but always it knowingly is a broken image, or image of brokenness. Whitman, still Emerson's strongest ephebe, caught the inevitable tropes for this wounded image of American voice:

> —and from this bush in the dooryard,
> With delicate-color'd blossoms and heart-shaped leaves of rich green,
>   A sprig with its flower I break.

In the swamp in secluded recesses,
A shy and hidden bird is warbling a song.

Solitary the thrush,
The hermit withdrawn to himself, avoiding the settlements,
Sings by himself a song.

Song of the bleeding throat,
Death's outlet song of life, (for well dear brother I know,
If thou wast not granted to sing thou would'st surely die.)

The breaking of the tally, of the sprig of lilac, is one with the wounding of the hermit thrush's throat, the breaking of voice, of the call, of prophetic vocation. Because it is broken, castrated, it remains an image of voice and of life, not the unbroken image of writing and of death. Whitman knows, even in *extremis*, because his father Emerson knew, and both knowings are fallings forward. What any philosophical knowing necessarily is or isn't I scarcely know, but I can read Emerson because every knowing I do know is part of a thrownness, a synecdoche for what Emerson wanted to call "victory" or "freedom." Was it not Emerson's peculiar strength that what to me seems catastrophe was to him—by the mad law of Compensation—converted to victory? What made him free was his Gnosis, and I move now into its center, his center, the image of voice that is self-reliance, at the high place of that rhapsody:

> ... It must be that when God speaketh he should communicate, not one thing, but all things; should fill the world with his voice; should scatter forth light, nature, time, souls, from the center of the present thought; and new date and new create the whole. Whenever a mind is simple and receives a divine wisdom, old Things pass away,—means, teachers, texts, temples fall; it lives now, and absorbs past and future into the present hour. All things are made sacred by relation to it,—one as much as another. All things are dissolved to their center by their cause....

Let us apply Whitman, since he was the strongest of the Emersonians. In *Specimen Days* he wrote:

> ... The best part of Emersonianism is, it breeds the giant that destroys itself. Who wants to be any man's mere follower? lurks

behind every page. No teacher ever taught, that has so provided
for his pupil's setting up independently—no truer evolutionist.

Emerson also then is a teacher and a text that must pass away if you or
I receive the Newness, a fresh influx of the image of voice. On Emerson's
precept, no man's Gnosis can be another's, and Emerson's images of voice are
fated to become yet more images of writing. Surely this is part of the lesson
of the Middle or Skeptical Emerson, warning us against all idolatries,
including my own deep temptation to idolize Emerson. Here is the
admonition of his greatest essay, *Experience*:

> ... People forget that it is the eye which makes the horizon, and
> the rounding mind's eye which makes this or that man a type or
> representation of humanity, with the name of hero or saint. Jesus,
> the "providential man," is a good man on whom many people are
> agreed that these optical laws shall take effect....

Emerson, unlike Whitman, hoped to evade the American version of
that "providential man." If no two disciples can agree upon Emerson's
doctrine, and they cannot, we can grant the success of his evasion. Yet there
is the center: evasion. Emersonianism, indeed like any Gnosis, moves back
and forth between negation and extravagance, and always by way of evasion
rather than by substitution. I will digress from Gnosis to Gnosticism, before
shuttling back to Emerson's passage through *Experience* to *Fate*, middle and
late essays no less modes of Gnosis than *Self-Reliance* is.

The way of evasion for the Gnostics meant freedom, and this was
freedom from the god of this world, from time, from text, and from the soul
and the body of the universe. Such freedom was both knowledge and
salvation, since the knowledge of saving self involved was one with the
knowledge of the alien true God and the Primal Abyss. How could so large
a knowing be known? Only by an image or trope of the self that transgressed
language through the most positive of negative moments. What Coleridge,
in his orthodox nightmare, dreads as the Positive Negation of *Limbo* is
known by the Gnostics as a being-there in the Pleroma, in the Place of Rest.
Coleridge's negative moment loses the self without compensation. Emerson,
in his 1838 Journal, slyly turning away from Coleridge, achieves a Gnostic
Sublime, a negative moment that is all gain and no loss, the truly American
moment of self-reliance:

> In the highest moments, we are a vision. There is nothing that
> can be called gratitude nor properly joy. The soul is raised over

passion. It seeth nothing so much as Identity. It is a Perceiving that Truth and Right ARE. Hence it becomes a perfect Peace out of the *knowing* that all things will go well. Vast spaces of nature the Atlantic Ocean, the South Sea; vast intervals of time years, centuries, are annihilated to it; this which I think and feel underlay that former state of life and circumstances, as it does underlie my present, and will always all circumstance, and what is called life and what is called death [my italics].

This passage is not so much an example of Gnostic rhetoric as it is part of a Gnosis of rhetoric, anti-epistemological without being vulnerable to the charge that it simply reverses an epistemological dilemma. In a transcendental hyperbole we mount beyond Coleridgean joy of the Secondary imagination because *we see nothing*. Instead, "we are a vision" and we know the identity between ourselves and our knowledge of ourselves. Space, time and mortality flee away, to be replaced by "the knowing." As always in Emerson, the knowing bruises a limit of language, and the impatient Seer transgresses in order to convey his "Perceiving that Truth and Right ARE," which compels the "ARE" to break through in capital letters. In its extravagance, this passage is nothing but tropological, yet its persuasive rhetoric achieves persuasion by the trick of affirming identity with a wholly discontinuous self, one which *knows* only the highest moments in which it *is* a vision. Emerson evades philosophy and chooses his Gnosis instead precisely because he is wary of the epistemological pitfalls that all trope risks. An image of voice is a fine tangle, well beyond logic, but it can testify only to the presence of things not seen, and its faith is wholly in the Optative Mood.

Yet if we move on from *Self-Reliance* first to *Experience* and then to *Fate*, we pass out of the Optative Mood and into the evidence of that world where men descend to meet, and where they cease to be a vision. But even in *Experience*, and then even more in *Fate*, we read not philosophy but Gnosis, a chastened knowing that is not chastened *as* knowing. Here is a single recovery from *Experience*:

> ... The partial action of each strong mind in one direction is a telescope for the objects on which it is pointed. But every other part of knowledge is to be pushed to the same extravagance, ere the soul attains her due sphericity....
>
> ... And we cannot say too little of our constitutional necessity of seeing things under private aspects, or saturated with our humors. And yet is the God the native of these bleak rocks. That need makes in morals the capital virtue of self-trust. We must

hold hard to this poverty, however scandalous, and by more rigorous self-recoveries, after the sallies of action, possess our axis more firmly.

Rather than comment upon this in isolation, I juxtapose it first with a more scandalous poverty of *Fate*:

> ... A man speaking from insight affirms of himself what is true of the mind: seeing its immortality, he says, I am immortal; seeing its invincibility, he says, I am strong. It is not in us, but we are in it. It is of the maker, not of what is made....

The fragment of *Experience* makes imaginative need, epistemological lack, itself into potential Gnosis, the potentia of power. But the resting-point of *Fate* is a more drastic Gnosis, for there the mind and the self have dissociated, in order to win the compensation of the self as spark of the uncreated. And in a coda to this discourse I now abandon Emerson for the giant of Emersonianism, for the question that is a giant himself. What does Emersonianism teach us about an American Gnosis, and what is it which makes that Gnosis still available to us?

The primary teaching of any Gnosis is to deny that human existence is a historical existence. Emerson's American Gnosis denies our belatedness by urging us not to listen to tradition. If you listen hard to tradition, as Walter Benjamin said Kafka did, then you do not see, and Emersonianism wants you to *see*. See what? That is the wrong question, for Gnosis directs *how* to see, meaning to *see earliest*, as though no one had ever seen before you. Gnosis directs also in stance, in taking up a place from which to see earliest, which is one with the place of belated poetry, which is to say, American poetry in particular.

In poetry, a "place" is *where* something is *known*, while a figure or trope is *when* something is willed or desired. In belated poetry, as in any other Gnosis, the place where knowing is located is always a name, but one that comes by negation; an unnaming yields this name. But to un-name in a poem, you first mime and then over-mime and finally super-mime the name you displace. Emerson and Gnosticism alike seek the terrible burden of a super-mimesis. The American poet must overthrow even Shakespeare, a doomed enterprise that shadows *Moby Dick*, despite our generous overpraise of the crippling of Melville's greatness by *King Lear*. Whitman must be the new Adam, the new Moses, and the new Christ, impossible aspirations that astonishingly he did not disappoint wholly. An imaginative literature that stems from a Gnosis, rather than a philosophy, is both enhanced and ruined by its super-mimetic teleologies. In every work of genius—in the Bible, Shakespeare, Spenser, Milton, Wordsworth—just there Hawthorne, Melville, Whitman, Thoreau, Dickinson, Henry James learned to recognize their own rejected thoughts. Frost, Stevens, Hart Crane, Faulkner and so many more later encountered their rejected thoughts coming back to them with a certain alienated majesty, when they read their American nineteenth-century precursors. Plato entered the agon with Homer to be the mind of Greece, but here in America we had no Homer. The mind of America perhaps was Emersonian even before Emerson. After him, the literary, indeed the religious mind of America has had no choice, as he cannot be rejected or even deconstructed. He *is* our rhetoric as he is our Gnosis, and I take it that, his sly evasion of both Hegel and Hume deprived us of our philosophy. Since he will not conclude haunting us, I evade concluding here, except for a single hint. He was an interior orator, and not an instructor; a vitalizer and not an historian. We will never know our own knowing, through or despite him, until we learn the lesson our profession refuses. I end therefore by quoting against us an eloquence from the essay *History*, which the seer rightly chose to lead off his essays:

> ... Those men who cannot answer by a superior wisdom these facts or questions of time, serve them. Facts encumber them, tyrannize over them, and make the men of routine, the men of *sense*, in whom a literal obedience to facts has extinguished every spark of that light by which man is truly man....

That, in one dark epiphany, *is* Emerson's Gnosis.

BARBARA L. PACKER

The Curse of Kehama

How shall we face the edge of time? We walk
In the park. We regret we have no nightingale.
We must have the throstle on the gramophone.
Where shall we find more than derisive words?
When shall lush chorals spiral through our fire
And daunt that old assassin, heart's desire?
—Wallace Stevens, "A Duck for Dinner"

"EXPERIENCE"

Emerson's final version of the Fall story is his shortest and most epigrammatic. It is remarkable not so much for its content as for its tone, and the startling nature of the "facts" it is invented to explain. The voice we hear in "Experience" has neither the rhapsodic intensity of the Orphic chants, nor the chill impersonality of the axis-of-vision formula, nor the militancy of "The Protest" or "Circles." It is instead the voice of a man of the world: urbane, rueful, a little weary. "It is very unhappy, but too late to be helped, the discovery we have made that we exist. That discovery is called the Fall of Man."

From *Emerson's Fall.* © 1982 by Continuum Publishing Company.

Equating self-consciousness with the Fall is of course one of the commonest Romantic ways of allegorizing the story of Genesis. And the myth of ossification, with its insistence that the conscious intellect was the enemy of that central power accessible only by surprise or abandonment, may be regarded as containing or at least implying this final myth (which we may call the myth of *reflection*).

But this new version differs from its predecessors in two significant respects. It is considerably more pessimistic in its implications (there is no suggestion that the catastrophe of self-consciousness is either potentially or temporarily reversible), and the evidence adduced to support it is more shocking, in its quiet way, than anything Emerson had ever written. In *Nature* he had based his argument for the original divinity of the Self on its surviving capacity for ecstasy; in "Circles," on its refusal to accept limitation. In "Experience" what is taken as proof of the "ill-concealed Deity" of the Self is neither its joy nor its zeal but simply its ruthlessness:

> There are moods in which we court suffering, in the hope that here at least we shall find reality, sharp peaks and edges of truth. But it turns out to be scene-painting and counterfeit. The only thing grief has taught me, is to know how shallow it is. That, like all the rest, plays about the surface, and never introduces me into the reality, for contact with which we would even pay the costly price of sons and lovers.

> We believe in ourselves as we do not believe in others. We permit all things to ourselves, and that which we call sin in others is experiment for us. It is an instance of our faith in ourself that men never speak of crime as lightly as they think; or that every man thinks a latitude safe for himself which is nowise to be indulged to another.... No man at last believes that he can be lost, or that the crime in him is as black as in the felon.

Emerson had once wanted to write a book like the Proverbs of Solomon; "Experience" sounds more like the *Maxims* of La Rochefoucauld.

The necessary ruthlessness of the Self had been a corollary of the doctrine of self-reliance from the beginning, of course; it is implicit in Emerson's exhortation to "shun father and mother and wife and brother" when genius calls, even if it causes them pain. And it is avowed even more frankly in "Circles," where Emerson argues that "men cease to interest us when we find their limitations. The only sin is limitation. As soon as you once come up with a man's limitations, it is all over with him." As individuals, we are always in the position of the disappointed child in "Experience" who asks his mother why the story he enjoyed yesterday fails to please him as much the second time around. And the only answer Emerson can give us is the one he offers the child: "will it answer thy question to say, Because thou wert born to a whole and this story is a particular?" This information is hardly an unmixed blessing. If our hunger for "sphericity" is on the one hand the only defense we have against the soul's tendency to ossification, it is on the other hand the restlessness that "ruins the kingdom of mortal friendship and of love."

Emerson's deliberate emphasis in essays like "Circles" and "Experience" on the ruthlessness and secret cruelty of the Self shocks us, and is meant to. It is not merely (as Firkins guesses) "that a parade of hardness may have seemed to him a wholesome counterpoise to the fashionable parade of sensibility,"[1] though that was doubtless an added attraction. Emerson says these unpleasant things chiefly because he thinks they are true. Of course it would be easier for us and for society as a whole if they were not true, if there were some way of living without the ruinous ferocity of desire, which never ceases to torment us in thought, even if our outward behavior is decorous. Our mortal condition would be easier to endure if the divine Providence had *not* "shown the heaven and earth to every child and filled him with a desire for the whole; a desire raging, infinite; a hunger, as of space to be filled with planets; a cry of famine, as of devils for souls"—as Emerson puts it in a memorable passage in "Montaigne." That desire sends us off on a perpetual quest through the world of experience, and at the same time foredooms the quest to failure, since each particular satisfaction can only frustrate a being whose desire is for the whole. As questers, we are partly like Tennyson's Ulysses—

.... all experience is an arch wherethrough
Gleams that untravelled world whose margin fades
For ever and for ever when I move ... [2]

but even more like Tennyson's Percivale—

"Lo, if I find the Holy Grail itself
And touch it, it will crumble into dust."[3]

Romance—the glamour or beauty that could transmute life's baser metals into gold—is always somewhere else, somewhere just beyond our grasp. "Every ship is a romantic object, except that we sail in. Embark, and the romance quits our vessel and hangs on every other sail in the horizon." Or, as he had put it in the earlier essay "Love": "each man sees his own life defaced and disfigured, as the life of man is not, to his imagination."

Sensible people, hearing these confessions of frustration and despair, counsel renunciation of the Self's imperial ambitions. But Emerson denies that any permanent renunciation is possible. For one thing, that glimpse of the whole we were granted as children survives in adult life as more than a memory. Just when we have, as we think, managed to adjust our desires to reality, the old vision reappears to tantalize us:

> How easily, if fate would suffer it, we might keep forever these beautiful limits, and adjust ourselves, once for all, to the perfect calculation of known cause and effect.... But ah! presently comes a day, or is it only a half-hour, with its angel-whispering,—which discomfits the conclusions of notions and years!

And this reminder, while it distresses us, calls to our attention something we cannot safely ignore. The desire that torments us is also the only "capital stock" we have to invest in the actions and relationships of life. The man who tried to conduct his business on the principles of common sense alone "would quickly be bankrupt. Power keeps quite another road than the turnpikes of choice and will; namely the subterranean and invisible tunnels and channels of life."

These meditations on power and ruthlessness are an important part of the essay "Experience." They constitute a sort of ground bass heard at intervals beneath the constantly varying melodies of the essay, and contribute not a little to the impression of toughness it makes on the reader's mind. Yet toughness is hardly the essay's most significant characteristic. What is strikingly new about "Experience" is the voice that is heard in its opening paragraph, a voice neither powerful nor ruthless, but instead full of bewilderment, exhaustion, and despair:

> Where do we find ourselves? In a series of which we do not know the extremes, and believe that it has none. We wake and find ourselves on a stair; there are stairs below us, which we seem to have ascended; there are stairs above us, many a one, which go upward and out of sight. But the Genius which according to the old belief stands at the door by which we enter, and gives us the lethe to drink, that we may tell no tales, mixed the cup too strongly, and we cannot shake off the lethargy now at noonday. Sleep lingers all our lifetime about our eyes, as night hovers all

day in the boughs of the fir-tree. All things swim and glitter. Our life is not so much threatened as our perception. Ghostlike we glide through nature, and should not know our place again.

When Dr. Beard, in his *American Nervousness*, wanted a phrase that would convey to a popular audience an accurate sense of the new disease he had identified and named *neurasthenia*, he instinctively chose a metaphor Emerson would have admired: "nervous bankruptcy."[4] In the peculiar lassitude of the prose here—so different from the militant assertiveness of "Circles" or "Self-Reliance"—Emerson has managed to create a stylistic correlative to the "Feeling of Profound Exhaustion" Dr. Beard found characteristic of the nervously bankrupt.[5] Insufficiency of vital force is in fact Emerson's chief complaint in this opening passage.

> Did our birth fall in some fit of indigence and frugality in nature, that she was so sparing of her fire and so liberal of her earth that it appears to us that we lack the affirmative principle, and though we have health and reason, yet we have no superfluity of spirit for new creation? We have enough to live and bring the year about, but not an ounce to impart or invest. Ah that our Genius were a little more of a genius! We are like the millers on the lower levels of a stream, when the factories above them have exhausted the water. We too fancy that the upper people have raised their dams.

No reader of Emerson's journals can be unfamiliar with the mood described here. Recurrent laments over want of stamina and of animal spirits, over feelings of exhaustion and despair, punctuate the earliest notebooks. "I have often found cause to complain that my thoughts have an ebb & flow," he noted in one of them. "The worst is, that the ebb is certain, long, & frequent, while the flow comes transiently & seldom." A few pages earlier, a pious composition intended as a meditation "Upon Men's Apathy to their Eternal interests" turns into a meditation upon apathy of a more personal sort—a meditation whose systematic hopelessness, coming from a youth of nineteen, almost raises a smile:

> In the pageant of life, Time & Necessity are the stern masters of ceremonies who admit no distinctions among the vast train of aspirants.... And though the appetite of youth for marvels & beauty is fain to draw deep & strong lines of contrast between one & another character we early learn to distrust them & to

acquiesce in the unflattering & hopeless picture which
Experience exhibits.

This grim lesson Emerson hastens to apply to his own disappointing life:

> We dreamed of great results from peculiar features of Character.
> We thought that the overflowing benevolence of our youth was
> pregnant with kind consequences to the world; that the agreeable
> qualities in the boy of courage, activity, intelligence, & good
> temper would prove in the man Virtues of extensive &
> remarkable practical effect.

The passage is revealing; it provides a glimpse of what Emerson's boyhood
ambition had really been—not to become a reclusive scholar and occasional
lecturer, but to be a public figure, an eloquent mover of men, like his hero
Daniel Webster. The disinterest of his elders in his visionary schemes of
regeneration had not dampened his personal ambitions; if anything, it had
increased them. "The momentary ardour of childhood found that manhood
& age were too cold to sympathise with it, & too hastily inferred that its own
merit was solitary & unrivalled & would by and by blaze up, & make an era
in Society." But this childhood ardor, like Wordsworth's "visionary gleam,"
eventually died away of its own accord:

> Alas. As it grew older it also grew colder & when it reached the
> period of manhood & of age it found that the waters of time, as
> they rolled had extinguished the fire that once glowed & there
> was no partial exemption for itself. The course of years rolls an
> unwelcome wisdom with them which forcibly teaches the vanity
> of human expectations.

And he concludes: "The dreams of my childhood are all fading away &
giving place to some very sober & very disgusting views of a quiet mediocrity
of talents & condition."

The intellectual revolution of the early 1830s—the discovery of the
God within—liberated Emerson from the hopelessness that had oppressed
his young manhood, but it could not do much for his stamina. He
circumvented the limitations of his constitution by carefully husbanding his
time and strength, and he learned to make the best of his alarming *"periods
of mentality"* ("one day I am a doctor, & the next I am a dunce") by means
of the unique method of composition he had already perfected by the mid-
thirties. He spent his mornings barricaded in his study, writing isolated

paragraphs in his journal when the spirit was upon him. When a longer composition was needed—a sermon or a lecture—he quarried in these journals for material and, as Chapman says, "threw together what seemed to have a bearing on some subject, and gave it a title." Chapman adds, correctly, I think, that what keeps this method from resulting in an "incomprehensible chaos" is Emerson's single-mindedness:

> There was only one thought which could set him aflame, and that was the unfathomed might of man. This thought was his religion, his politics, his ethics, his philosophy. One moment of inspiration was in him own brother to the next moment of inspiration, although they might be separated by six weeks.[6]

What keeps this procedure from resulting in monotony for the reader, is first, the sheer power and felicity of Emerson's prose; next, the perpetual surprise of his observations (who else would have thought of comparing readers at the Boston Athenaeum to flies, aphids, and sucking infants?); and finally, his unflinching honesty, which will not let him rest until he has subjected his claim for the unfathomed might of man to every shred of negative evidence that can reasonably be urged against it. The combination of his single-mindedness and his insistence upon recognizing all the "opposite negations between which, as walls, his being is swung" is responsible for the curious fact about his work noticed long ago by Firkins. "Emerson's wish to get his whole philosophy into each essay tended toward sameness and promiscuity at once; it made the *essays similar* and the *paragraphs diverse*."[7] (It is also responsible for the fact that while his paragraphs are extraordinarily easy to remember word for word, they can be almost impossible to locate. Anything can be anyplace. The most time-consuming feature of being a student of Emerson is the necessity it places one under of repeatedly rereading half the collected *Works* and *Journals* in the maddening pursuit of some paragraph one can remember but not find.)

But his habits of composition, though they enabled him to produce a body of written work that would be remarkable enough for even a vigorous man, probably contributed to his sense of the unbridgeable gap between the life of the soul and the life of the senses, between the Reason and the Understanding. His ecstasies were carefully reserved for his study; the price he paid for them was an abnormally lowered vitality for the acts and perceptions of everyday life. He repeatedly complains of the "Lethean stream" that washes through him, of the "film or haze of unreality" that separates him from the world his senses perceive. How to transfer "nerve capital" (as a follower of Dr. Beard termed it[8]) from the column of the

Reason to the column of the Understanding seemed to him life's chief insoluble problem. In "Montaigne" he writes:

> The astonishment of life is the absence of any appearance of reconciliation between the theory and practice of life. Reason, the prized reality, the Law, is apprehended, now and then, for a serene and profound moment amidst the hubbub of cares and works which have no direct bearing on it; is then lost for months and years, and again found for an interval, to be lost again. If we compute it in time, we may, in fifty years, have half a dozen reasonable hours. But what are these cares and works the better? A method in the world we do not see, but this parallelism of great and little, which never discover the smallest tendency to converge.

Or, as he had once laconically observed: "Very little life in a lifetime."

Yet despite this discouraging arithmetic Emerson had always refused to abandon his insistence that the visionary moments constituted our *real* life, the one in which we felt most truly ourselves. This insistence is not quite as suicidal as it sounds, for the visionary moments, however brief they may be when measured by the clock; have a way of expanding while they are occurring into an eternal present that makes a mockery of duration. In a paragraph of "Circles" that looks forward to Thoreau's parable of the artist of Kouroo, Emerson had written:

> It is the highest power of divine moments that they abolish our contritions also. I accuse myself of sloth and unprofitableness, day by day; but when these waves of God flow into me, I no longer reckon lost time. I no longer poorly compute my possible achievements by what remains to me of the month or the year; for these moments confer a sort of omnipresence and omnipotence, which asks nothing of duration, but sees that the energy of the mind is commensurate with the work to be done, without time.

With this proviso in mind it is easier to understand why Emerson could speculate in his journal that "in the memory of the disembodied soul the days or hours of pure Reason will shine with a steady light as the life of life & all the other days & weeks will appear but as hyphens which served to join these."

In "Experience" Emerson tries for the first time in his career to describe life as it looks from the standpoint of the hyphens rather than the heights, from the "waste sad time" (as Eliot calls it) separating the moments of vision rather than from the moments themselves. It is his attempt to confront the only form of suffering he recognized as genuinely tragic, because it was the only one for which his imagination could discover no answering compensation—the haze of unreality that sometimes suggested to him that we were "on the way back to Annihilation."

Emerson had originally planned to call the essay "Life." At first glance the difference between the two titles does not seem very great. Everything that happens in life can be described as an experience: a visionary moment as much as a bump on the head. Emerson himself uses the word this way in "The Transcendentalist" when he says that a transcendentalist's faith is based on a "certain brief experience" that surprises him in the midst of his everyday worries and pursuits.

Yet the word "experience" also had a technical meaning in empirical philosophy, where it refers to that portion of the world accessible to the senses, the world of time and space. This is the meaning it has in the works of Hume, whose skepticism had provoked the young Emerson into his first spiritual crisis during the decade of the 1820s. "Experience" is the weapon Hume uses to demolish belief in miracles and the argument for God's existence based on inferences from the evidence of design in the universe. If one accepted Hume's thesis—that "we have no knowledge but from Experience"—it was difficult to avoid his conclusion—that "we have no Experience of a Creator & therefore know of none." Hume could also use arguments from experience to shake belief in more fundamental assumptions: in the existence of matter, in the relationship of cause and effect, in the stability of personal identity. Emerson puzzled over these problems. In a high-spirited letter to his Aunt Mary written in 1823 he confessed that the doubts raised by this "Scotch Goliath" were as distressing to him as worries about the origin of evil or the freedom of the will. "Where," he asked rhetorically, "is the accomplished stripling who can cut off his most metaphysical head? Who is he that can stand up before him & prove the existence of the Universe, & of its Founder?" All the candidates in the "long & dull procession of Reasoners that have followed since" only proved, by their repeated attempts to confute Hume, that Hume had not been confuted.

Here, it is evident, Emerson is still accepting his teachers' argument that an attack on the existence of the material universe led inevitably to an attack on the existence of God. Whicher points out that "though Berkeley had denied the existence of matter independent of perception to confute sceptical materialism," to the Scottish Realists whose philosophical works dominated the Harvard scene in Emerson's youth, "the end product of the Ideal Theory was the scepticism of Hume."[9]

Emerson's discovery of "the God within" released him from the necessity of clinging to proofs of the existence of matter, since once the confirmation of the truths of religion had been made a purely intuitive affair, no longer dependent for its ratification on miracles perceivable by the senses, the "Ideal Theory" no longer seemed dangerous. The endless, fussy debates about whether we could trust the testimony of the Apostles who claimed to have witnessed the miracles of Jesus, about how the immutable laws of nature could have been temporarily suspended (e.g., whether Jesus made the water he walked on temporarily solid or himself temporarily weightless), about whether the gospels in which these events were recorded were genuine or spurious, neutral historical records or (as the German Higher Critics alleged) legendary or mythological narratives, could all be dispensed with in one liberating gesture. "Internal evidence outweighs all other to the inner man," Emerson wrote in 1830. "If the whole history of the New Testament had perished & its teachings remained—the spirituality of Paul, the grave, considerate, unerring advice of James would take the same rank with me that now they do." It is the truth of the doctrine that confirms the truth of the miracle, not the other way round. If it were not so, Emerson frankly confesses, he would probably "yield to Hume or any one that this, like all other miracle accounts, was probably false."

Hume's argument against the possibility of miracles had rested on the observation that our opinions about the reliability of testimony and about the probability of matters of fact are both drawn from experience. We usually believe the testimony of honorable witnesses, because we have found from experience that such men usually tell the truth. But we also form our opinions about the probability of matters of fact from our experience: whether it is likely to snow in July, whether a man can walk on water or rise from the dead. "The reason, why we place any credit in witnesses and historians, is not derived from any *connexion*, which we perceive *a priori*, between testimony and reality, but because we are accustomed to find a conformity between them. But when the fact attested is such a one as has seldom fallen under our observation, here is a contest of two opposite experiences; of which the one destroys the other, as far as its force goes, and the superior can only separate on the mind by the force, which remains."[10]

Emerson's mature position can best be characterized by saying that he accepts Hume's argument but reverses his conclusions. When the testimony involved is not the testimony of witnesses but the testimony of consciousness, the "superior force" clearly belongs to consciousness. Experience and consciousness are indeed in perpetual conflict: "life is made up of the intermixture and reaction of these two amicable powers, whose marriage appears beforehand monstrous, as each denies and tends to abolish the other." When an irreconcilable conflict occurs, it is consciousness, not experience, whose testimony we believe. Hence Emerson's delight in the "scientific" equivalent to this assertion: the law he attributed to the Swiss mathematician Euler and quoted in the "Idealism" chapter of *Nature*. "The sublime remark of Euler on his law of arches, 'This will be found contrary to all experience, yet it is true;' had already transferred nature into the mind, and left matter like an outcast corpse."

Idealism had always held a secret attraction for Emerson, which had survived unchanged even during the years when his teachers were telling him to regard it as dangerous. In a letter to Margaret Fuller in 1841 he writes: "I know but one solution to my nature & relations, which I find in the remembering the joy with which in my boyhood I caught the first hint of the Berkleian philosophy, and which I certainly never lost sight of afterwards." What Emerson means by the "Berkleian philosophy," as Whicher notes, is not Berkeley's particular system but

> simply the "noble doubt ... whether nature outwardly exists." The seductive reversal of his relations to the world, with which the imagination of every child is sometimes caught, transferring his recurrent sense of a dreaminess in his mode of life to outward nature, and releasing him in his imagination into a solitude peopled with illusions, was scepticism of a special kind—

but a kind that increasingly seemed not the murderer of faith but rather its midwife.[11] The man who believes that the mind alone is real, matter only a phenomenon, is easier to convince of spiritual realities than the empiricist who continually demands sensible proofs. "Idealism seems a preparation for a strictly moral life & so skepticism seems necessary for a universal holiness," Emerson noted in an early journal. Indeed, if what he asserts in "Montaigne" is correct—that "belief consists in accepting the affirmations of the soul; unbelief, in denying them"—it is the empiricist, not the idealist, who deserves the title of skeptic. With this in mind, the history of philosophy begins to look very different. The classical skeptics no longer look frightening—Emerson quotes with approval de Gérando's opinion that Sextus Empiricus' skepticism had been directed only at the external world, not at metaphysical truths. Even the Scotch Goliath begins to look less formidable. "Religion does that for the uncultivated which philosophy does for ~~Hume~~ Berkeley & Viasa; makes the mountains dance & smoke & disappear before the steadfast gaze of Reason." Emerson crossed out Hume's name (enlisting Hume as an ally of religion was presumably too radical an idea for Emerson at this point in his career, though the Emerson of "Circles" would have found it plausible), but that he thought of Hume in context at all is significant enough.

But Idealism as a doctrine was more than philosophically important to Emerson; it was emotionally important as well. *Nature* as originally planned was to have ended with the chapter "Idealism"; and in that chapter he suggests some of the chief attractions the doctrine possessed. When "piety or passion" lifts us into the realm of Ideas, "we become physically nimble and lightsome; we tread on air; life is no longer irksome, and we think it will never be so. No man fears age or misfortune or death in their serene company, for he is transported out of the region of change." "The best, the happiest moments of life are these delicious awakenings of the higher powers, and the reverential withdrawing of nature before its God."

No wonder Emerson seized eagerly upon every philosopher whose system tended toward idealism of one kind or another: Plato, Plotinus, Berkeley, Kant, Fichte, Schelling. Religious doctrines, too, he tends to judge by their approximations to idealism. In an early journal he notes with approval that idealism seems to be a primeval theory, and quotes from the Mahabharata (one of the sacred books of India) a sentence that neatly inverts the Peripatetic formula (*nihil in intellectu quod non ante fuerit in sensu*) upon which Locke had based his philosophy. "The senses are nothing but the soul's instrument of action, *no knowledge can come to the soul by their channel*" (emphasis added).

I have made this digression into Emerson's philosophical interests for a reason: the essay "Experience" cannot, I think, be fully understood without some grasp of the metaphorical ways in which he employs the technical vocabulary of epistemology to talk about things like grief, guilt, ruthlessness, and isolation. Stanley Cavell sees in Emerson the only thinker who can be said to have anticipated the Heidegger of *Being and Time* in an attempt "to formulate a kind of epistemology of moods":

> The idea is roughly that moods must be taken as having at least as sound a role in advising us of reality as sense-experience has; that, for example, coloring the world, attributing to it the qualities "mean" or "magnanimous," may be no less objective or subjective than coloring an apple, attributing to it the colors red and green. Or perhaps we should say: sense-experience is to objects what moods are to the world.[12]

What makes this difficult subject more complicated still is Emerson's own recognition that the various epistemological theories proposed by every philosopher from Plato to Kant might themselves be little more than metaphorical equivalents of moods or habitual ways of taking the world. "I fear the progress of Metaphysical philosophy may be found to consist in nothing else than the progressive introduction of apposite metaphors," Emerson had dryly remarked in an early journal. "Thus the Platonists congratulated themselves for ages upon their knowing that Mind was a dark chamber whereon ideas like shadows were painted. Men derided this as infantile when they afterwards learned that the Mind was a sheet of white paper whereon any & all characters might be written." The real difficulty in arriving at an epistemology of moods is that moods are likely to dictate beforehand the shape of one's epistemology. A soul in a state of exaltation will instinctively incline to the mystical idealism of the Mahabharata; a soul in a state of depression, to the skepticism of Hume. A healthy but nonreflective man might find the epistemology of the Scottish Realists sufficiently convincing; a more introspective man might not rest content until he had seen the relation between subject and object given transcendental ground in the philosophy of Kant.

Words like "experience" and "idealism" have different meanings in each of these systems, and different from any are the meanings they have acquired in popular use, where "idealism" is taken to mean any rosy or elevated estimate of human possibilities, and "experience" the process by which that estimate is lost. In "Experience" Emerson does not so much attempt to introduce order into this confusion as to exploit its ironies. If the essay, like life itself, is a "train of moods" or succession of "many-colored lenses which paint the world their own hue," each showing only what lies in its focus, then one of the chief ways of arriving at an epistemology of moods is by studying the shadings these words take on as the paragraphs pass by. From some moods within the essay, "experience" looks like a neutrally descriptive word; from others, a term of bitterness or contempt; from others still, the most savage of ironies. And the same thing holds true for "idealism," as one can see from the sentence (which may be the bitterest Emerson ever wrote) taken from the paragraphs of the essay that deal with the death of his son: "Grief too will make us idealists."

From the beginning of the essay the concept of experience is already involved in ironies. The opening image, which compares life to the climbing of an endless staircase, has reminded more than one critic of a Piranesi engraving, and Porte has pointed out that Emerson's references to "lethe" and "opium" recall a passage in DeQuincey's *Confessions of an English Opium-Eater*, where Piranesi's *Carceri d'Invenzione* is explicitly mentioned.[13] But DeQuincey was describing dreams induced by an actual drug; Emerson is describing the ordinary waking consciousness, life as it presents itself to the senses.

Hume, who thought that all knowledge came through experience, divided the contents of the mind into "IMPRESSIONS and IDEAS," the former derived from sensation (whether from external nature or the passions themselves), the latter the "faint images" of the former.[14] Since the two are different not in kind but only in degree, he pauses at the beginning of the *Treatise of Human Nature* to consider whether the two can ever be confused. He admits that in madness or fever or dreams ideas may become almost as lively as impressions, and that conversely there are some states in which "it sometimes happens, that our impressions are so faint and low, that we cannot distinguish them from our ideas."[15] What Emerson suggests in the opening paragraph of "Experience" is that the state Hume admitted as exceptional is in fact closer to being the norm: our impressions are most of the time as faint as our ideas, and a system of philosophy that separated one from the other according to the "degrees of force and liveliness, with which they strike upon the mind"[16] would very shortly lose the power to tell reality from phantasmagoria. The first irony we can record about experience is that it chiefly menaces the very philosophical system supposed to revere it. The exhaustion that attends it numbs the mind so that all the things we perceive "swim and glitter" like apparitions—a condition that, as Emerson accurately says, threatens not so much our life as our perception.

The second paragraph of the essay lodges a different complaint: the fact that experience and whatever wisdom can be derived from it are never coincident. Our life becomes meaningful only retroactively. "If any of us knew what we were doing, or where we are going, then when we think we best know! We do not know today whether we are busy or idle. In times when we have thought ourselves indolent, we have afterwards discovered that much was accomplished and much was begun in us." The most valuable experiences Wordsworth discovered in his childhood as he looked back on it were not the incidents a biographer would be likely to record but rather certain uncanny moments of heightened perception that occurred unexpectedly in the midst of ordinary childish sports—ice skating, robbing birds' nests, going for a night ride in a stolen boat—just as the most significant experience during the European tour he made as a young man turned out to be not the visions of sublime Alpine scenery but the vague feeling of depression that had succeeded the peasant's revelation that he and his companion had passed the highest point on their Alpine journey without recognizing it. Life and the meaning of life can never be apprehended simultaneously; like Pandarus in *Troilus and Criseyde* we can all justly complain "I hoppe alwey byhynde."[17]

Nor can any illumination ever prove final. "What a benefit if a rule could be given whereby the mind could at any moment *east* itself, & find the sun," Emerson had written in his journal. "But long after we have thought we were recovered & sane, light breaks in upon us & we find we have yet had no sane moment. Another morn rises on mid-noon." That final Miltonic allusion (along with its demonic counterpart, "under every deep a lower deep opens") may be regarded as a slightly more cheerful version of the staircase image that opens "Experience": it combines the suggestion of interminability with the suggestion that with each new layer of experience there is at least a widening of circumference or gain in wisdom. As Emerson says later on in the essay, "the years teach much that the days never know." Unfortunately, this wisdom clarifies only the past; each new situation finds us blundering like novices. "The individual is always mistaken." This melancholy but resigned conclusion resembles the opinion Yeats expresses in *Per Amica Silentia Lunae*, that since no disaster in life is exactly like another, there must always be "new bitterness, new disappointment";[18] it is perhaps even closer to the remark made by a contemporary Zen master, Shunryu Suzuki, to the effect that the life of a Zen master in pursuit of enlightenment "could be said to be so many years of *shoshaku jushaku*—'to succeed wrong with wrong,' or one continuous mistake."[19]

It is important to realize that at this point in the essay Emerson is *not* contrasting the wisdom that comes from experience with the higher wisdom that comes from consciousness. He is exploring a curious paradox that exists within experience itself. "All our days are so unprofitable while they pass, that 'tis wonderful where or when we ever got anything of this which we call wisdom, poetry, virtue. We never got it on any dated calendar day." The contrast between the pettiness of our daily lives and the accumulated wisdom that somehow results from them is so vast that even a resolute empiricist will be driven to mythology or fiction to account for it. "Some heavenly days must have been intercalated somewhere, like those that Hermes won with the dice of the Moon, that Osiris might be born."

Yet the cruelest feature of experience is the power it possesses of alienating *us* not only from our perceptions and our interpretations but even from our own sorrows:

> What opium is instilled into all disaster! It shows formidable
> as we approach it, but there is at last no rough rasping friction,
> but the most slippery sliding surfaces; we fall soft on a thought;
> *Ate Dea* is gentle,—
>
> > "*Over men's heads walking aloft,*
> > *With tenderfeet treading so soft.*"

People grieve and bemoan themselves, but it is not half so bad
with them as they say. There are moods in which we court
suffering, in the hope that here we shall find reality, sharp peaks
and edges of truth. But it turns out to be only scene-painting and
counterfeit. The only thing grief has taught me, is to know how
shallow it is. That, like all the rest, plays about the surface, and
never introduces me into the reality, for contact with which we
would even pay the costly price of sons and lovers. Was it
Boscovich who found out that bodies never come in contact?
Well, souls never touch their objects. An innavigable sea washes
with silent waves between us and the things we aim at and
converse with. Grief too will make us idealists. In the death of my
son, now more than two years ago, I seem to have lost a beautiful
estate,—no more. I cannot get it nearer to me. If tomorrow I
should be informed of the bankruptcy of my principle debtors,
the loss of my property would be a great inconvenience to me,
perhaps, for many years; but it would leave me as it found me,—
neither better nor worse. So it is with this calamity; it does not
touch me; something which I fancied was a part of me, which
could not be torn away without tearing me nor enlarged without
enriching me, falls off and leaves no scar. It was caducous. I grieve
that grief can teach me nothing, nor carry me one step into real
nature. The Indian who was laid under a curse that the wind
should not blow to him, nor fire burn him, is a type of us all. The
dearest events are summer-rain and we the Para coats that shed
every drop. Nothing is left us now but death. We look to that
with a grim satisfaction, saying, There at least is a reality that will
not dodge us.

I have quoted the whole of this magnificent passage because it is chiefly in its
cumulative force that it achieves its great and disturbing power over us. I
have never yet read a commentary on it that I thought did justice to the
peculiar kind of shock it administers to the reader who is encountering the
essay for the first time. The casual brutality of the sentence in which
Emerson introduces the death of his son *as an illustration* is unmatched by
anything I know of in literature, unless it is the parenthetical remark in which
Virginia Woolf reports the death of Mrs. Ramsay in the "Time Passes"
section of *To the Lighthouse*.

Not that the unreality or numbness Emerson reports is itself shocking.
Many writers before and after Emerson have said as much. A similar
experience forms the subject of Dickinson's chilling lyric, "After great pain,

a formal feeling comes"; it is also analyzed in a passage of Sir Thomas Browne's *Hydrotaphia* from which Emerson had copied sentences into one of his early journals. "There is no antidote against the Opium of time," Browne reminds us, and then goes on to say:

> Darknesse and light divide the course of time, and oblivion shares with memory a great part even of our living beings; we slightly remember our felicities, and the smartest stroaks of affliction leave but short smart upon us. Sense endureth no extremities, and sorrows destroy us or themselves. To weep into stones are fables. Afflictions induce callosities, miseries are slippery, or fall like snow upon us, which notwithstanding is no unhappy stupidity. To be ignorant of evils to come, and forgetfull of evils past, is a mercifull provision in nature, whereby we digest the mixture of our few and evil dayes, and our delivered senses not relapsing into cutting remembrances, our sorrows are not kept raw by the edge of repetitions.[20]

The whole passage, even down to the details of its tactile imagery, is a striking anticipation of "Experience." Yet the differences are as noteworthy as the similarities. The slipperiness of misery, which Browne calls a "mercifull provision in nature," is for Emerson "the most unhandsome part of our condition." And this is so because Emerson, unlike Browne, sees in the unreality of grief only an intensification of our normal state of alienation or dislocation from the world our senses perceive. This distance—the "innavigable sea" that washes between us and the world—is the real torture. If grief could relieve it, if suffering could introduce us to the reality behind the glittering and evanescent phenomena, we would welcome it. For contact with that reality we would be *willing* to pay (as Emerson says in what is surely the most chilling of all his hyperboles) "even the costly price of sons and lovers."

But grief proves to be as shallow as everything else. In a letter written a week after the death of his son Emerson laments: "Alas! I chiefly grieve that I cannot grieve; that this fact takes no more deep hold than other facts, is as dreamlike as they; a lambent flame that will not burn playing on the surface of my river. Must every experience—those that promised to be dearest & most penetrative,—only kiss my cheek like the wind & pass away? I think of Ixion & Tantalus & Kehama." "Kehama" is an allusion to Robert Southey's long narrative poem *The Curse of Kehama*, in which a virtuous character named Ladurlad is laid under a curse by the wicked ruler Kehama, who, though himself a mere mortal, has learned to wrest such power from the gods that he is able to send a burning fire into Ladurlad's heart and brain, and at the same time order the elements to flee from him. As Ladurlad laments:

> The Winds of Heaven must never breathe on me;
>   The Rains and Dews must never fall on me;
> Water must mock my thirst and shrink from me;
>   The common earth must yield no fruit to me;
> Sleep, blessed Sleep! must never light on me;
>   And Death, who comes to all, must fly from me,
> And never, never set Ladurlad free.[21]

Ladurlad is the "Indian" mentioned in "Experience": in making him a "type of us all" Emerson gives us his grimmest assessment of the human condition: an endless, goalless pilgrimage, driven by an inner but unquenchable fire through a world that recedes perpetually before the pilgrim. The bitter lesson we learn from experience is the soul's imperviousness to experiences. The traumas are not traumatic. "The dearest events are summer-rain, and we the Para coats that shed every drop." If we look forward with a "grim satisfaction" to death, it is because it is the one event in life that we can be sure will not slip through our fingers. "There at least is a reality that will not dodge us."

Yet the central portion of the passage is the most explicitly self-lacerating. In observing that grief, like poetry or religion, convinces us of the insubstantiality of the phenomenal world, in offering as evidence for this assertion his own imperviousness to the death of his son, whose loss he likens, with deliberate vulgarity, to the loss of an estate, Emerson is indulging in a candor so "dreadful" (as Bishop puts it) that it has driven more than one critic to suppose that he either did not mean what he said or else was unaware of his meaning.[22]

Part of the problem comes from the difficulty of determining Emerson's tone in the passage. Bishop has pointed out Emerson's fondness for what he calls "tonal puns." He instances a sentence from *The Conduct of Life*: "Such as you are, the gods themselves could not help you." Bishop says: "One can hear a voice that says this insultingly and another voice, intimate and quiet, that says it encouragingly."[23] But he confesses that sentences like "*Ate Dea* is gentle" and "Grief too will make us idealists" and "I cannot get it nearer to me" leave him puzzled. Are they straightforward or ironical, desperate or resigned?[24] The answer, I think, is that we *can* imagine a voice that says all of these things with bitter irony, but that we can also imagine them being said in a voice as toneless and detached as that of a witness giving evidence in a war crimes trial, or that of the wasted and suffering discharged soldier whom Wordsworth questions about his experiences in Book IV of *The Prelude*:

> ... in all he said
> There was a strange half-absence, as of one
> Knowing too well the importance of his theme
> But feeling it no longer.[25]

Emerson is driven to offer his testimony by an inner necessity. I admire Maurice Gonnaud's fine remark about this compulsion: "The greatness of an essay like 'Experience' lies, I suggest, in our sense of the author's being engaged in a pursuit of truth which has all the characters of faith except its faculty of radiating happiness."[26]

What sharpens the sting of the revelations is Emerson's tacit acknowledgment, through his phrasing and imagery, that fate itself has retroactively conferred upon some brave assertions of the past the one kind of irony it was beyond his power to intend. Thus "grief too will make us idealists" both echoes and answers a journal entry of 1836 in which Emerson was working out the concepts that later became part of the sixth chapter of *Nature*: "Religion makes us idealists. Any strong passion does. The best, the happiest moments of life are these delicious awakenings of the higher powers & the reverential withdrawing of nature before its god." His remark that his relationship to his son proved to be "caducous" recalls a happy declaration, made after the departure of some friends in August of 1837, that he had faith in the soul's powers of infinite regeneration: "these caducous relations are in the soul like leaves ... & how often soever they are lopped off, yet still it renews them ever." Even more chilling is the prophetic remark he made to Jones Very during the latter's visit in 1838: "I told Jones Very that I had never suffered, & that I could scarce bring myself to feel a concern for the safety & life of my nearest friends that would satisfy them: that I saw clearly that if my wife, my child, my mother, should be taken from me, I should still remain whole with the same capacity of cheap enjoyment from all things." There is a kind of self-contempt in this passage; Emerson had already survived so many losses that he felt confident in predicting his response to more. But this passage was written when little Waldo was barely two. In the intervening years—years in which Emerson had delightedly recorded his small son's doings and sayings in his otherwise austerely intellectual journal—he had evidently come to hope that this relationship was somehow different, that it was something that "could not be torn away without tearing me nor enlarged without enriching me."

Alas. Though Elizabeth Hoar's brother Rockwood "was never more impressed with a human expression of agony than by that of Emerson leading the way into the room where little Waldo lay dead,"[27] Rusk tells us, Emerson discovered to his sorrow that the prophecy he had made in 1838 was true. In his young manhood he had been greatly stirred by the remark of a Methodist farmer he worked with one summer that men were always praying and that their prayers were always answered. "Experience" records Emerson's grim awareness that the price you pay for invulnerability is invulnerability.

The passages here recanted were all confined to Emerson's private journals—a fact that helps explain why the opening pages of "Experience," almost alone among Emerson's works, give the impression of being not heard but overheard. But these privately recorded passages are not the only ones to be so retracted. Nearly every critic of the essay has pointed out the connection between some detail of its imagery or argument and those of an earlier work that it systematically recants or retracts. Thus the opening question—"Where do we find ourselves?"—when compared to the boldness of *Nature*'s opening—"Let us inquire, to what end is nature?"—suggests the bewilderment that has overtaken this latter-day Oedipus as he turns from riddle solving to self-examination. The opening image of an endless staircase recalls the "mysterious ladder" of "Circles," but where the latter saw a new prospect of power from every rung, "Experience" sees only repetition and exhaustion. Idiosyncrasy or subjectivity, which in "Self-Reliance" was felt to be the source of one's chief value, now becomes part of the limitation of temperament, which shut us out from every truth our "colored and distorting lenses" cannot transmit. The horizon that in "Circles" was a promise of perpetual expansion has now become merely a metaphor for frustration: "Men seem to have learned of the horizon the art of perpetual retreating and reference." In *Nature* Emerson was a Transparent Eye-ball; in "Experience" he is shut in "a prison of glass which [he] cannot see." The "noble doubt" whether nature outwardly exists, the exhilarating suggestion that perhaps the whole of the outward universe is only a projection from the apocalypse of the mind, has become in "Experience" the Fall of Man.[28]

But if "Experience" is in one way a palinode, it is in another way a continuation, under grimmer conditions, of the faith Emerson had never relinquished. That faith first enters the essay only as a kind of recoil against the reductiveness of the argument in the section devoted to temperament. Life is a string of moods, each showing only what lies in its focus; temperament is the iron wire on which these beads are strung. "Men resist the conclusion in the morning, but adopt it as the evening wears on, that temper prevails over everything of time, place, and condition, and is inconsumable in the flames of religion."

Yet in the midst of this determinism Emerson suddenly pauses to note the "capital exception" every man makes to general or deterministic laws—that is, himself. Although every man believes every other to be "a fatal partialist," he never sees himself as anything other than a "universalist." (In a similar passage later on in the essay Emerson will observe that we make the same exception to moral laws, which is why no man can believe that "the crime in him is as black as in the felon.") In "Circles" Emerson had noted that "every man supposes himself not to be fully understood; and if there is any truth in him, if he rests at last on the divine soul, I see not how it can be otherwise. The last chamber, the last closet, he must feel was never opened; there is always a residuum unknown, unanalyzable. That is, every man believes he has a greater possibility." However much we may appear to one another as creatures limited by a given temperament, bound by the "links of the chain of physical necessity," the very fact that our consciousness rebels utterly at such a description of *ourselves* is the best evidence we have of the falsity of the doctrine. On its own level—the level of nature, of experience—temperament may be final, relativism inescapable.

> But it is impossible that the creative power should exclude itself. Into every intelligence there is a door which is never closed, through which the creator passes. The intellect, seeker of absolute truth, or the heart, lover of absolute good, intervenes for our succor, and at one whisper of these high powers we awake from our ineffectual struggles with this nightmare. We hurl it into its own hell, and cannot again contract ourselves to so base a state.

Yet this recovery, though it suggests the direction the essay will take, is by no means a final triumph over the lords of life. After Temperament there is Succession, by which Emerson means both the succession of "moods"—which he has already discussed—and the succession of "objects." The succession of moods is something we suffer; the succession of objects is something we choose. "We need change of objects." Our hunger for the whole keeps us restlessly searching through the world of experience in pursuit of a final consummation forever denied us. But if there are no final satisfactions, there are at least partial ones. In *The American Scholar* Emerson had compared inspiration to the "one central fire which flaming now out of the lips of Etna, lightens the capes of Sicily; and now out of the throat of Vesuvius, illuminates the towers and vineyards of Naples." The image he uses in "Experience" is considerably less apocalyptic, but the faith it expresses is the same: "Like a bird which alights nowhere, but hops

perpetually from bough to bough, is the Power which abides in no man and
no woman, but for a moment speaks from this one, and for another from that
one."

The essay by this point seems to have established a pattern—a dip into
despair, followed by a recoil of hope. But suddenly and unexpectedly
Emerson turns on himself and his method: "what help from these fineries or
pedantries? What help from thought? Life is not/dialectics." This yawing
back and forth between despair and hope is not, after all, how we spend most
of our time. "Life is not intellectual or critical, but sturdy." Some way must
be found to redeem the time, to treat it as something other than an emptiness
separating moments of vision. "To fill the hour,—that is happiness; to fill the
hour and leave no crevice for a repentance or an approval. We live amid
surfaces, and the true art of life is to skate well on them." In these sentences
we hear a different voice emerging, a voice that will become stronger in
"Montaigne" and dominant in a book like *English Traits*. It is the voice of
strong common sense, giving a view of the world Emerson had indeed
expressed earlier, in things like the "Commodity" chapter of *Nature* and in
essays like "Prudence" and "Compensation," but had never before offered as
a serious *alternative* to the world of Reason. Now, for the first time, he
proposes the "mid-world" as something other than a step on the way to
vision.

Yet the mid-world offers no permanent anchorage either; moments of
illumination will return whether we want them to or not, upsetting all our
resolutions to keep "due metes and bounds." "Underneath the inharmonious
and trivial particulars, is a musical perfection, the Ideal journeying always
with us, the heaven without rent or seam." This region is something we do
not make, but find, and when we find it all the old exhilaration returns. We
respond with joy and amazement to the opening of "this august
magnificence, old with the love and homage of innumerable ages, young with
the life of life, the sunbright Mecca of the desert. And what a future it opens!
I feel a new heart beating with the love of the new beauty. I am ready to die
out of nature and be born again into this new yet unapproachable America I
have found in the West."

For a vision of life that assessed man only from the platform of
"experience" would leave out half his nature. "If I have described life as a flux
of moods, I must now add that there is that in us which changes not and
which ranks all sensations and states of mind." This something is the "central
life" mentioned at the end of "Circles," the center that contains all possible
circumferences. "The consciousness in each man is a sliding scale, which
identifies him now with the First Cause, and now with the flesh of his body;
life above life, in infinite degrees." Different religions have given this First

Cause different names—Muse, Holy Ghost, *nous*, love—but Emerson confesses that he likes best the one ventured by the Chinese sage Mencius: "vast-flowing vigor." Asked what he means by this, Mencius describes it as the power that can "fill up the vacancy between heaven and earth" and that "leaves no hunger." With this definition we have come as far as possible from the terminal exhaustion and depletion of the essay's opening paragraphs: "we have arrived as far as we can go. Suffice it for the joy of the universe that we have arrived not at a wall, but at interminable oceans. Our life seems not so much present as prospective; not for the affairs on which it is wasted, but as a hint of this vast-flowing vigor."

But if this is the end of the dialectic, it is not the end of the essay, which—like life itself—will not let us remain in any state of illumination for long. We are brought back to the mid-world in a paragraph that summarizes all that has come before:

> It is very unhappy, but too late to be helped, the discovery we have made that we exist. That discovery is called the Fall of Man. Ever afterwards we suspect our instruments. We have learned that we do not see directly but mediately, and that we have no means of correcting these colored and distorting lenses which we are, or of computing the amount of their errors. Perhaps these subject-lenses have a creative power; perhaps there are no objects. Once we lived in what we saw; now, the rapaciousness of this new power, which threatens to absorb all things, engages us. Nature, art, persons, letters, religions, objects, successively tumble in, and God is but one of its ideas.

As Michael Cowan notes, this investigation of Subjectiveness in some ways "represents a spiralling back to the lord of Illusion, but now seen from the viewpoint of the saved rather than the damned imagination."[29] What has made the difference is the discovery that there is an irreducible something in the soul that rebels fiercely at any attempt to reduce it to a mere "bundle of perceptions," and that is hence the best proof that any such definition is false. Knowing that the soul retains even in its grimmest moments "a door which is never closed, through which the creator passes" is the saving revelation that transforms the hell of Illusion into the purgatory of Subjectiveness. We are still unable to transcend the limitations of our vision, but now we seem not so much cut off from the real as the unconscious progenitors of it. Our "subject-lenses," unlike the object-lenses of a telescope or microscope, do not merely magnify reality, they determine its characteristics: "the chagrins which the bad heart gives off as bubbles, at once take form as ladies and gentlemen in the street, shopmen or barkeepers in hotels, and threaten or insult whatever is threatenable or insultable in us." This is a trivial example of a principle, anything but trivial, whose gradual triumph one can witness in the history of the race. Realism is the philosophical system of every primitive tribe, but as civilization advances, men come gradually to suspect that as it is the eye that makes the horizon, so it is the beholder who creates the things he perceives.

It is not to be denied that there is something melancholy about such self-awareness. In a lecture entitled "The Present Age," delivered in 1837, Emerson expresses the traditional Romantic envy of those luckier ages that lived in what they saw:

> Ours is distinguished from the Greek and Roman and Gothic ages, and all the periods of childhood and youth by being the age of the second thought. The golden age is gone and the silver is gone—the blessed eras of unconscious life, of intuition, of genius.... The ancients were self-united. We have found out the difference of outer and inner. They described. We reason. They acted. We philosophise.

The act of reflection severs us as with an "innavigable sea" from the "things we aim at and converse with," and at the same time plants in our minds the suspicion that these things, which *feel* so distant, may not be "out there" at all. On this point modern empiricism and idealism coincide. Hume wrote: "Let us fix our attention out of ourselves as much as possible: Let us chace our imagination to the heavens, or to the utmost limits of the universe; we can never really advance a step beyond ourselves, nor can conceive of any kind of existence, but those perceptions, which have appear'd in that narrow compass."[30] As Emerson remarked of a similar passage from the materialist Condillac, "what more could an idealist say?"

This imprisonment has some lamentable consequences, as Emerson is the first to acknowledge, for the kingdoms of mortal friendship and of love. "Marriage (in which is called the spiritual world) is impossible, because of the inequality between every subject and every object.... There will be the same gulf between every me and every thee as between the original and the picture." For the soul, though it incarnates itself in time as an ordinary mortal with ordinary limitations, is in fact "of a fatal and universal power, *admitting no co-life*" (emphasis added). To say this is to push one's philosophy considerably beyond antinomianism; it ought logically to lead to a state in which everything—theft, arson, murder—is permitted. Emerson does not attempt to refute this objection. Instead (in what is surely one of the more audacious gestures in American literature) he coolly embraces it. That crime occurs at all is the best evidence we have of our unshakable belief in the divinity of the self. "It is an instance of our faith in ourselves that men never speak of crime as lightly as they think.... Murder in the murderer is no such ruinous thought as poets and romancers will have it; it does not unsettle him or fright him from his ordinary notice of trifles; it is an act quite easy to be contemplated." Our reasons for abstaining from murder are (by a nice irony) purely empirical, derived from experience: "in its sequel [murder] turns out to be a horrible confounding of all relations." Emerson's own version of the categorical imperative derives from the same ontology. Just as the highest praise we can offer any artist is to think that he actually possessed the thought with which he has inspired us, so the highest tribute we can pay to a fellow human being is to assume that his exterior—which must remain to us merely a part of the phenomenal—conceals a Deity as central to itself as our own. "Let us treat the men and women well; treat them as if they were real; perhaps they are."

We have here reached the shadowy ground where philosophy and psychology merge. In the letter to Margaret Fuller quoted earlier Emerson had claimed that the Berkleian philosophy was the clue to his nature *and relations*. Idealism as a philosophical doctrine appealed to him partly because it offered a credible way of accounting for the loneliness and isolation to which he felt temperamentally condemned. In 1851, after a rambling talk with Thoreau in which both of them had "stated over again, to sadness, almost, the Eternal loneliness," Emerson exclaimed, "how insular & pathetically solitary, are all the people we know!" We are inclined to try to find excuses for our separation from others, but in more honest moments we admit the grimmer truth: "the Sea, vocation, poverty, are seeming fences, but Man is insular and cannot be touched. Every man is an infinitely repellent orb, and holds his individual being on that condition." Existence for each of us is a drama played out in a private theater that admits only one spectator:

> Men generally attempt early in life to make their brothers first, afterwards their wives, acquainted with what is going forward in their private theater, but they soon desist from the attempt on finding that they also have some farce or perhaps some ear- & heart-rending tragedy forward on their secret boards on which they are intent, and all parties acquiesce at last in a private box with the whole play performed before him Bolus.

The same haunting notion prompts the question that closes this section of "Experience": "How long before our masquerade will end its noise of tambourines, laughter and shouting, and we will find it was a solitary performance?"

It is true, as Emerson says, that the muses of love and religion hate these developments. But our inescapable subjectivity has its own compensations. The "sharp peaks and edges of truth" we had hoped to find in reality we discover at last in the soul. God himself is "the native of these bleak rocks," an insight that "makes in morals the capital virtue of self-trust. We must hold hard to this poverty, however scandalous, and by more vigorous self-recoveries, after the sallies of action, possess our axis more firmly. The life of truth is cold and so far mournful; but it is not the slave of tears, contritions, and perturbations. It does not attempt another's work, nor adopt another's facts." As James Cox notes, "if 'Self-Reliance' was a ringing exhortation to trust the self, 'Experience' turns out to disclose that, after the last disillusion, there is nothing to rely on *but* the self.[31]

And the sunbright Mecca of the West? The New Jerusalem, the kingdom of man over nature? What has become of it? In a journal Emerson had once noted sadly that "it takes a great deal of elevation of thought to produce a very little elevation of life.... Gradually in long years we bend our living to our idea. But we serve seven years & twice seven for Rachel." In "Experience" Emerson admits that he has served his time—"I am not the novice I was fourteen, nor yet seven years ago"—and still must be content only with Leah. "Let who will ask, Where is the fruit? I find a private fruit sufficient." This private fruit is, as Yoder says, "consciousness without correspondent results"[32]—but I think it is not quite true to say that it is the only paradise offered us after the circuitous journey of "Experience." The view from Pisgah is as clear as it ever was.

In a letter to Margaret Fuller written to mark the second anniversary of his son's death Emerson declared himself no closer to reconciling himself to the calamity than when it was new, and compared himself to a poor Irishman who, when a court case went against him, said to the judge, "I am not satisfied." The senses have a right to perfection as well as the soul, and the soul will never rest content until these "ugly breaks" can be prevented. The attitude of defiance and the feeling of impotence recall a famous journal entry written a few months after his son's death. Speaking of Christ's sacrifice, he says:

> He did well. This great Defeat is hitherto the highest fact we
> have. But he that shall come shall do better. The mind requires a
> far higher exhibition of character, one which shall make itself

good to the senses as well as the soul. This was a great Defeat. We demand Victory.

If it is not clear how long we will have to wait for this victory, how wide is the distance between ourselves and the Promised Land, Emerson refuses to give up hope. "Patience and patience, we shall win at the last." Experience may counsel only despair, "but in the solitude to which every man is always returning" there is a "sanity" that gives a very different kind of advice. "Never mind the ridicule, never mind the defeat; up again, old heart!—it seems to say." The "romance" that fled from our ship at the beginning of "Experience" returns at the end to become the goal of our weary but still hopeful pilgrimage. The "true romance which the world exists to realize"— the point at which desire and fact, the pleasure principle and the reality principle, will coincide "will be the transformation of genius into practical power.

Yet the ending of "Experience," if it restates the old hope—or at least restates the impossibility of giving it up—hardly leaves us cheered. As Firkins says, "the victory is gained in the end, idealism is reestablished, but the world in which its authority is renewed looks to the common eye like a dismantled, almost a dispeopled, universe."[33] After such knowledge, what consolation?

Emerson develops two main answers to his question in the decade of the 1840s, one of them given in "The Poet," the other in "Montaigne." Both are attempts to find some sort of "paradise within" to compensate the individual for his loss of Eden and for his failure to reach the New Jerusalem. One is designed to satisfy the Reason, the other the Understanding. (The very fact that this distinction still remains is a sign that the consolations offered are clearly thought of as *second bests*.[34]) And both essays, in their imagery and structure, show that by now Emerson's four fables— contraction, dislocation, ossification, and reflection—have become a system of significances as useful to him as the Biblical stories had been to his ancestors: a series of types or analogies by which the chaotic impressions of experience could be ordered and understood.

NOTES

1. Firkins, *Ralph Waldo Emerson*, p. 112.

2. Alfred Lord Tennyson, "Ulysses," lines 18–21, in *The Poems of Tennyson*, ed. Christopher Ricks (New York: W. W. Norton & Co., 1972), p. 563.

3. "The Holy Grail," lines 438–439, from *Idylls of the King*, in *Poems of Tennyson*, p. 1674.

4. Beard, American Nervousness, p. 9.

5. George M. Beard, A Practical Treatise on Nervous Exhaustion (Neurasthenia) Its Symptoms, Nature, Sequences, Treatment (New York: William Wood & Co., 1880), p. 66.

6. Chapman, *Selected Writings*, p. 163.

7. Firkins, *Ralph Waldo Emerson*, p. 239.

8. Albert Abrams, *The Blues (Splanchnic Neurasthenia): Causes and Cures*, 2nd. ed., enlarged (New York: E. B. Treat & Co., 1905) p. 16.

9. Whicher, *Freedom and Fate*, p. 15.

10. David Hume, "Of Miracles," in *An Enquiry Concerning Human Understanding*, in: *Essays, Moral, Political, and Literary*, ed. T. H. Green and T. H. Grose, 2 vols. (London: Longmans, Green, & Co., 1875), I, 91–92.

11. Whicher, *Freedom and Fate*, p. 16.

12. Cavell, *The Senses of Walden*, p. 125.

13. Porte, *Representative Man*, p. 181, n. 10.

14. David Hume, A Treatise of Human Nature, Being an Attempt to Introduce the Experimental Method of Reasoning into Moral Subjects, ed. T. H. Green and T. H. Grose, 2 vols. (London: Longmans, Green, & Co., 1898), I, 311.

15. Ibid., I, 311–312.

16. Ibid., I, 311.

17. Chaucer, *Troilus and Criseyde*, Bk. 2, line 1107.

18. W. B. Yeats, *Per Amica Silentia Lunae* (London: Macmillan & Co., 1918), p. 41.

19. Shunryu Suzuki, *Zen Mind, Beginner's Mind*, ed. Trudy Dixon, with an introduction by Richard Baker (New York: John Weatherhill, 1970), p. 35.

20. Hydrotaphia: Urne-Burial, or, A Brief Discourse of the Sepulchral Urnes Lately Found in Norfolk (1658), in Sir Thomas Browne: Selected Writings, ed. Sir Geoffrey Keynes (Chicago: University of Chicago Press, 1968), pp. 150, 152. Among the sentences Emerson copied were "There is no antidote against the Opium of time," and "miseries are slippery, or fall like snow upon us, which notwithstanding is no unhappy stupidity." See JMN, III, 219–220.

21. *The Poetical Works of Robert Southey*, 10 vols. (London: Longman, Orme, Brown, Green, & Longmans, 1840), VIII, 21.

22. Bishop, *Emerson on the Soul*, p. 198.

23. Ibid., p. 139.

24. Ibid., pp. 196–197.

25. Wordsworth, *The Prelude*, 1850 version, Bk. 4, lines 442–445.

26. Gonnaud, *Emerson: Prophecy*, pp. 121–122.

27. Rusk, *Life*, p. 294.

28. See Bishop, *Emerson on the Soul*, pp. 193–194; Porte, *Representative Man*, p. 182; Whicher, *Freedom and Fate*, p. 121. For additional examples, see Yoder, *Orphic Poet*, pp. 45, 48.

29. Michael Cowan, *City of the West: Emerson, America, and Urban Metaphor* (New Haven, Conn.: Yale University Press, 1967), p. 120. Cowan's reading of "Experience" is excellent.

30. Hume, Treatise of Human Nature, p. 371.

31. Cox, *Emerson: Prophecy*, p. 80.

32. Yoder, *Orphic Poet*, p. 46.

33. Firkins, *Ralph Waldo Emerson*, p. 194.

34. Whicher points out that Emerson's later thought is "characteristically an affirmation of a *second best*." *Freedom and Fate*, p. 126.

JULIE ELLISON

Detachment and Transition

I have followed Emerson's example in describing in Romantic terms the sensations produced by reading his prose. For just as he knowingly reflects on his anti-authoritarian hermeneutics in certain of his fables, so he represents, in other parables, ideas about composition and style that utilize a variety of Romantic aesthetic notions. The relationship between the drama of interpretation enacted throughout the essays and the thematic values Emerson ascribes to stylistic features is very close. His fluctuating emotions about the nature and extent of the author's intellectual control of his tradition are repeated in allegories about the interaction between words and thoughts, discontinuity and teleology, purposiveness and surprise. He manages to convince me, at least, that his style successfully gratifies his desire for both conscious power over his material and the feeling of being surprised by it. He addresses our sense of the apparent randomness of his prose by repeatedly telling us what randomness signifies; he advances but also skeptically criticizes periodic claims to order. Such meditations focus on the metaphoric opposition of objects and energy and, analogously, of detachment and transition.

These patterns emerge in a characteristic fable. Emerson justifies his own practice of assembling essays from journal entries by attributing this

From *Emerson's Romantic Style*. © 1984 by Princeton University Press.

method to all artists. Initially, he praises stylistic discontinuity resulting from
the separate origins of a work's parts:

> by a multitude of trials & a thousand rejections & the using &
> perusing of what was already written ... a poem made that shall
> thrill the world by the mere juxtaposition & interaction of lines
> & sentences that singly would have been of little worth & short
> date. Rightly is this art named composition & the composition
> has manifold the effect of the component parts. The orator is
> nowise equal to the evoking on a new subject of this brilliant
> chain of sentiments, facts, illustrations whereby he now fires
> himself & you. Every link in this living chain he found separate;
> one, ten years ago; one, last week; some of them he found in his
> fathers house or at school when a boy; some of them by his losses;
> some of them by his sickness; some by his sins. The Webster with
> whom you talk admires the oration almost as much as you do, &
> knows himself to be nowise equal, unarmed, that is, without this
> tool of Synthesis to the splendid effect which he is yet well
> pleased you should impute to him.
>
> No hands could make a watch. The hands brought dry sticks
> together & struck the flint with iron or rubbed sticks for fire &
> melted the ore & with stones made crow bar & hammer these
> again helped to make chisel & file, rasp & saw, piston & boiler, &
> so the watch & the steam engine are made, which the hands could
> never have produced & these again are new tools to make still
> more recondite & prolific instruments. So do the collated
> thoughts beget more & the artificially combined individuals have
> in addition to their own a quite new collective power. The main
> is made up of many islands, the state of many men. The poem of
> many thoughts each of which, in its turn, filled the whole sky of
> the poet was day & Being to him. (*JMN*.V.39–40)

Journal keeping—"the using & perusing of what was ... written ... ten years
ago" or "last week"—initiates the "art named composition." Sentences record
"sentiments, facts, illustrations" that have been lifted out of the continuum of
experience, have "filled the whole sky of the poet," were "day & Being to
him." The author must link these in a "living chain" without diminishing
their individual integrity as moments. The separate genesis of "lines &
sentences" makes possible juxtaposition, in which they creatively clash with
each other and generate the "power" that "fires" the reader or listener.

This parable metaphorically represents the interaction of subject matter and imagination as the symbiotic relationship between objects and energy. Fragments of experience ("sentiments, facts, illustrations") and of prose ("lines & sentences") correspond to raw materials: dry sticks, flint, iron, stones, tools. Authorial intelligence is represented by energy: hands, fire, steam. The "living chain" of imaginative prose is a chain reaction between the two. Later in the passage, the ocean's flow, a collective political will, the poet's active mind transform into new wholes isolated islands, men, and thoughts. But Emerson's metaphor undergoes a significant change as he feels his way through this meditation. "Mere juxtaposition" gives way to "Synthesis" and an allegory of technological progress. He begins by celebrating the "splendid effect" of random combination. But open-ended process becomes teleological through shifts in metaphor. Oscillation becomes progressive, as in the famous dictum from "Self-Reliance": "Power ... resides in the moment of transition from a past to a new state, in the shooting of the gulf, in the darting to an aim" (*CW*.II.40). The privileged term ceases to be "transition" and becomes "aim."

In a lecture of the same year as the "tool of Synthesis" passage, Emerson criticizes Bacon's failure to use that tool:

> Bacon's method is not within the work itself, but without. This might be expected in his *Natural History* but ... in his *Essays* it is the same. All his work lies along the ground a vast unfinished city. He did not arrange but unceasingly collect facts. His own Intellect often acts little on what he collects. Very much stands as he found it—mere lists of facts.... The fire has hardly passed over it and given it fusion and a new order from his mind. It is sand without lime ... thrown together; the order of a shop and not that of a tree or an animal where perfect assimilation has taken place and all the parts have a perfect unity. (*EL*.I.335)

Again we find the dichotomy between matter and fire, "facts" and intellect. Their ideal relationship is the organic fusion of a tree's or an animal's "perfect assimilation." The opposite image of a "vast unfinished city" bears witness to repeated beginnings never completed, a nightmare vision of the technological miracles praised in the other passage. Nostalgia for the organic enters in response to an unending series like the desire for the unifying absolute of the sublime. We glimpse the anxiety that frequently leads Emerson to recommend organic synthesis rather than the contrived alternation that potentially leads to "mere lists."

The impulse to sheer away from the constructed nature of his own work surfaces in his equivocations on the writer's self-consciousness. The idea that "composition" involves "a multitude of trials & a thousand rejections & the using & perusing of what was already written" implies that revision is the most creative phase of writing. Our examination of Emerson's own methods bears this out. Yet he then claims that his successes are inadvertent. The author "admires the oration almost as much as you do & knows himself to be nowise equal ... to the splendid effect which he is yet well pleased you should impute to him." The passage shuffles between method and accident, intention and automatism, as he attributes energy to the artist's own mind, then to a spirit within or behind things. "Juxtaposition" generates sparks that surprise even the author. Tools—emblems of human inventiveness—produce effects beyond his control. The brilliant synopsis of technological development from the Stone Age to the Industrial Revolution conveys our perpetual unpreparedness in the face of our "recondite and prolific instruments."

The journal entry written at Nantasket Beach in July 1841 and partly quoted in my introduction brings together with marvelous complexity Emerson's simultaneous desire for knowledge and power, which he represents as repetition and surprise:

> We have two needs Being & Organization. See how much pains we take here in Plato's dialogues to set in order the One Fact in two or three or four steps & renew as oft as we can the pleasure the eternal surprize [sic] of coming at the last fact as children run up steps to jump down or up a hill to coast down on sleds or run far for one slide or as we get fishing tackle & go many miles to a watering place to catch fish and having caught one & learned the whole mystery we still repeat the process for the same result though perhaps the fish are thrown overboard at the last. The merchant plays the same game on Change, the card lover at whist, and what else does the scholar? He knows how the poetry he knows how the novel or the demonstration will affect him no new result but the oldest of all, yet he still craves a new book & bathes himself anew with the plunge at the last. The young men here this morning who have tried all the six or seven things to be done, namely, the sail, the bowling alley, the ride to Hull, and to Cohasset, the bath & the spyglass, they are in a rage just now to *do* something these itching fingers, this short activity, these nerves, this plasticity or creativeness accompanies forever & ever the profound Being. (*JMN*.VIII.12–13)

Emerson's explanation posits an economy of psychic forces. The last sentence suggests that repetition is a discharge of energy. Young men "in a rage ... to *do* something" are flooded with the suprapersonal force of Being, of which they are not conscious and which is consequently beyond their control. They "rage" because they have not yet discovered the pleasures of recurrence. But if they are governed by involuntary motion ("itching fingers" and "nerves"), the scholar "organizes" the pure dynamism of Being by *electing* to repeat himself. Repetition is a complex episode in which consciousness manages to surprise itself—a perfectly ironic and perfectly sublime event. As always in Emerson's writings, surprise is a conscious strategy to replicate unself-consciousness, a borderline state contained in the oxymoron, "eternal surprize." The reader "knows the poetry ... will affect him" with "the oldest of all results" yet "bathes himself anew." An instantaneous change of state yields a split second of illusory newness which, later, he knows as renewal. It is as though there is a momentary lag when memory has not yet caught up to sensation.

As Nietzsche proclaimed in "The Use and Abuse of History" (1873), one of his most Emersonian polemics, "Forgetfulness is a property of all action";[1] Emerson was quite right to assert, in "Memory," "We forget .. according to beautiful laws" (*W*.XII.107). He clearly attributes repetition to the workings of a pleasure principle; he repeats to "renew ... the pleasure, the eternal surprize." "This metonymy, or seeing the same sense in things so diverse, gives a *pure pleasure*," *he writes elsewhere*. "Every one of a million times we find a charm in the metamorphosis" (*W*.VIII.25; emphasis added). Pleasure is a compound of motion and power. The mind's leap in repeated transition is play for its own sake. As with the card player's or financier's calculations, the winnings are irrelevant; "perhaps the fish are thrown overboard at last." Stevens, writing against Freud, would later celebrate the same pleasure in repetition and difference: "Two things of opposite nature seem to depend / On one another.... This is the origin of change / ... cold copulars embrace / and forth the particulars of rapture come" ("Notes toward a Supreme Fiction," Part II, canto iv, ll. 1–6).[2]

Emerson's need for a distance or difference between subject and object, mind and world, reveals how unlike Coleridge he was. Despite the importance of Coleridge to his intellectual development, he never absorbed the English Romantic's desire to interinvolve subject and object organically; rather, he thrives on the almost conflictual difference between them. In another parable, which favors teleology over sheer transition, the action of energy on matter once again represents imaginative process. "Is not poetry the little chamber in the brain," he asks, "where is generated the explosive force which, by gentle shocks, sets in action the intellectual world?" He answers himself by illustrating how consciousness takes up nature and converts it into words in a process which both requires and frees the mind's energy:

> the beholding and co-energizing mind sees the same refining and ascent to the third, the seventh or the tenth power of the daily accidents which the senses report, and which make the raw material of knowledge. It was sensation; when memory came, it was experience; when mind acted, it was knowledge; when mind acted on it as knowledge, it was thought.

"Explosive force" acts on "raw material." When objects are "melted" in the "Promethean alembics" of the mind, they "come out men, and then, melted again, come out words, without any abatement, but with an exaltation of power!" (*W*.VIII.64, 24, 16).

Emerson summarizes his metaphoric system in "Experience": "A subject and an object,—it takes so much to make the galvanic circle complete." The authorial subject is "the conductor of the whole river of electricity" (*W*.III.80, 40). His objects are fragments of writing, the "boulders" or "infinitely repellent particles" that he knows make for his "lapidary style" (*CEC*.185, 303). Emerson's journal entries are substantial, even material, entities. Each of his sentences is "a cube, standing on its bottom like a die, essential and immortal" (*J*.IX.423). It is while writing to Carlyle that he most often objectifies his language. Usually these metaphors are self-deprecating, part of the exchange of apologies and curiously mutual stylistic insults sprinkled throughout their letters. "I dot evermore in my endless journal," he reports, "a line on every unknowable in nature; but the arrangement loiters long, & I get a brick kiln instead of a house." The "little raft" of *Essays, First Series* is "only boards & logs tied together." Carlyle agrees. His correspondent's sentences do not "rightly stick to their foregoers and their followers: the paragraph [is] not as a beaten *ingot*, but as a beautiful square bag of *duck-shot* held together by canvas!" (*CEC*.278, 291, 371).

Emerson restates the metaphor of objects and energy cognitively in terms of the mind's acts of "detachment" and "transition," two of the key terms of his poetics. His artist's first task is identifying and fixing the points between which he will move. "And thou shalt serve the god Terminus, the bounding Intellect, & love Boundary or Form," he instructs the poet (*JMN*.VIII.405). In the following selection from "Art," the starting point can be object, thought, or word, so long as it be detached:

> The virtue of art lies in detachment, in sequestering one object from the embarrassing variety. Until one thing comes out from

the connection of things, there can be enjoyment, contemplation, but no thought.... It is the habit of certain minds to give an all-excluding fulness to the object, the thought, the word, they alight upon, and to make that for the time the deputy of the world.... The power ... to magnify by detaching is the essence of rhetoric in the hands of the orator and the poet. (*CW*.11.211)

Rhetorical power originates in an epiphanic experience of the object when the poet's attentiveness climaxes in a moment of "all-excluding fulness." Having made "a pigment of thought ... palpable and objective," the artist can launch himself toward another position. The "fact" created by objectification becomes a "fulcrum": "Transition is the attitude of power. A fact is only a fulcrum of the spirit. It is the terminus of a past thought, but only a means now of new sallies of the imagination and new progress of wisdom" (*W*.XII.59).

Emerson's ambivalence about detachment is characteristic of Romantic notions of creative thought. Coleridge attributes something like the powers of detachment and transition to the imagination. The secondary imagination, we recall,

dissolves, diffuses, dissipates, in order to re-create; or where this process is rendered impossible, yet still, at all events, it struggles to realize and to unify. It is essentially *vital*, even as all objects (as objects) are essentially fixed and dead.[3]

Coleridge is pessimistic about the possibility of total "recreation." He implies (more darkly than is usually noticed), that "this process" is frequently "rendered impossible." Still, when the imagination cannot win, it should "at all events" struggle with its material. If the Coleridgean imagination fails, what remains is Emerson's terminology of energy (vitality), "fixed and dead" objects, and the continuous oscillation (struggle) between them. Coleridge prefers to focus on the successful acts of re-creation that effect unity in poems, nations, and Christians. But his vision of what happens when the secondary imagination breaks down seems to prophesy the poet who detaches objects rather than dissolves them and juxtaposes thoughts and things instead of "diffusing" them. Emerson's habit of distinguishing objects from energy reverses the strategy of most English Romantics, who envisioned language as living matter or incarnate spirit.[4] He desires the contest between idealizing mind and recalcitrant objects which, to Coleridge, was a poor second best. Like a good American, he identifies power with struggle, self-reliance with rebellion. The poet as liberator cannot afford to "diffuse" his adversary.

In his emphasis on detachment and objectification, Emerson comes closer to the German Romantics than to the English. Detachment was frequently discussed as both a perceptual and an historical phenomenon, "the path along which the individual, as well as the race, must pass." For Schiller, disunity is the moral equivalent of the fall of man. In the naive state, man enjoyed "an undivided sensuous unity." But "once [he] has passed into the state of civilization," art "divides and cleaves him in two."[5] Detachment is agonizingly felt as self-division but is absolutely essential for art. For Schelling, detachment, "definiteness of form," is "never negation but always an affirmation." It is not an historical process but an attribute of nature and the works that seek to represent her: "without bound the boundlessness could not be manifested ... if unity is to be made palpable, this can only be done through singularity, isolation and conflict."[6]

The notion of the detached fragment leads Emerson, as it led Schlegel, to a celebration of irony. Emerson's translation of "Witz" is "whim of will." He characterizes the fragment as an aggressive, self-reliant individual. It is no accident that in "Fate," his exemplar of the sublime is a human fragment, a baby. "I know not what the word *sublime* means," he writes in that essay, "if it be not the intimations, in this infant, of a terrific force.... A little whim of will to be free gallantly contending against the universe of chemistry!" (*W*.VI.29). Compression increases energy, and diminution is an index of heroism, it seems, in people as in prose. The speaker of "Experience" expects to be admired for telling us, "I know better than to claim any completeness for my picture. I am a fragment, and this is a fragment of me" (*W*.III.83).[7] Emerson's irony informs the peculiarly blithe tone of many passages in "Fate": "The way of Providence is a little rude." "The more of these drones perish, the better for the hive." "[I]t would be ... the speediest way of deciding the vote, to put the selectmen or the mayor and aldermen at the hay-scales." "The German and Irish millions, like the Negro, have a great deal of guano in their destiny" (*W*.VI.7, 14, 16). This essay, which is supposed to express the darkening mood of Emerson's middle and later years, is, in fact, dryly humorous. The tension between the themes of repetition (the determinism of fate) and of discontinuity (the human will that defies necessity) results in a celebration of sublime irony:

> here they are, side by side, god and devil, mind and matter, king and conspirator, belt and spasm, riding peacefully together in the brain of every man.

> A man must ride alternately on the horses of his private and his public nature, as the equestrians in the circus throw themselves

nimbly from horse to horse, or plant one foot on the back of one
and the other foot on the back of the other. (*W*.VI.22–23, 47)

In "The Comic," we recall, the "double consciousness" exposes "the radical
joke of life, and then of literature." The simultaneous perception of freedom
and fate is a "radical joke," not tragic knowledge.

In intensifying the struggle between mind and matter, Emerson drew
on quite a different set of sources, nineteenth-century varieties of linguistic
fundamentalism and primitivistic conceptions of the word. In
Swedenborgian cosmology, ideas and words tend toward the condition of
matter but remain sharply distinguished from each other, for correspondence
requires a triple parallelism of nature, thought, and language. The French
Swedenborgian, Oegger, for example, advanced a theory of literal
correspondence between nature and Scripture, even providing a table of
"Hieroglyphic Keys" to facilitate a reading of nature's text.[8] Sampson Reed
dreamed of an ideal state of language in which ideas are one with words and
words "one with things." Human language "being as it were resolved into its
original elements, will lose itself in nature."[9] It is but a short step from the
correspondence of words and things to conceiving of words as thinglike.
Attributing substance to words implies that ideas, too, are discrete entities.

Emerson's conception of detachment combines or reacts to elements of
all these speculations. From the philosophers, he receives the fundamental
notion of detachment as the origin of art and, like them, regards it as both
loss and gain. In order to emphasize transition between detached
perceptions, he increases the materiality of thoughts and words.
Swedenborgianism provides a convenient vocabulary for this, although
Emerson's "transition," as a differentiating movement, undoes the
Swedenborgians' correspondential links. The demand for objects to react
against comes from an antithetical rather than synthetic or Coleridgean
imagination. Emerson's need to represent the unlikeness of words and mind
(objects and energy) reveals the crucial role of difference in repetition. What
is repeated is the "struggle" between different qualities, which strongly
suggests that the motive for repetition is antagonism.

One result of Emerson's conception of the encounter between mind
and matter is that every object comes to stand for the term, "matter." The
aggressive imagination turns the world into a collection of metaphors, all
vehicles for the same tenor. The alternating current of transition can take
place between any two places, things, or persons, if sufficiently detached:

Our strength is transitional, alternating; or, shall I say, a thread of
two strands. The sea-shore, sea seen from shore, shore seen from

sea; the taste of two metals in contact; and our enlarged powers
at the approach and at the departure of a friend; the experience of
poetic creativeness, which is not found in staying at home, nor yet
in travelling, but in transitions from one to the other, which must
therefore be adroitly managed to present as much transitional
surface as possible. (*W*.IV.55–56)

Sea and shore, two metals, two persons must be separate. When the artist
moves through the spaces created by detachment, he cannot be precisely
located. He evades those who would define him and in this elusive freedom
discovers the "enlarged powers" which make possible "the experience of
poetic creativeness." Yet his termini are related by resemblance. Intellect
masters an "embarrassing variety" of objects by discovering that they typify
the same thing. Intense scrutiny transforms the object into a figure for the
world's "central nature." The underlying affinity between the end points of
transition permits Emerson to conceive of transition as metaphor making.

The metamorphosis of nature shows itself in nothing more than
this that there is no word in our language that cannot become
typical to us of nature by giving it emphasis.... The world is a
Dancer; it is a Rosary; it is a Torrent; it is a Boat; a Mist; a Spider's
Snare; it is what you will, and the metaphor will hold, and it will
give the imagination keen pleasure.... [T]he ear instantly hears, &
the spirit leaps to the trope. (*JMN*.VIII.23)

"Emphasis"—that is, detachment or objectification—makes any word
"typical ... of Nature." Detachment entails the perception of the inherently
metaphoric character of words and things which, thus fixed, become the
objects between which "metamorphosis" occurs. (We remember the
connection, in the "Transition" collation, between "transit" and "trope" in
the mind of the reader [*JMN*.X.160].) In "Prospects" at the end of *Nature*,
Emerson announces that the mystery of man's life lies in the "tyrannizing
unity in his constitution, which evermore separates and classifies things,
endeavoring to reduce the most diverse to one form" (*CW*.1.39–40). This
splendidly succinct definition, which ricochets between unity and separation,
reduction and diversity, under the pressure of his drive to embrace them
simultaneously, shows us what metaphor does. A unifying impulse separates
in order to conform what has been sundered to its own vision of unity.
Imagination thus generates discontinuities that only it can heal, a solipsist
exulting in its own deconstructive and reconstructive powers. We can see
how metaphor fits into the paradigm of language as objectification that

"separates and classifies" and as "tyrannizing, endeavoring" energy. This energy enables the writer to contain opposites in the close verbal quarters of a metaphor, where their interaction generates the "explosive force" of language (*W*.VIII.64).

The physics of detachment and transition replicates the strategy we observed at the outset of "The Poet" and other essays. Emerson sets himself against one figure in order to propel himself toward another. He attacks, we found, not in order to attain the object of his desire, but to restore or strengthen his self-regard. In opposition, he feels free, distinct, and individual. His theory of transition accomplishes the same thing. With a remarkable awareness of the thematics of style, he makes fixity a necessary attribute of figurative language. The sensation of power comes in the transition between one momentarily frozen percept and the next, in the instant of undoing their artificial importance. "Man is made for conflict, not for rest," he exclaims. "In action is his power; not in his goals but in his transitions man is great" (*W*.XII.60). In acting to connect two objects, intellect becomes aware of its own energy. Self-consciousness, in turn, brings on "an exaltation" or redundancy "of power" (*W*.VIII.16). The mind discovers that it is greater than the thoughts it entertains; between two ideas is a field of force that contains them both. By continuously separating and rejoining consciousness and its contents, energy and matter, Emerson simultaneously enjoys freedom from and mastery of facts.

The association of transition with power is, of course, conventional. Sudden, even violent transitions between the parts of the ode (turn, counter-turn, stand) had long been thought to be essential to the reader's astonishment and wonder. In the Romantic lyric, the association between discontinuity and greatness persists. Blair found it difficult to condone the fact that the sublime poet is "so abrupt in his transitions; so eccentric and irregular in his motions." But Wordsworth hoped his readers would find in "the transitions and the impassioned music of the versification" of "Tintern Abbey" "the principal requisites" of the ode. [10]

Although in Emerson's formula perpetual transition seems to be brought about by an unlimited supply of metaphoric vehicles, the availability of these vehicles actually depends on the author's "ulterior intellectual perception": "*once seen* ... [metamorphosis] does not stop" (*W*.III.20, 30; emphasis added). Metaphor is not a property of the object but of the observer who

> perceives the independence of the thought on the symbol, the stability of the thought, the accidency and fugacity of the symbol. As the eyes of Lyncaeus were said to see through the earth, so the

poet turns the world to glass, and shows us all things in their right series and procession. (*W*.III.20)

The metaphoric chain reaction is an ongoing act of mastering the object world. Once things are seen through, we are free from them; that is why symbols have the "power of emancipation" and "liberty" for all men (*W*.III.30, 32). Since any word or image can "represent the world," and since transition can occur between any two words or images, the chain reaction can go on forever, fueled by an infinite number of possible substitutions. Emerson "deprives himself of any brake on the transmutation of form," but this is not what bothers him.[11] When he knows himself capable of transition, he can contemplate the possibility of its endless repetition with perfect equanimity. But a series of unrelated objects not bound by organizing energy, the "vast unfinished city" that "lies along the ground," is a different matter. At one moment, detachment is "the measure of all intellectual power" (*W*.XII.39) and at another, an "immense deduction from power" (*W*.XII.44). Pessimistic versions of his fable of mind show us detachment without transition. In these passages, we can trace how he alters his parable to compensate for transit's frequent cessation.

In the absence of energy, solid objects become oppressive. "[I]t is the inert effort of each thought having formed itself into a circular wave of circumstance ... to heap itself on that ridge, and to solidify and hem in the life." The writer cannot muster sufficient force to overcome the inertia of his raw material. "Alas for this infirm faith," Emerson laments, "this will not strenuous, this vast ebb of a vast flow!" (*CW*.II.180–82). He feels that enormous intervals, as well as hypostasis, prevent him from making contact with his material and thus from manipulating it in transitional play. For example, the writings that make up "Natural History of Intellect," from which I cited passages that show his delight in the mind's detaching power, also contain passages like these:

> the discontinuity which perception effects between the mind and the object paralyzes the will.... That indescribably small interval is as good as a thousand miles, and has forever severed the practical unity.... Affection blends, intellect disjoins subject and object. For weal or woe we clear ourselves from the thing we contemplate. We grieve but are not the grief; we love but are not love.

> Continuity is for the great.... what we want is consecutiveness. 'T is with us a flash of light, then a long darkness, then a flash again.

Ah! could we turn these fugitive sparkles into an astronomy of
Copernican worlds. (*W*.XII.44, 52–53)

In good Romantic fashion, he blames self-consciousness ("perception" or
"intellect") for his debility. An "indescribably small interval" appears
immense ("as good as a thousand miles") because the will to span it is
paralyzed. The verbal result of this condition is the remoteness of words
from things; its visual effect, the lack of coincidence between "the axis of
vision" and "the axis of things" (*CW*.1.43).

Frequently, he represents the curse of detachment in compressed
synopses of the passage from a naive to a sentimental condition. In his little
cosmogony in *Nature* ("Man is the dwarf of himself"), the Orphic poet
describes an "interval" that is both spatial and temporal:

> having made for himself this huge shell, his waters retired; he no
> longer fills the veins and veinlets; he is shrunk to a drop. He sees
> that the structure still fits him, but fits him colossally. Say, rather,
> once it fitted him, now it corresponds to him from far and on
> high. (*CW*.I.42)

The same parable that describes the poor fit of man to nature illustrates his
linguistic predicament:

> Language clothes nature as the air clothes the earth, taking the
> exact form & pressure of every object. Only words that are new
> fit exactly the thing, those that are old like old scoriae that have
> been long exposed to the air & sunshine have lost the sharpness
> of their mould & fit loosely. (*JMN*.7.246)

The yearning to eliminate all distance whatsoever by taking "the exact form
and pressure" of the world is the opposite of the enjoyment of voluntary
detachment Emerson recommends elsewhere.

These last two passages exhibit the structure of the "alienated majesty"
motif in its diachronic manifestations (*CW*.II.27). When Emerson longs for
something, he tends to locate it in the past or future. He may draw, in the first
instance, on fables of the Fall, Romantic primitivism, and theories of an original
language in which words were one with things. In the second case, he makes use
of the prophetic conventions and millennial imagery found in the closing
paragraphs of "The Poet." He is fully aware that these mythic projections are
representations of inaccessible mental states. With considerable humor, he
pictures the nostalgic impulse as a mildly senile but benevolent old man:

The Spirit of Humanity finds it curious & good to leave the arm-
chair of its old age ... & go back to the scenes of Auld Lang Syne,
to the old mansion house of Asia ... where the faculties first
opened, where youth first triumphed in the elasticity of strength
& spirits & where the ways of Civilization & thought (then
deemed infinite) were first explored.

"It may be," he comments after this flight of fancy, "this emotion will be only
occasionally felt for though the grandeur is real, it is ever present, as the
firmament is forever magnificent but is only felt to be so when our own
spirits are fresh" (*JMN*.II.218). Even as a very young man (this was written
when he was twenty-one) he understood the dynamics of desire well enough
to know that it projects its objects in time and space: "the world lacks unity
and lies broken and in heaps ... because man is disunited with himself"
(*CW*.I.43).

But this awareness does not defend him against feeling that the
condition of detachment unredeemed by transition is one of loss. Loss, in
turn, activates the desire for future resolution he has criticized as a wishful
illusion. He compensates for the failure of transitional energy by introducing
teleology into his fables, as we have already seen. Separate insights, images,
and sentences are defined, not as the termini of energetic oscillation, but as
parts evolving in the direction of wholeness. The unifying element is an
anticipated retrospection, as hope replaces power:

I write anecdotes of the intellect; a sort of Farmer's Almanac of
mental moods....

I cannot myself use that systematic form which is reckoned
essential in treating the science of the mind. But if one can say so
without arrogance, I might suggest that he who contents himself
with dotting a fragmentary curve, recording only what facts he
has observed, without attempting to arrange them within one
outline, follows a system also—a system as grand as any other,
though he does not interfere with its vast curves by prematurely
forcing them into a circle or ellipse, but only draws that arc which
he clearly sees, or perhaps at a later observation a remote curve
of the same orbit, and waits for a new opportunity, well assured
that these observed arcs will consist with each other. (*W*.XII.11)

Keeping an "Almanac" of daily "anecdotes" demonstrates his faith that life is
taking shape, that time itself bestows form. When self-reliance wavers, future

closure gives the present its significance. Transition originates in freely willed detachment. Its reward is the sensation of mastery that occurs in the rapid apprehension of unlikeness when, as in all forms of the sublime, the mind recognizes its superiority to its objects. When incapable of transition, Emerson feels that he has lost control. Detachment has been imposed, not elected. The movement between dissimilar elements is not his own, aggressive and quick, but the impersonal, slow purposiveness of nature or of the soul's instinct.

The fluctuation between the two versions of detachment and transition repeats the alternating moods of desire and power analyzed in Part II. Emerson is proud of his bravely unconventional prose and scorns the critic who would protest. In this he is right in line with theorists and practitioners of the sublime who, beginning with Longinus, have legitimated breaking the rules of style.[12] But at times, he looks on discontinuity as failure. To the extent that he shares them, he feels himself at the mercy of his readers' expectations of thematic unity and stylistic continuity. One of the most complex manifestations of Emerson's ambivalence occurs in a journal entry recorded in the fall of 1841. The heading indicates that its purported theme is "Criticism," not the act of criticizing, as it turns out, but the effect of criticism on the writer (one is tempted to say "victim"). The passage begins by recounting a dream or dreamlike fable and proceeds to interpret it:

Into one of the chambers of hell came a man with his head under his arm, then several men carrying their heads under their arms. Well I suppose a man will come to that in his time also to cut up his brain & his heart neatly in a box to carry, and put his irritabilities aloof from him as a fact, out of which the interpretation of the dream was also to be extorted. But why do I write another line, since my best friends assure me that in every line I repeat myself? Yet the God must be obeyed even to ridicule. The criticism of the public is, as I have often noted, much in advance of its invention. The ear is not to be cheated. A continuous effect cannot be produced by discontinuous thought and when the eye cannot detect the juncture of the skilful mosaic, the Spirit is apprised of disunion simply by the failure to affect the Spirit. This other thing I will also concede,—that the man Fingal is rather too swiftly plastic, or, shall I say, works more in the spirit of a cabinet maker, than of an architect. The thought which strikes him as great & Dantesque, & opens an abyss, he instantly presents to another transformed into a chamber or a neat parlor, and degrades ideas. (*JMN*.VIII.95–96)

The passage exhibits two kinds of detachment or "disunion" which correspond to two visions of hell. The effect of criticism is the same as the effect of man's fall into self-consciousness. "[A]n intellectual man has the power to go out of himself and see himself as an object," he writes in "Powers and Laws of Thought." "Intellectual perception severs once for all the man from the things with which he converses" (*W*.XII.44). Criticism exacerbates these operations and causes the artist to perform them on himself. He literally contains himself, boxing up his brain, his heart, and his anger. He has betaken himself voluntarily to a hell where his punishment reenacts his sin. Assuming that style is a true image of spirit, he accepts decapitation as an image of psychic "disunion" that no rhetorical surface can mask. He attempts to excise the organ that he blames for provoking criticism by disassociating himself from his irritabilities (putting them "aloof"), but this only creates more drastic division. Having been censured for excessive repetitiveness, he confronts duplicates of himself: "a man with his head under his arm" turns into "several men carrying their heads under their arms."

Emerson defends himself against criticism by agreeing with it. He accepts the judgment of his "best friends" and "the public," which he credits with critical astuteness "much in advance of its inventions." The irritability which he disavows is almost certainly exasperation at such friendly advice. The question "why do I write another line," and his answer, "The God must be obeyed," show him to be restless in his acquiescence. But the reference to Fingal (a figure for Emerson) occasions more self-criticism, and he confesses to being fanciful rather than imaginative. But even as he chastises his "too swiftly plastic" talent, his "god" inspires "the thought which strikes him as great and Dantesque and opens an abyss." Having imagined the hell of criticism, he recalls the hell Dante created. The wish to match Dante's powers, suppressed throughout as he tries to make concessions to his critics, breaks out in an acknowledgment of the thrill of disunion and the sublimity of the abyss. But what came to him as a sublime image, he receives "in the spirit of a cabinet maker." In the end, he boxes up inspiration as he boxed up his brain and heart in the "dream."

Two models of imagination, composition, and reading, each with radically different criteria for success, are implicit in this entry. According to the dominant conventional view, "discontinuous thought," an imaginative flaw, produces a regrettably discontinuous prose. Even where disjunction is not manifested stylistically, the "failure to affect the reader's Spirit" betrays the author's spiritual condition. Penetrating the rhetorical surface, spirit speaks to spirit; the reader is disappointed and the writer exposed. Reacting to this condition, the artist goes to the other extreme, producing graceful, "plastic" prose with all the aesthetic virtues of a "neat parlor." The reference to a "Dantesque thought" suggests an opposite interpretation of the same facts. The poet does indeed think discontinuously—his idea "opens an abyss." But as Dante's readers find his abyss to be sublime, so Emerson recognizes his thought as "great." In this light, the urge to domesticate and decorate with an excessively continuous style "degrades" the vision of the abyss. Both reader and writer would prefer less unity and more power.

This exercise in defensive self-interpretation is a meditation on the compositional habits we examined in the last chapter. Repetition and discontinuity are genetically related, and their effects are clearly intentional. But they result in a form of sublimity that defies conventional expectations of continuity and resolution. The thought of failing in the judgment of his public and anxiety about his mind's power to control and organize its material (which is to say, the thought of failure, period) makes sublimity a source of distress as well as of gratification. Emerson works out his mixed feelings by inventing elaborate metaphoric representations of his style which are alternately defensive and desirous. In the reading of his dream, he rebels against the expectations of the conventional reviewer and insists that his text is inspired. The author turns interpreter and retroactively makes the dream in which he was damned represent an imaginative victory; he changes it from an image of his failure into a figure for his will.

NOTES

1. Friedrich Nietzsche, *The Use and Abuse of History*, translated by Adrian Collins (Indianapolis: Bobbs-Merrill, 1949, 1957), p. 6.

2. Wallace Stevens, *The Collected Poems of Wallace Stevens* (New York: Alfred A. Knopf, 1954), p. 392.

3. Samuel Taylor Coleridge, *Biographia Literaria*, I, 202.

4. Gerald L. Bruns, *Modern Poetry and the Idea of Language: A Critical and Historical Study* (New Haven: Yale University Press, 1974), pp. 43–55.

5. Friedrich von Schiller, *Naive and Sentimental Poetry and On the Sublime*, translated by Julias A. Elias (New York: Ungar, 1966), pp. 111–12; *On the Aesthetic Education of Man*, translated by Reginald Snell (New York: Ungar, 1974), p. 39.

6. Friedrich Wilhelm von Schelling, "Concerning the Relation of the Plastic Arts to Nature," translated by Michael Bullock, in Herbert Read, *The True Voice of Feeling: Studies in English Romantic Poetry* (New York: Pantheon Books, 1953), pp. 334, 342.

7. The lines of Emerson's poems seem to be formed by the same urge to intensify by compression. A complex thought is squeezed into the fewest possible words, which are forced out of their normal order to accommodate a surplus of meaning. The discontinuity of the poems is caused by the cryptic quality that results from compression rather than by the fissures between the repetitive expansions of the prose. In the former, discourse is forced to fit a space too small for it; in the latter, it is permitted such an unlimited expanse that gaps appear between parts. Is the poetic motto that precedes each essay a fragment requiring the more discursive prose to complete and explain it, or is the essay contained

in—reduced to—its motto? Their inverse structures seem to require each other. For the reader, the gnomic motto is a puzzle. He turns to the essay for the relief of interpretation but finds that Emerson's prose is aphoristic and proverbial. It aspires, in other words, to the condensation of the motto.

8. Guillaume Oegger, *The True Messiah*, translated by Elizabeth P. Peabody (Boston: E. P. Peabody, 1842), rpt. in Kenneth Walter Cameron, *Young Emerson's Transcendental Vision* (Hartford, Conn.: Transcendental Books, 1971), p. 338.

9. Sampson Reed, Observations on the Growth of the Mind (Boston, 1826), rpt. in Cameron, Young Emerson's Transcendental Vision, p. 316.

10. *Wordsworth and Coleridge: Lyrical Ballads, 1798*, edited by W.J.B. Owen, 2nd ed. (London: Oxford University Press, 1969), p. 148.

11. Feidelson, Symbolism and American Literature, p. 150.

12. Monk, *The Sublime*, pp. 15–17, 26–27.

MARK EDMUNDSON

Emerson and the Work of Melancholia

Emerson claimed that he read for the "lustres," and yet most of his best twentieth-century critics, beginning with Stephen Whicher, have told the story of Emerson's progressive darkening, as he moves from "Self-Reliance" to worship of the "beautiful Necessity." Even as they have located, for themselves and for us, Emerson's early brightnesses, they have focused their narratives on his later disavowal of Romanticism. These critics, among whom one could include the recent Harold Bloom and Barbara Packer, and the much earlier Stephen Whicher, write exemplary prose—keenly dialectical and inventive. And it is of course an Emersonian prose: the Sage of Concord seems to direct the tides of their thought. Yet what they have imbibed on the level of style, these critics seem compelled to repudiate in their narratives, which return perpetually to the drama of Emerson's fall. One feels at times that some of Emerson's devoted readers need to disown what they find most Emersonian and Romantic in themselves, which in its most reductive form is the urge to make claims upon life that it cannot sustain, so that the retelling of Emerson's story becomes a method of personal exorcism, a way of avoiding the later disillusionment that Emerson himself suffered.

Yet this sort of exorcism is itself Emersonian, characteristic of his later stance, where he uses the technique, against appearances and contrary to the

From *Raritan* 6, no. 4 (Spring 1987): 120–36. © 1987 by *Raritan: A Quarterly Review*.

apprehensions of his committed scholars, to in vent a fresh high Romanticism. This essay urges a new reading of Emerson's late mode, finding in his critics' need to exorcise him a hint about Emerson's own methods of self-recreation through crisis. I will focus, then, on Emerson's evolving response to the problem of loss and his development of a fresh Romantic sublime through what Freud would call "the work of melancholia."

Most readers of American literature know the story of Emerson's refusal to mourn. His first wife Ellen died in 1831, when she was nineteen. Five years later he lost Charles, the brother to whom he was closest. Yet, as James Cox has shown in a brilliant essay, "The Circles of the Eye," an undeniable influx of affirmative energy came to Emerson following both of the deaths. "Getting over the deaths of loved ones is no tired or traditional 'spiritual' vision for Emerson precisely because it is a literal breathing in, or inspiration, of the death in life," Cox writes. Indeed, the refusal to mourn is central to Emerson's first high Romantic phase. Considered in its broadest Emersonian sense, to mourn is to misplace one's energies in customs, conventions, usages, and laws that oppress the soul because they are, for all purposes, dead. We tend to deny our own gifts, and to overestimate culture, great men, and, most destructively, the wealth of the past. The object of life, as Emerson would see it, is to redeem our grief over what we are not and have not, "to bring the past for judgment into the thousand-eyed present, and live ever in a new day." In this enlarged sense, mourning assimilates all of the self-inflicted repressions against which Emerson inveighs in the essay "Self-Reliance," his declaration of prophetic independence. Envy, imitation, reticence, craven consistency, prayer, regret, in short, conformity in all of its guises is evidence of a desire to give our bounty to the dead.

In Emerson misdirected grief is evidence of our spiritual bondage:

> The objection to conforming to usages that have become dead to you is, that it scatters your force. It loses your time and blurs the impression of your character. If you maintain a dead church, contribute to a dead Bible society ... I have difficulty to detect the precise man you are. And, of course, so much force is withdrawn from your proper life.

And later in the same essay,

> Why drag about this corpse of your memory, lest you contradict somewhat [sic] you have stated in this or that public place?

Emerson excoriates our tendency to "lament the past" and our "mortifying" social smiles. His fable of choice about the soul's resurrection is that of the sot, "dead drunk," who wakens to his princely estate. The more that you imitate, that is the more that you attempt to shape your present moment in the image of the private or the cultural past, the more you consign yourself to leading a death-in-life. From this awareness comes one of Emerson's best-known formulations: "imitation is suicide." "Self-Reliance" is populated with figures who represent the dangers of succumbing to the ethos of mourning, and they are, in various ways, death figures. In the first paragraph of the essay, Emerson introduces us to the "stranger" who says "with masterly good sense precisely what we have thought and felt all the time," and thus usurps our original impulse. Later we encounter the giant who stalks Emerson to remind him that travel, that is, the urge to find novelty outside of himself, is a method of turning away from the burden of being original, and thus also a form of mourning or death-in-life. In fact, all of those who constitute what Emerson calls "the firmament of bards and sages"—including, for instance, Moses, Plato, and Milton,—are finally instances of this stranger. The more we exalt them, the more we sacrifice our own vitality. The masterly stranger is Emerson's equivalent to the interior antagonist with which many of the English Romantics contended. Blake calls his the spectre; Keats speaks of the identity; for Coleridge it is a variety of versions of the intrusive man from Porlock who halts the composition of "Kubla Khan." Part of what is moving about Emerson, I think, is his love for the masterly stranger, particularly when the stranger is Milton or Plato or the promise of travel, coupled with the awareness that, nonetheless, he must rather ruthlessly reject everything the stranger represents.

Yet Emerson doesn't just preach against mourning. He offers a philosophy of aggressive perpetual motion by which we can throw off circumstances before they have become confining. This strategy of ceaseless self-creation, which, it should be added, is always accomplished through the systematic destruction of the existing self, is the subject of a remarkable passage from the essay "Compensation."

> Every soul is by ... intrinsic necessity quitting its whole system of things, its friends, and home, and laws, and faith, as the shell-fish crawls out of its beautiful but stony case, because it no longer admits of its growth, and slowly forms a new house. In proportion to the vigor of the individual, these revolutions are frequent, until in some happier mind they are incessant.... And such should be the outward biography of man in time, a putting off of dead circumstances day by day.... But to us, in our lapsed

estate, resting, not advancing, resisting, not cooperating with the divine expansion, this growth comes by shocks.

To Emerson, the mind always seeks to record its transformations in some outward form, be it a religious rite, a social usage, or a literary text. Our chief sorrow lies in our tendency to inhabit those forms as though they were ultimate truths. The spirit flashes and burns, and we, hungry for stabilities, make of the ashes that remain a faith. To begin dwelling in received forms is, for Emerson, to enter the house of mourning.

And yet, the power to produce in the reader this false sense of ultimates is inseparable from poetic genius. The test of visionary power for Emerson is the capacity to force an impression upon the reader, to establish his "character." That is, the sublime poet is he who unlooses so compelling a force of tropes that his reader takes them for literal revelation and lives them out. He is made over "in the image of the imagery," in Kenneth Burke's phrase. The reader so constituted will find this received vocabulary inevitable, which is to say that he will have involuntary recourse to it in moments of crisis. Emerson knows that even as he preaches self-reliance, he is dispensing a series of figures for the enfranchised spirit on which his readers may slavishly rely. Such a paradox is, to Emerson himself, of no particular consequence. What does matter is his tendency to respond to his own tropes as if they were absolute truths and so to become his text's inert reflection—nothing more than a cold type. Thus the effort of the creative mind is perpetually to reimagine its true poverty, its clinging creative forms, as the motive for self-reinvention.

When we fail to do so, our "growth comes by shocks." Unexpectedly, fate intervenes to deprive us of an unacknowledged prop and shame us by exposing our dependencies. Mourning, which for Emerson begins the moment we rely upon any external object, then enters its painful and debilitating phase, though it has, from the beginning, scattered our force. Aggressive perpetual motion is the only cure:

> Life only avails, not the having lived. Power ceases in the instant
> of repose; it resides in the moment of transition from a past to a
> new state, in the shooting of the gulf, in the darting to an aim.
> This one fact the world hates, that the soul *becomes*.

Life thus faces us with two choices: leap or be shoved. And the Emersonian leap, a self-willed free flight, is by far the better option. Yet if our tendency is groundward, toward the inorganic, piling on dead forms until we become sadly vulnerable from the weight of our own defenses, by what means do we rise up and shoot the gulf, cut ourselves loose from the binding labor of grief?

Eloquence is Emerson's chief weapon against mourning. His true units of composition in the early work are his sentences, "barbed and winged" as O. W. Firkins, the author of a distinguished book on Emerson, called them. The Emersonian utterance, at its most formidable, has a dual purpose: it is a barbed irony and a metaphor conducive to flight. The ironic charge severs a draining attachment. It locates an unconsciously maintained idealization ("a dead church, ... a dead Bible-society") or an easy reduction and undoes it with a rhetorical thrust. But coeval with this detachment is an injunction to make a new commitment, to return the proper energies of the spirit to the self or to fresh objects that are truly conducive to power. Each effective sentence embraces availing life and purges the "having lived."

Yet to Emerson, the spirit is most vital in the midspace—"in the moment of transition from a past to a new state"—when energies have been withdrawn in a sudden curtailment of mourning, but be fore the new investment has been made. Then is "the shooting of the gulf ... the darting to an aim." It is this state of empowered suspension that reveals to us how, as Wordsworth writes in *The Prelude*, "The mind is lord and master—outward sense / The obedient servant of her will." Yet to Wordsworth these instances will be rare, "spots of time." The Emersonian injunction is that we find in every passing moment the "renovating virtue," which is to say that a rhetoric of perpetual crisis dominates his early texts.

Yet the midspace, as Emerson knew to his sorrow, is not forever. We are so constituted—our influxes of power being temporary—that we must seek new forms to invest. Finding these new forms is the metaphorical objective of Emerson's sentences. Metaphor locates fresh commitments, less insistently final because more easily apprehended as "vehicular and transitive." Thus to leave the rock-built church and worship mutable nature discourages the spirit's tendency to inertia, but Emerson at his most radical goes even further and invests nothing but the fact (and not even the principle) of transition. All established forms—institutions, rites, and usages—almost everything that we tend to value as humanistic culture, appears to Emerson, in certain moods, as nothing better than a communal act of mourning.

Nietzsche, who learned a great deal from Emerson, was, I believe, thinking of him when he called the tendency to turn perpetually against the past and the immediately given situation "the spirit of revenge," or "the will's ill-will against time and its it was." He saw that the kind of perpetual motion that Emerson commended would result in obsessive repetition, as one set of terms and commitments was replaced by the next ad infinitum. This repetition could in itself become as deadening as the stasis or compulsive mourning that it sought to overcome. Nietzsche's solution to the problem posed by the "spirit of revenge" is that we might learn to affirm repetition by willing the eternal recurrence of the same, and in so doing triumph over our desire to revise the past. Yet this response is, it seems to me, one that Emerson fully anticipates in a key passage from the essay "Circles."

> For it is the inert effort of each thought, having formed itself into a circular wave of circumstance,—as, for instance, an empire, rules of an art, a local usage, a religious rite,—to heap itself on that ridge, and to solidify and hem in the life. But if the soul is quick and strong, it bursts over that boundary on all sides, and expands another orbit on the great deep, which also runs up into a high wave, with attempt again to stop and to bind. But the heart refuses to be imprisoned; in its first and narrowest pulses, it already tends outward with a vast force, and to immense and innumerable expansions.

Though Emerson's circles do "expand" outward on "the great deep," no commitment to progress is necessarily implied here. One set of rules, usages, or rites need be no better than the previous one. Rather, the passage records Emerson's own shrewd reading of his ethos of perpetual motion. He sees himself committed to recurrence as one "circular wave" displaces the next, but he then exuberantly proclaims that embracing this process can keep the spirit vital. Here Emerson prefigures not only Nietzsche but the Wallace Stevens who writes: "The man-hero is not the exceptional monster, / But he that of repetition is most master."

There is also a significant compatibility between Emerson's injunction that the spirit be mobile and the ethos that seems implicit in Freud's 1914 formulation of the narcissistic ego. Beginning with the essay "On Narcissism," Freud conceives of the ego as being itself constituted by libidinal investment. Thus, there is no firm distinction between the energy that is the ego and that which "invests" or "occupies" objects in the world. It follows, then, that the subject's allocation of libido, which is finite, is depleted by every external investment. But self-enclosure is not a solution: "a strong egoism is a protection against falling ill, but in the last resort we must begin to love in order not to fall ill, and we are bound to fall ill if, in consequence of frustration, we are unable to love." From this pronouncement comes Philip Rieff's formulation of the Freudian ethic: "The therapy of all therapies, the secret of all secrets, the interpretation of all interpretations, in Freud, is never to attach oneself exclusively or too passionately to any one particular meaning or object." The ethic is as characteristic of Emerson as it is of Freud.

Yet Emerson differs significantly from the founder of psychoanalysis in his implicit denial that the erotic component is constitutive of every human engagement. The Emersonian soul exists somewhere beyond the vicissitudes of erotic experience (or, perhaps more accurately, power subsumes eros always in Emerson). But it is precisely the Freudian dilemma of having made poorly comprehended investments, and then paying for them with an attenuation of one's proper force, from which Emerson attempts to free himself by way of symbolic action. His assurance that imagination—an influx of power that is made manifest through a surprising piece of eloquence—can sever commitments and redeploy force is, of course, a surpassing naivete in Freudian terms. Freud's strongest insights about the mortal state involve the grim resolve with which we conserve our libidinal positions. Even when reality testing has shown the object to be lost, Freud observes, the psyche will not function on behalf of its own economic welfare and quickly choose another. Rather, we disassociate ourselves from the world and undertake the labor of grief (*Trauerarbeit*). The early Emerson, Freud would say, underestimates the stubbornness of the psyche, its cruel inertia. That a flash of rhetorical judo, which turns the bulk of fate against itself, can set us instantly free, sorely underestimates how much the strength of our first crucial attachments lingers on into what is called adult life and adult love.

Later, Emerson develops this kind of Freudian sense of the inadequacies of a condensed dialectic of liberation. The Emersonian refusal to mourn may indeed disappear in 1842, the year his young son Waldo died, but it is not replaced by acquiescence to "the beautiful Necessity." Rather, Emerson devises a new spiritual strategy of self-recreation, one whose process becomes more arduous out of a deepened sense of the conservatism of the drives. Yet the goal of the quest remains unchanged: it is to reinvent the self and to revise his readers, make them possible only as Emersonians. In a sense, the effect of Emerson's shift in strategy reaches as far ahead as to a nonreader, to Freud. (Perhaps it is more accurate to say that Freud read his Emerson indirectly—through Nietzsche.) For if Freud provides the terms for the limits of the early Emerson's stance, Emerson will allow us to undo one of Freud's most guarded idealizations, the normative "work of mourning."

The critical consensus, of course, is that 1842 marks the point of turning in Emerson's career, what he calls in "Threnody" his "lordly man's down-lying." Stephen Whicher, whose *Freedom and Fate* remains the most influential book on Emerson, conceives that Emerson's high Romantic aspirations perished on the crossroads of his boy's death. Henceforth

Emerson teaches submission to fate and her iron laws, turns his podium into an altar to "beautiful Necessity," and dispenses the sacraments of circumstance. This final submission to fate—Freud would call it a sane acquiescence to the Reality Principle—occurs against considerable resistance: there is something in Emerson that still refuses to be conquered. A week after Waldo's death, Emerson writes to his friend Caroline Sturgis: "Alas! I chiefly grieve that I cannot grieve; that this fact takes no more deep hold than other facts, is as dreamlike as they; a lambent flame that will not burn playing on the surface of my river." Then there is the withering passage from "Experience," published in 1844:

> Grief too will make us idealists. In the death of my son, now more than two years ago, I seem to have lost a beautiful estate,—no more. I cannot get it nearer to me. If tomorrow I should be informed of the bankruptcy of my principal debtors, the loss of my property would be a great inconvenience to me, perhaps, for many years; but it would leave me as it found me,—neither better nor worse. So it is with this calamity: it does not touch me: some thing which I fancied was a part of me, which could not be torn away without tearing me, nor enlarged without enriching me, falls off from me, and leaves no scar. It was caducous.

Yet the grief for Waldo's death, we are told, eventually makes its full weight known by way of a delayed reaction. At the time of the boy's death, Emerson put aside his journal (lettered *J*), saving it for his recollections of his son. He returned to the journal in April to begin "Threnody," the elegy for Waldo, which was completed and published in 1846. And there, the received understanding goes, we see the authentic toll of Emerson's loss. Until this point, he has cast himself in the image of Hegel's *belle âme*, lacking "the power of alienation, the power to make himself a thing and support being." In *The Conduct of Life*, published in the year Lincoln was elected president, 1860, and particularly in the seminal "Fate," this story continues: we can see how Emerson has adapted himself to the new stance. He recognizes his place in the world and understands that fate, not spirit, is the dominant force in his and every life.

Yet the crucial passage from "Experience" on Waldo's death may not signal a refusal of grief, but rather that the spiritual labors of mourning have been in some way completed. Emerson's shocking figuration of his loss in material terms—of a beautiful estate, bankruptcy, property, debt, and enrichment—darkly anticipates Freud's own economic tropes for the psyche. (Though Freud, the European, prefers liquid assets to Emerson's real estate.)

In an excellent recent essay on Emerson, Sharon Cameron attempts to mitigate the ostensible cruelty of the "Experience" passage. She writes that "the vulgarity of alluding to these losses as if they were comparable is meant to replicate the vulgarity of experience's obliviousness to any niceties of human perception. The man who must sacrifice not simply his child but also his belief that the sacrifice has special meaning replicates the failure of discrimination by which he sees himself victimized." Yet Emerson is rarely so elaborate an ironist; his chief stylistic attribute is rather a primitive force, which is part of what made him mean what he did to writers like Whitman, Thoreau, and Nietzsche. I take it, rather, that to have achieved this vocabulary in which grief is so severely objectivized stands, for Emerson, as a symbolic representation that the loss has been surpassed, and that, in Freud's terms, "the ego has become free and uninhibited again." But this is only an isolated moment. The entire drama of self-recreation is only fully recorded in the text of "Threnody."

"Threnody" is a Wordsworthian poem whose concerns and strategies of Romantic argument owe their first debt to the "Intimations Ode." Emerson's burden is the burden of all great imaginative dualists, poets of loss, from Milton to Wordsworth, Keats and Coleridge—what to make of a diminished thing. Emerson, in "Threnody," is diminished not only by the loss of his boy, but by the failure of his own earlier hopes—not his hopes to become a poet of the first order, for this he has accomplished (though, as he says, his poetic voice is a hoarse and rugged one most itself in prose), but to transform his rude nation, to be the true prophet of American life. Those aspirations have, along with his dear son, faded into the light of common day, leaving the merest memory:

> The gracious boy, who did adorn
> The world whereinto he was born,
> And by his countenance repay
> The favor of the loving Day,—
> Has disappeared from the Day's eye;
> Far and wide she cannot find him;
> My hopes pursue, they cannot bind him.

These lines are from the beginning of the poem; yet it will not be long before the departed Waldo becomes associated with his father's own wounded aspirations:

> 'Tis because a general hope
> Was quenched, and all must doubt and grope,

For flattering planets seemed to say
This child should ills of ages stay,
By wondrous tongue, and guided pen,
Bring the flown Muses back to men.
Perchance not he but Nature ailed,
The world and not the infant failed.
It was not ripe yet to sustain
A genius of so fine a strain,
Who gazed upon the sun and moon
As if he came unto his own,
And, pregnant with his grander thought,
Brought the old order into doubt.

The "old order" still stands firm in 1846 despite Emerson's efforts to make all of America's children into prophets. "Threnody" embraces that failure along with Waldo's death and pursues both losses through their every effect, much the way Wordsworth works through his grief at the failure of his "visionary gleam" up to the turning of "Intimations." The irony of both poems is the massive irony of situation, the negative gap between expectation and event. And it is precisely this overwhelming irony that permits Wordsworth and Emerson to suspend local qualification or the kinds of specific ironies that are commonly manifest in tonal ambiguities, and to write with a full, uninhibited force of feeling. This is the painful freedom of the elegist, who even attenuates his grief to preserve the right to speak in an idiom of originary force. For tonal irony may be nothing more than evidence of the abiding awareness that it all has happened before and will again. Thus, in the Romantic elegy (and many of the great Romantic lyrics are indeed elegies) an achieved eloquence redeems grief somewhat, preventing a too thorough identification with the dead. "The intellect ... converts the sufferer into a spectator," Emerson writes in his essay on tragedy, "and his pain into poetry. Hence also the torments of life become tuneful tragedy, solemn and soft with music, and garnished with rich dark pictures."

The double labor of grief in "Threnody," for Waldo and for the Waldo who was the author himself before he became a name, became Emerson, might be approached by way of Freud's great paragraph in "Mourning and Melancholia":

In what, now, does the work which mourning performs consist? I do not think there is anything far-fetched in presenting it in the following way. Reality-testing has shown that the loved object no longer exists, and it proceeds to demand that all libido shall be withdrawn from its attachments to that object. This demand arouses understandable opposition—it is a matter of general observation that people never willingly abandon a libidinal position, not even, indeed, when a substitute is already beckoning to them. This opposition can be so intense that a turning away from reality takes place and a clinging to the object through the medium of a hallucinatory wishful psychosis. Normally, respect for reality gains the day. Nevertheless its orders cannot be obeyed at once. They are carried out bit by bit, at great expense of time and cathectic energy, and in the meantime the existence of the lost object is psychically prolonged. Each single one of the memories and expectations in which the libido is bound to the object is brought up and hypercathected, and detachment of the libido is accomplished in respect of it. Why this compromise by which the command of reality is carried out piecemeal should be so extraordinarily painful is not at all easy to explain in terms of economics. It is remarkable that this painful unpleasure is taken as a matter of course by us. The fact is, however, that when the work of mourning is completed the ego becomes free and uninhibited again.

This passage contains two quite radical implications, one of which, in his desire to enforce certain distinctions between mourning and melancholia, Freud conceals from his readers and perhaps from himself. The first implication is submerged in Freud's compound "*Trauerarbeit*," the "work of mourning." To figure mourning as "work" is to issue, however subtly, an ethical injunction that we undertake mourning economically, proceed to work thoroughly but without waste, cut the failed investment, and suspend losses. This motive is one which Emerson fully anticipates in the symbolic action of "Threnody." Though his loss is too grievous to convert to gain in the space of a single utterance with a rhetorical flourish, the objective remains an expeditious freeing of the energies of the self, their orderly withdrawal from a bankrupt object. (Recall the broker's rhetoric in the central passage from "Experience.") Here, though, Freud's darker insight comes into play. Freud has equated the "work of mourning" with summoning up and hyperinvesting the lost object. Yet this would be closer to a formula for falling in love by engraving the image deeper. The insight that Freud evades is, I take it, that the object is brought up, born into the psyche, precisely in order to be dismissed, done away with, slain by the subject. This labor of grief, for Freud and for the Emerson who in "Threnody" calls up a sequence of images of his boy in order, symbolically, to slay each one, is compellingly described by Nietzsche. It is the labor of transforming "Thus it was" into "Thus I willed it." The strategy here is not, as it was in Emerson's early works, to sunder deadening commitments with a single stroke of invention. It is, rather, inventively to reproduce the actions of fate, and in the inspired reinvention or representation of the "it was" to make the past, symbolically, into a function of one's own imaginative will. By repeatedly representing the birth and death of the lost object, the poet becomes imaginatively identical with fate. "'Tis paltry to be Caesar / Not being Fortune," says Shakespeare's Cleopatra, and yet the sacrifice for becoming, in one's own mind, "Fortune," is humane grief for what has been loved and lost.

This understanding of the dynamics of loss leaves us less perplexed by the moment of turning in "Threnody" in which an appallingly revised version of the Over-Soul intervenes:

> The deep Heart answered, "Weepest thou?
> Worthier cause for passion wild
> If I had not taken the child."

Surely "the deep Heart" is crucially Emerson's, but it is also the agent of fate, that which has "taken the child." The symbolic action of the poem, the representation and sacrifice of the image, makes the poetic imagination identical with fate, an identification that Emerson, unlike Freud, is willing to acknowledge and to sustain in the interest of his abiding project, the acquisition of power. In Emerson the power that matters the most is, always, the power to reinvent the self at the expense of whatever conformity impedes quickened life. Thus, the death of Waldo is mastered, assimilated in "Threnody" to the imagery of self-surpassing that crowns the pivotal essay "Circles":

> "And know my higher gifts unbind
> The zone that girds the incarnate mind.
> When the scanty shores are full
> With Thought's perilous whirling pool;
> When frail Nature can no more,
> Then the Spirit strikes the hour:
> My servant Death, with solving rite,
> Pours finite into infinite."

And what force now takes responsibility for having broken the circle that was constituted by Waldo's life? The answer is as disturbing as it is unavoidable.

Freud defends himself against such broodings not from any tenderheartedness, but, I would suggest, sheerly as a maneuver for protecting the ritual of therapy, or rather that aspect of the ritual in which the therapist transfers his influence to the subject under treatment. For the great Freudian essay on loss meditates indirectly but unremittingly on the termination of therapy and on the fate of the internalized imago of the physician. In the idealized condition of "mourning" the patient desexualizes the imago, making over his own ego and superego in its image, sustaining its influence. Yet a stronger resistance against intrusion, an Emersonian resistance, slays the ingested other rather than preserving him. What Freud calls "de-sexualization" is a method of assimilation. Through "desexualization" the self establishes binding relations to the past, coming to resemble more closely crucial figures of authority and to perpetuate the values of venerable institutions. This is the process by which we assimilate ourselves to humanistic culture. It is, to Emerson, suicidal. Emerson thus prefigures and subverts the Freudian category of "normal mourning," committing himself instead to that remorseless activity of self-creation Freud called "melancholia." Toward the close of his essay, having failed to draw a clear distinction between mourning and melancholia, Freud becomes franker about what is at stake in the latter:

> Just as mourning impels the ego to give up the object by declaring the object to be dead and offering the ego the inducement of continuing to live, so does each single struggle of ambivalence loosen the fixation of the libido to the object by disparaging it, denigrating it and even as it were killing it.... The ego may enjoy in this the satisfaction of knowing itself as the better of the two, as superior to the object.

It is this struggle, not to be constituted by the lost object, that Emerson undertakes in "Threnody," and that Freud, as a proponent of the authority of the psychoanalyst and of psychoanalysis in general, finds most troubling. The insight which Freud finally evades is that "mourning" is a normative fiction: pragmatically there are only varying degrees of melancholia.

Given this reading of "Threnody," we might go on to conceive of Emerson's great essay, "Fate," which we are told is the bitter proof of his final acquiescence, in more audacious terms. Quite radically, perhaps, I want to suggest that Emerson, having internalized fate in "Threnody," proceeds in his essay to submit fate itself to the work of melancholia. Like "Threnody," "Fate" moves toward a massive turning, a dialectical swing at its midpoint, where Emerson can rise up and say that "Fate has its lord; limitation its limits ..." and leave us in little doubt as to who that lord might be. This turning is achieved rhetorically by a sequence of superb refigurings of fate, until the agency becomes, imaginatively, a function of Emerson's powers of verbal invention. All through the first half of the essay, Emerson shows us how fate can be summoned forward, figured and dismissed, slain as it were, in the gap between sentences, then brought freshly to life at the whim of the creator. And we would not be wrong to equate this rhythm of willful creation and destruction with the rhythm of melancholia. Consider a representative affirmation of limits from the opening section of the essay:

> In different hours, a man represents each of several of his ancestors, as if there were seven or eight of us rolled up into each man's skin,—seven or eight ancestors at least,—and they constitute the variety of notes for that new piece of music which his life is.

Surely this is close to anticipating Freud's remark that the ego is "a precipitate of abandoned object cathexes, and that it contains the history of those object-choices," and yet the exuberance of the image, the sprightly transformation of the ancestors into notes, makes of Emerson the finer composer, the master of mastery. In Freud's terms, what Emerson is doing here is wildly dangerous: he is using the imagination to de-mystify the Reality Principle. That is, Emerson is returning to his conviction voiced at the end of his first book, *Nature*, that "'Nature is not fixed but fluid. Spirit alters, moulds, makes it. The immobility or bruteness of nature, is the absence of spirit; to pure spirit, it is fluid, it is volatile, it is obedient.'" Here, as in "Fate," Emerson is teaching us that the imagination is a more startling power, more promising and more dangerous, than anything in nature. But now he knows just how costly such a belief can be and will continue to be. Such knowledge renders more convincing his faith that a commitment to the merely given (to the Reality Principle) is inadequate to what we are.

Yet perhaps the dangers involved in Emerson's new Romanticism only add to the grandeur of the turning passage in "Fate," which I quote now more fully.

> Thus we trace Fate, in matter, mind, and morals,—in race, in retardations of strata, and in thought and character as well. It is everywhere bound. or limitation. But Fate has its lord; limitation its limits; is different seen from above and from below; from within and from without. For, though Fate is immense, so is power, which is the other fact in the dual world, immense. If Fate follows and limits power, power attends and antagonizes Fate. We must respect Fate as natural history, but there is more than

natural history. For who and what is this criticism that pries into the matter? Man is not order of nature, sack and sack, belly and members, link in a chain, nor any ignominious baggage, but a stupendous antagonism, a dragging together of the poles of the Universe.

Freud would perhaps stigmatize this exuberance as mania, the exultation which follows upon an achieved work of melancholia, when "a large expenditure of psychical energy, long maintained or habitually occurring has at last become unnecessary, so that it is available for numerous applications and possibilities of discharge...." Let me close with a contrary suggestion. What Freud characterizes as the progression from narcissistic attachment to melancholia to mania is the movement central to the great Romantic lyrics of Wordsworth, Coleridge, Browning, Tennyson, Emerson, Whitman, and Stevens, to all of the poets of certain loss and qualified restitution. Freud, against his own wishes, has provided us with a map of that process in which the self is constituted by powers not its own, and initiates a self-wounding drama of exorcism and incorporation whose final issue will be nothing better than a motive to begin the process once again. This unfolding act of self-destroying self-invention, which is at odds with our humanistic ethical principles, may in fact be the driving force within what we have come to call the Romantic sublime.

DAVID BROMWICH

Emerson and the Ode to W.H. Channing

Emerson wrote successful poems of at least three kinds. The most familiar is the Concord Poem, or sociable ramble. Here he is often charming, and much closer to the style of his time and place than he lets himself appear elsewhere, in either verse or prose. In a very different mode, the Wordsworthian elegy or meditation, he writes with enough ease to rival Bryant, but with a power of invention that makes us want to ignore all other claims and think of him as the first American poet. Finally, Emerson is himself a pioneer of the sort of poem he calls for in "Merlin," the shocker or far-fetcher, the prophetic blast that we hear as the "strokes of fate," and see as "Sparks of the supersolar blaze." These classifications turn out to be a hindrance in reading, however, because so few of the poems are willing to stay put and respect the boundaries. "Monadnoc" is a ramble that leaps into prophecy, and then tip-toes back; "Bacchus" is an elegy, modeled on the Immortality Ode, which opens up an apocalyptic prophecy of renewal; "The Snow-Storm" is a *Wordsworthian* ramble. The only point of beginning like this is to warn ourselves against inferring much about Emerson's poetry from the discussion of a single poem: with him, even more than with most poets, any conclusion drawn about his "characteristic" tone or strategy is pretty certainly going to be false. In the following remarks on the "Ode Inscribed to W. H. Channing," I assume only that it is an unsettling poem which we

From *A Choice of Inheritance: Self and Community from Edmund Burke to Robert Frost.* © 1989 by the President and Fellows of Harvard College.

125

have not yet begun to make our peace with, and that Emerson would have placed it with "Uriel" as the most serious of his prophecies.

Here is the poem:

Though loath to grieve
The evil time's sole patriot,
I cannot leave
My honied thought
For the priest's cant,
Or statesman's rant.

If I refuse
My study for their politique,
Which at the best is trick,
The angry Muse
Puts confusion in my brain.

But who is he that prates
Of the culture of mankind,
Of better arts and life?
Go, blindworm, go,
Behold the famous States
Harrying Mexico
With rifle and with knife!

Or who, with accent bolder,
Dare praise the freedom-loving mountaineer?
I found by thee, O rushing Contoocook!
And in thy valleys, Agiochook!
The jackals of the negro-holder.

The God who made New Hampshire
Taunted the lofty land
With little men;—
Small bat and wren
House in the oak:—
If earth-fire cleave
The upheaved land, and bury the folk,
The southern crocodile would grieve.
Virtue palters; Right is hence;

Freedom praised, but hid;
Funeral eloquence
Rattles the coin-lid.

What boots thy zeal,
O glowing friend,
That would indignant rend
The northland from the south?
Wherefore? to what good end?
Boston Bay and Bunker Hill
Would serve things still;

Things are of the snake.
The horseman serves the horse,
The neatherd serves the neat,
The merchant serves the purse,
The eater serves his meat;
'Tis the day of the chattel,
Web to weave, and corn to grind;
Things are in the saddle,
And ride mankind.

There are two laws discrete,
Not reconciled,—
Law for man, and law for thing;
The last builds town and fleet,
But it runs wild,
And doth the man unking.

'Tis fit the forest fall,
The steep be graded,
The mountain tunnelled,
The sand shaded,
The orchard planted,
The glebe tilled,
The prairie granted,
The steamer built.

Let man serve law for man;
Live for friendship, live for love,
For truth's and harmony's behoof;

The state may follow how it can,
As Olympus follows Jove.

　　Yet do not I implore
The wrinkled shopman to my sounding woods,
Nor bid the unwilling senator
Ask votes of thrushes in the solitudes.
Every one to his chosen work;—
Foolish hands may mix and mar;
Wise and sure the issues are.
Round they roll till dark is light,
Sex to sex, and even to odd;—
The over-god

Who marries Right to Might,
Who peoples, unpeoples;—
He who exterminates
Races by stronger races,
Black by white faces,—
Knows to bring honey
Out of the lion;
Grafts gentlest scion
On pirate and Turk.

The Cossack eats Poland,
Like stolen fruit;
Her last noble is ruined,
Her last poet mute:
Straight, into double band
The victors divide;
Half for freedom strike and stand;—
The astonished Muse finds thousands at her side.

We know enough about Concord in the 1840s to reconstruct the occasion of this poem. Through much of 1845 and 1846, Emerson was working against the odds to find strength in solitude, while Texas was annexed, the war of persuasion between the slave and free states grew heated, and America embarked on its imperial war against Mexico. Thoreau went to jail rather than pay taxes for the war, and Channing, in league with other neighbors or friends, sought to extract from Emerson some comparable gesture of public defiance. It would be wrong to view Channing and

Emerson as natural allies. Channing was convinced that all progress must come from unified movements; he had objected to Emerson's thinking as early as the Divinity School Address: "You deny the Human Race. You stand, or rather seek to stand, a complete Adam. But you cannot do it."[1] In the background of the Ode we thus have three temperaments, each occupying a distinct position: Channing, the man of great public causes, who denounces the war on principle; Thoreau, the disciple of self-reliance, who resists the war as an invasion of his privacy; and Emerson, who so far has taken no public stand, though from time to time he confides in his journal.

Emerson's conduct during this crisis would have been a familiar story to anyone who knew him well. His pattern generally was to withhold himself from the fray until the last possible moment, when the force of a calamity became unendurable. Then, at the beckoning of others, he would make his statement. Once he had played the part, he would confess to a sense of having been besmirched, or somehow cheated of himself, in the course of making his eloquence serviceable to a cause. When, for example, President Van Buren's sham-treaty with the Cherokees first contracted for the exchange of all Cherokee lands and the transportation of the entire tribe beyond the Mississippi River, Emerson's friends prevailed on him to write an open letter of protest to Van Buren. It is an eloquent but also a curiously personal document, in which a long stream of interrogatives is suddenly closed tight: "A crime is projected that confounds our understandings by its magnitude—a crime that really deprives us as well as the Cherokees of a country." With this letter Emerson satisfied, the cause while speaking not as the agent of a cause but as a private citizen. Yet after writing it, he says in his journal that on all such occasions, "my genius deserts me"—and he adds, "It is like dead cats around my neck."

We now come to a moment eight years later, with nothing changed in Emerson. Once again, the question he has to ask himself is, How, given my purity of self-reliance, can I ever ally myself with the common sentiments of men, and not feel besmirched by having consummated the alliance in public? The Ode shows us what it looks like when he tries to meet the question head-on. The poem is a very mixed success, in an area where Emerson's ideas seem to have ruled out any kind of success whatever; but it is an important poem to the American imagination, for reasons that have nothing to do with our search for masterpieces. To explain its importance we need to return to three of Emerson's favorite words: *commodity*, *spirit*, and *power*.

The Ode exhibits a cleavage that Emerson had often sought to deny or repair, between commodity and spirit; and it impresses us more strongly than ever with his tendency to mistake them for each other, especially when they were joined by the pivotal third term, power. We are conscious of power in our sovereignty over the realm of commodity and our liberty in the realm of spirit. As we discover in *Nature*, commodity has a very low place on the Emersonian scale of being, and spirit the highest place. Since, however, it is power that gives us access to both realms, the two can look dangerously alike. Because they can, and because we find the resemblance attractive, we risk forgetting our end in the infatuation with our means: we become sovereigns of commodity and call it spirit. The Ode, I think, exemplifies this confusion but does not surmount it; and my conclusion, which I will try to keep in sight as I proceed, is that there can be no convincing resolution of the quarrel between Emerson's scholarly interpreter, Henry Thoreau, and his national interpreter, Henry Ford. Both tell us what they mean, and in both cases the name of what they mean is Emerson.

The journal entries around the time of the Ode are haunted by the evils a nation can do, and adroit in baffling their impulse to condemn with a nervous suspicion of all motives. "Mr. Webster," writes Emerson, "told [us] how much the war cost, that was his protest, but voted the war, and sends his son to it. They calculated rightly on Mr. Webster. My friend Mr. Thoreau has gone to jail rather than pay his tax. On him they could not calculate. The Abolitionists denounce the war and give much time to it, but they pay the tax." Webster's position is wrong, and yet Thoreau's protest—with its incidental reward of allowing him to be seen as an incalculable—is too idiosyncratic to be repeated or bear consequences. On the other hand, the very brazenness of the American government testifies to its strength of will, which almost looks like self-will, and compels us to recognize its power, which part of us wants to admire. "These—rabble—at Washington are really better than the snivelling opposition. They have a sort of genius of a bold and manly cast, though Satanic."[2]

In another entry of roughly the same period, the calculability of the abolitionists has ceased to be a warrant for rejecting their cause, and we find Emerson oppressed by the weight of soul-sickening events. He admits to himself that his only reason for keeping silent is the still greater oppression that would come if he allowed his anger to settle on an easy target. "Really," he writes, "a scholar has too humble an opinion of the population, of their possibilities, of their future, to be entitled to go to war with them, as with equals. This prison is one step to suicide. He knows that nothing they can do will ever please him. Why should he poorly pound on some one string of discord, when all is jangle?"[3] These are the words of a man whose temperament will permit him neither to pursue his calling in spite of public events nor to join the crowd that tries to effect a change in them. From the jail, suicide is but a step away; but one feels that for Emerson, as he writes, total paralysis is but a step in the opposite direction: few passages in his journals have this one-tone grimness. And, after this, we find it impossible to believe that Emerson could credit, or long be happy with, his remark that "The annexation of Texas looks like one of those events which retard or retrograde the civilization of ages. But the World Spirit is a good swimmer, and storms and waves cannot easily drown him. He snaps his fingers at laws."[4]

I have quoted these three entries out of sequence because, in their present order, they reproduce the movement of the Ode. We begin with the disagreeable summoning to public. speech, the refusal to supply eloquence for the occasion, and the rather anxious speculation on the motives of others who do speak. There follows the survey of America's estate, with the admission that evil it abroad in the land, but an evil that has come to dominate nature itself, to the point where all action is equally useless and equally blameless. Finally, about-face; the World Spirit is a good swimmer. The end of the poem is made inevitable not by a master-stroke of dialectical cunning, or because Emerson has convinced even himself of its propriety. It has only the claim of necessity. There was nothing else for Emerson to do if he wanted to go on writing.

Emerson speaks the first two stanzas, and Channing—or whatever in Emerson is embarrassable by Channing—the next three. Emerson gets pretty much the rest of the poem, his mind ranging far and wide to produce new contradictions while his stomach labors hard to digest the old. At the outset Emerson wants only to defend the solitude a poet builds so that poetry will visit him; abridge your solitude at the urging of society, and the "angry Muse" puts confusion in your brain. This would seem to require no apology. But in the third, fourth, and fifth stanzas Channing quickly gets the better of it: "While you preen yourself with fine talk about culture, one of your hapless neighbors is being assaulted in a back-alley of the Republic." And the pollution of slavery covers everything: "I found by thee, O rushing Contoocook! / And in thy valleys, Agiochook! / The jackals of the negro-holder." We have expected a different climax— something more like, "I found by thee ... / The flower that grows no other-where." Emerson loves these place-names; they belong to his New England, and mean as much to him as Monadnoc, or the troop of colonists in a famous opening line: "Bulkeley, Hunt, Willard, Homer, Meriam, Flint." The jackals are not here yet, but you can smell them in the air; the Fugitive Slave Law is on its way; and this is a betrayal of the intransigence that the very names were meant to convey. In the fifth stanza New Hampshire's men are seen as unworthy of the sublime landscape they inhabit: they are full of ambition, mean egotism, and complicity, and the land towers over them in gigantic scorn.

Yet, as this stanza continues, something strange is happening to the logic of the poem. A specific revulsion from those who would countenance slavery is generalized into universal disenchantment. The saber-rattling of the abolitionists is really just coffin-rattling; in such a time all eloquence becomes merely funereal. Channing's argument has touched an extreme at which it plays into Emerson's hands. The mode of much of the fifth stanza—beginning with "Small bat and wren / House in the Oak"—is close to Blakean satire, and we see that political remedies of the usual sort are out of the question. "Things are of the snake." Therefore, render unto Caesar what is Caesar's; and while you do it there will be plenty of time for debate.

The debate that occupies the rest of the poem ought to interest students of American politics as much as students of Emerson. *Service* has been on Emerson's mind from the start: whether or not to be pressed into service for a cause, whether to say his "I will not serve" to Channing or to the rabble in Washington. Now he observes that the right disposition of service has been inverted throughout nature: the horseman serves the horse, the eater serves his meat, "things are in the saddle, / And ride mankind." This happens because, of the "two laws discrete," "Law for man and law for thing," the second runs wild and "Doth the man unking." When I first read the Ode and came to the ninth stanza, I took it to be straight irony, a demonstration of how law for thing runs wild. But after all, *it is we that feel the irony*. What Emerson knew was that he needed two stanzas; one each, to demonstrate the proper functioning of law for thing and law for man. And law for thing includes: cutting down forests, building steamers, annexing new lands. Emerson is writing this poem to attack at the root the man–thing confusion that has tricked us into war. Yet the perfected man that he envisions has agreed neither to leave things alone nor to serve law for man. On the contrary, the march of technological optimism brings us back where we began, at the annexation of Texas, and determines it to have been legal in a more than political sense. We can see what the trouble is. Down this path a little way, things get in the saddle, and we are in Mexico with the rifle and the knife.

For "thing" let us temporarily substitute "commodity." Emerson writes in *Nature*:

> Under the general name of commodity, I rank all those advantages which our senses owe to nature.... [But] Nature, in its ministry to man, is not only the material but is also the process and the result. All the parts incessantly work into each other's hands for the profit of man.... The useful arts are reproductions or new combinations by the wit of man, of the same natural

benefactors. He no longer waits for favoring gales, but by means of steam, he realizes the fable of Aeolus's bag, and carries the two and thirty winds in the boiler of his boar.[5]

Commodity thus includes both the thing and what man does to the thing—which is understood as part of the thing itself, its final cause. In *Nature* as in the Ode, we can gauge Emerson's high spirits by the catalogue of things which he regards as a wonder requiring no comment. And yet the chapter in *Nature* closes with an admonition: "This mercenary benefit [conferred by nature with the help of man's skill] is one which has respect to a farther good. A man is fed, not that he may be fed, but that he may work." And if we are set to work on deeper tunnels and vaster prairies—what then? Work, after all, implies self-reliance only for a scholar.

The truth is that Emerson had a lover's quarrel with commodity, and liked to speak of its advancement in the language of manifest destiny. His journals portray it as an energy-giver to man, who may require coaxing to unleash his genius; and as the maker of harmony in those vicissitudes where man can hear only jangle. "By atoms, by trifles, by sots, Heaven operates. The needles are nothing, the magnetism is all." This is simple enough, as one instance of a monism that Emerson never leaves unqualified for long. (But the needles, I suspect, are the lives of individual men.) More amusing, and a good deal more puzzling, is the entry that runs: "Alcott should be made effective by being tapped by a good suction pump."[6] Here Alcott is to be understood as either inflated, or constipated, or both. The suction pump will make his genius serviceable. But something else is happening too. The machine is turning Alcott into a *thing*, and Emerson is expressing a certain satisfaction in the fact. It is fitting. The machine was made to do this to Alcott, and he needed to have this done to him. Which is in the saddle?

For "man" let us now substitute "spirit." Again, in the relevant chapter of *Nature*, we discover an admonition: "You cannot freely admire a noble landscape if laborers are digging in the field hard by." In the sight of bare commodity you do not participate in spirit. But what of a large mountain with a tunnel through it, when the laborers have gone away? If commodity may be assimilated to nature as the steamboat to Aeolus, the mountain-with-tunnel can plausibly become one of the hieroglyphs we read in identifying ourselves with spirit, and the power we feel in contemplating it is not to be wholly severed from the power the laborers spent in gouging it from rock. Perhaps when the scholar of nature does come to speak of spirit, he will see the lofty land taunting little men. But it is the same scholar who tells us that the land ought not to be left alone. Power occupies a landscape or nation as naturally as it fills a stanza. When, in a journal entry of 1846, Emerson transforms his distinction between our engine power over commodity and our contemplative power of spirit into an ethical distinction, between the politician who serves things and the poet who serves men, he gives us this:

> *Amalgam.* The absolutist is good and blessed, though he dies without sight of that paradise he journeys after; and he can forgive the earthworms who remain immersed in matter and know not the felicities he seeks. But not so well the middle man who receives and assents to his theories and yet, by habit and talent formed to live in the existing order, builds and prospers among the worldly men, extending his affection and countenance all the time to the absolutists. Ah, thou evil, two-faced half-and-half! how can I forgive thee? Evil, evil hast thou done. Thou it is that confoundest all distinctions. If thou didst not receive the truth at all, thou couldst do the cause of virtue no harm. But now the men of selfishness say to the absolutist, Behold this man, he has all thy truth, yet lo! he is with us and ours,—Ah, thou damnable Half-and-Half? choose, I pray you, between God and the Whig Party, and do not longer strew sugar on this bottled spider.
>
> Yes; but Confucius. Confucius, glory of the nations, Confucius, sage of the Absolute East, was a middle man. He is the Washington of philosophy.[7]

The face Emerson had before him when he spoke of Half-and-Half must have been Webster's. But Webster turns into Confucius quite effortlessly, and Emerson thought of himself now and then as a sage of the Absolute East. To the sentence at the end of this passage one wants to add: yes, and America is the Washington of nations; and the Ode is in this sense a thoroughly American poem.

In the penultimate stanza the over-god appears, bringing the honeycomb from out of the lion but also doing rather bloodier work: it is he that peoples and unpeoples, exterminates races by stronger races. He is the subtlest of artificers and, like the gardener of *The Winter's Tale*, "Grafts gentlest scion / On pirate and Turk." But another allusion, at once more strange and less remote, is also at work in these lines. Emerson was returning, for the iron will and martial cadence, to Wordsworth's "Ode: 1815," which had addressed an unequivocal prayer to the God who

> guides the Pestilence—the cloud
> Of locusts travels on his breath;

The region that in hope was ploughed
His drought consumes, his mildew taints with death

—the God, that is, of victory in battle:

But Thy most dreaded instrument
In working out a pure intent,
Is Man—arrayed for mutual slaughter,
—Yea, Carnage is thy daughter.

Wordsworth later softened and qualified this terrible utterance; yet it belonged to the eccentric canon of poems that mattered greatly to Emerson; it makes an ambiguous legacy, which Emerson was too honest to deny and yet too canny to welcome by its original name. It is curious to reflect that his summons to the over-god observes all the forms of a war-whoop for the allied adventure against Napoleon, in the very depth of the winter of democracy in England.

Having given over the discreteness of laws to the keeping of the over-god, Emerson retreats once again to his solitude—this time, however, accompanied by an army of thousands who stand ready to fight for liberty *and* solitude. One of Emerson's best known early poems, "Each and All," ends with the line: "I yielded myself to the perfect whole." Here we would have to alter it to read: "Aided by the over-god, I caused nature to yield a perfect whole, to which all in turn must yield." Emerson was of course shocked by the Russian invasion of Poland; but in the poem it seems hardly worse than a boyish trespass; the atmosphere in which the over-god subsists has converted everything to its own terms, and worked an eerie change on the words we use for good and evil. The muse, we remember, grew angry when Emerson deserted her for a cause. Now she is astonished because the cause has joined her. With some assistance from both her and the over-god, Emerson has won his right to stand alone. But at what cost? In the final sentence of "Experience" he wrote: "the true romance which the world exists to realize will be the transformation of genius into practical power." Every reader on coming to this sentence at the end of that somber essay will have felt certain of one thing: Emerson could not have known exactly what he meant. And anyone who knows Emerson well may feel certain of another: he was not speaking metaphorically. The iron in the soul of the Channing Ode is that a part of Emerson is in deep and unacknowledged sympathy with Channing's enemies and his own.

Poetry like history has its afterthoughts, the return in an almost penetrable disguise of an event too large to be easily recalled, and there is a troubling resemblance between the Ode and a more recent political poem, by another cunning respecter of "the angry Muse," Robert Frost's "Provide, Provide." Frost's occasion is a strike by the charwomen at Harvard, in the early years of the New Deal. He professes no sympathy for the strikers, and no shame or confusion about the sympathy withheld. The Abishag of his poem washes the steps "with pail and rag" after having fallen "from great and good," and we understand that no fall is without its cause. The poem affirms only that she should have planned her future with greater craft.

> Better to go down dignified
> With boughten friendship at your side
> Than none at all. Provide, provide!

When we provision ourselves with boughten friendship, we turn a spiritual good into a commodity; we know this, but are not less flattered and not less consoled for knowing it. The poem is delivered, as a kind of sermon, in the radically complacent tones of a Yankee minister, endeavoring at one stroke to confute every New England jeremiad that dared to lament the decline of a religion of faith into a habit of work. "What's the difference?" says this new and imperious voice of conscience. "If things are in the saddle, it is because we put them there. And what more have we ever desired, than to catch a trace of our own glory in the dazzle of theirs?" The Ode, "astonished" as it is, energetic and imperfect, may appeal to us more searchingly than the perfect freedom of satisfaction that we hear in Frost. But there can be no doubt that both poets had drunk deep from the same source.

NOTES

1. Quoted in *Selections from Ralph Waldo Emerson*, ed. Stephen E. Whicher (Boston, 1957). p. 505.

2. *Journal of Ralph Waldo Emerson*, ed. Edward Waldo Emerson and Waldo Emerson Forbes, 10 vols. (Cambridge, Mass., 1909–1914), VII, 219.

3. Ibid., p. 223.

4. Ibid., p. 26.

5. Emerson, *Works*, 12 vols. (Cambridge, Mass., 1903–1904), 1, 12–13.

6. Emerson, *Journals*, VII, 67, 39.

7. Ibid., pp. 125–126.

SHARON CAMERON

The Way of Life by Abandonment: Emerson's Impersonal

"Most of us have false beliefs about our own nature, and our identity, over time," Derek Parfit writes in *Reasons and Persons*, a book that challenges commonsense ideas about personal identity, and whose conclusions, I shall suggest, pertain directly to the writings of Ralph Waldo Emerson.[1] The false view, according to Parfit, centers on the idea that we are separately existing entities. We hold such a view because we mistake the psychological continuity of consciousness for the continued existence of a separately existing self in whom that consciousness inheres. But since experience gives no proof of this premise, we ought, Parfit writes, to reject it. We ought to accept what he calls the Reductionist claim that "the existence of a person just consists in the existence of his brain and body, and the doing of his deeds, and the occurrence of various other physical and mental events" (*RP*, p. 225). In other words, we ought to see there is no identificatory extra essence, distinct from our brains or bodies, on which a discrete or personal identity could be founded. I shall return to this characterization, described by Parfit as "impersonal," at the end of my discussion, but before leaving it I want to underline Parfit's understanding of the radical implications of his theory. Granting that personal identity does not matter is equivalent to, or has the consequence of, supposing that "if tomorrow someone will be in agony [it is] an empty question whether this agony will be felt by *me*," of seeing that "if I am about to lose consciousness, there may be no answer to the question 'Am I about to die?'" (*RP*, p. 280). What would it mean not to care if pain were *your* pain, to find the question empty? To find unanswerable the question of whether the loss of consciousness would mean *your* death? These are the central questions raised obliquely, one might even say unconsciously, by the centrally recurring idea of the impersonal in Emerson's essays.[2]

In the middle of "Nominalist and Realist" Emerson articulates his disillusion with the conventional idea that persons are separate and integral entities: "I wish to speak with all respect of persons, but sometimes I must pinch myself to keep awake, and preserve the due decorum. They melt so fast into each other, that they are like grass and trees, and it needs an effort to treat them as individuals."[3] The essay equivocates between belief in individuals and disbelief in them ("Though the uninspired man certainly finds persons a conveniency in household matters, the divine man does not respect them" ["NR," p. 580]), seeing this equivocation as a matter of shifting moods. But in the end Emerson's point of view is unambiguous, in favor of acknowledging what in "Montaigne" he names the "catholic sense," the "larger generalizations,"[4] in effect the impersonal, called by him "the Over-soul" in the most famous example: "In youth we are mad for persons. Childhood and youth see all the world in them. But the larger experience of man discovers the identical nature appearing through them all. Persons themselves acquaint us with the impersonal."[5] Impersonality is the antidote for the egotistical, the subjective, the solipsistic. It is so specifically because it refutes the idea that the mind is one's "property," that one's relation to being is that of ownership, on the one hand, and separate identity, on the other ("O," p. 390). From the perspective of the truth Emerson advocates in "The Over-soul," subjectivity and egotism are delusions about personal identity. From the vantage of the truth Emerson advocates in "The Over-soul," what defines "thoughts" as well as "events" is "alien energy," not "the will I call mine" ("O," p. 385). Thus the private will is overpowered by a force—variously named a "common heart" ("O," p. 386), and in others a "universal mind," an "identical nature"—that inhabits all.[6] By light of this identical nature, ownership is nonsensical; it is a mistake to call a talent, an idea, an achievement, or even a heart (and therefore a body) one's own, as it is a mistake to entertain the more abstract idea that persons have discrete identities. When Emerson in "The Over-soul" writes "we do not yet possess ourselves" ("O," p. 391), he means that we live out of synch with the truth of this impersonality. Yet to live *in* synch with it is to become indifferent to any fate one might conceivably call "mine" (the point ultimately made by the essay "Fate").

In part 1 of the following I examine formulations that elaborate the mechanics of impersonality, an examination necessary to specify how persons come in contact with the impersonal; in the second half of part 1 I examine Emerson's analysis of the way in which body and mind, counterintuitively, exemplify attributes of impersonality, as well as the way in which that "law," outside of body and mind, is equally said to epitomize it ("M," p. 708).

In part 2, I consider the features of the person who is expounding impersonality. I argue there is a connection between the anonymous voice of the speaker, the essays' stylistic singularity, and the compensating features of the erasure of personality. Throughout this and the following section I consider a series of concerns that threaten to produce a devastating critique of Emerson in any serious reading of him. Someone might reasonably feel that Emerson's idea of the impersonal is ethically illegitimate if not indeed simply delusional. If it is neither of these, what keeps it from being so? I understand such a question to mean: from what vantage could one relinquish the personal perspective one inevitably has as a delimited self? At the heart of the question is the issue of what licenses the abdication of a perspective one can't in some sense abdicate—what licenses it for oneself and what sanctions such a claim when it is made on another's behalf. For instance, when Emerson makes the following astonishing assertion, "If, in the hours of clear reason, we should speak the severest truth, we should say, that we had never made a sacrifice. In these hours the mind seems so great, that nothing can be taken from us that seems much. All loss, all pain, is particular; the universe remains to the heart unhurt.... It is only the finite that has wrought and suffered; the infinite lies stretched in smiling repose," this seems the sort of claim that cannot be made by one person for another ("SL," p. 305).

In part 3 I turn to "The Poet," the practitioner of impersonality—the poet being he who relinquishes the "jailyard of individual relations," who lays aside his private self so as to draw on "great public power ... by unlocking at all risks his human doors."[7] Although public power appears to require an indifference to persons, specifically to the distinction among persons, and especially to the particular status of the person who is writing, I argue that it does so at the peril of calling its own authority into question. Thus I claim that the deficiency in Emerson's representation of the impersonal lies peculiarly in the missing sense of a person.

1

How one gains access to the impersonal is a question that precedes all others in Emerson's essays. In "The Divinity School Address" it receives an explanation that initially differentiates between what "the preacher" is to do from what others are to do. The preacher is to decline any secondary relation to God: "to go alone; to refuse the good models ... and dare to love God without mediator or veil." Disavowing custom and authority, the preacher is "to live with the privilege of the immeasurable mind." He is to become visible to himself. The ocular image is Emerson's (in that the "immeasurable mind" is what the preacher will see when fashion, custom, authority, pleasure, money "are not bandages over [his] eyes"). When the preacher is visible to himself, he is enjoined to make himself visible to others, so that they will have a model. ("Let their doubts know that you have doubted, and their wonder feel that you have wondered.") What they will have a model *for* is precisely autonomy, which leads, in turn, to their ability to look within themselves, to do what the preacher does: like the preacher, "to go alone." From the preacher's point of view what's advocated is a theory of interpenetration: the self with "the immeasurable mind" and consequently with others. In this formulation inspiration turns inward and outward at once: to be visible to yourself is to make yourself visible to others, which will make visible the fact that what is in you is also in them. Such visibility will bequeath to them the autonomy that Emerson in his sermon is arguably bequeathing to the young students.[8]

The paradigm for access is somewhat different in "The American Scholar," where the self "going down into the secrets of his own mind ... has descended into the secrets of all minds." The American Scholar has access to others by having access to himself, unlike the "Divinity School" preacher who, having access to himself consequently (as opposed to identically), has access to others, and who therefore can show others how to have access to themselves. But the difference is without ultimate significance since (disappointingly from a pedagogic vantage) the lesson in both cases is that "the man has never lived that can feed us ever. The human mind cannot be enshrined in a person."[9]

In context this is an astonishing statement. It does not mean that no man is an exemplary, in the sense of adequate, incarnation, because each is partial (what it would mean in *Representative Men* or "Nominalist and Realist"). Nor does it precisely suggest that you should look to yourself rather than to others, though, like "The Divinity School Address," it also counsels autonomy, but for slightly different reasons. The American Scholar become autonomous will discover that no person (not even his own person) is adequate to enshrine the human mind. Thus while other persons produce a barrier to what "The Divinity School Address" calls "the immeasurable mind," so does one's own self understood in any conventional way. In effect, then, what self-reliance turns out to mean for Emerson is a strong recognition of the inadequacy of any person: other persons or this person.[10] And what the preacher and the American Scholar know how do is to break out of the tyranny of egotistical self-enclosure.

But what is meant by a person? And what is the alternative to supposing that the human mind can be "enshrined in a person"? "Compensation" provides one answer to the second of these questions. In this essay Emerson argues the need for recompense ("each thing is a half, and suggests another thing to make it whole"), on the one hand, and, on the other hand, the means of recompense ("We can no more halve things ... than we can get an inside that shall have no outside."[11] In this way a theory of dualism turns into a theory of ultimate totality). But the essay also wishes to illustrate some fact "deeper than" recompense that does not therefore require it: "The soul is not a compensation, but a life. The soul is. Under all this running sea of circumstance, whose waters ebb and flow with perfect balance, lies the aboriginal abyss of real Being. Essence, or God, is not a relation, or a part, but the whole" ("C," p. 299). Not part of the system of compensation (not necessitating it, not contributing to it), the soul is free of the drama of "More or Less" which is also the drama of "*His* and *Mine*" or, put differently still, free of the drama of the "inequalities of condition" and circumstance ("C," p. 301).

In "Compensation," then, the soul is free of particulars, good or bad; impersonality is a consequence of that liberation. The following paragraph from "Self-Reliance" elaborates the nature of this freedom. It does so by identifying the features of "real Being" ("Compensation"'s name for it), a state so stripped down that it is defined by negations. In such a state, characterized in the following passage as intuition without an object, one lives impersonally, that is, "in the present, above time" and "with God":

> And now at last the highest truth on this subject remains unsaid; probably cannot be said; for all that we say is the far-off remembering of the intuition. That thought, by what I can now nearest approach to say it, is this. When good is near you, when you have life in yourself, it is not by any known or accustomed way; you shall not discern the footprints of any other; you shall not see the face of man; you shall not hear any name;—the way, the thought, the good, shall be wholly strange and new. It shall exclude example and experience. You take the way from man, not to man. All persons that ever existed are its forgotten ministers. Fear and hope are alike beneath it. There is somewhat low even in hope. In the hour of vision, there is nothing that can be called gratitude, nor properly joy. The soul raised over passion beholds identity and eternal causation, perceives the self-existence of Truth and Right, and calms itself with knowing that all things go well. Vast spaces of nature, the Atlantic Ocean, the South Sea,—

long intervals of time, years, centuries,—are of no account. This which I think and feel underlay every former state of life and circumstances, as it does underlie my present, and what is called life, and what is called death.[12]

In the state Emerson describes, immediate experience is incomparable, not contingent on others' experience or on one's own experience. But what does it mean to get beyond others' and one's own experience? What is one *beyond*?

The answer offered by the passage has something to do with extrication from emotion, including all those emotions like hope, gratitude, joy, which one might suppose Emerson to wish to cultivate. Hope is under stood to be "low" presumably because, by definition, it supposes the inadequacy of the present state; gratitude, which is inspired by the sufficiency of the present, presumes, albeit implicitly, some alternative state that *wouldn't* be adequate. In effect it assumes a discrimination between the actual and an alternative to the actual. Joy especially implies the possibility of its opposite; moreover, the very meaning of joy, and the experiential sense of joy, presupposes an excess, a going beyond the bounds of bare awareness to which the soul has penetrated. Joy is a reaction, albeit a pleasant reaction. But the state Emerson describes is empty of reaction. That is its beneficence, its great gift. Vision undistracted by passion (by hope, gratitude, joy) is vision that is equanimous; Emerson calls it "calm." The passage asserts no reliable distinction between "what underlies" this present state of mind and what underlies either of those states supposed to be categorically other, between "what is called life, and what is called death."

If "this which I think and feel" is also foundational—is the *same* foundation—for "what is called life and what is called death," then the all-substantial present, the present made substantial by the clairvoyance of one's seeing of it ("the hour of vision"), is the predicative ground for what we suppose to be different in both magnitude and category. That is what we see when we see the present as it is: without passion, and without comparison, as if it alone were real.

Though it might seem surprising, the impersonal, as instantiated in the passages I have touched on, *leads* to the social in its highest form. In Emerson's words, the consciousness of divine presence "makes society possible" ("O," p. 392). Thus in Emerson's account the impersonal enables the social world it appears to eradicate. "The Over-soul" offers a rigorous analysis of how the impersonal is incarnated.

The Over-soul makes itself manifest through particular properties within particular persons, who act as its conduit. This Over-soul is not an entity, nor is it a property. Call it a manifestation, even always a particular manifestation, though not always the same particular manifestation:

> All goes to show that the soul in man is not an organ, but animates and exercises all the organs; is not a function, like the power of memory, of calculation, of comparison, but uses these as hands and feet; is not a faculty, but a light; is not the intellect or the will, but the master of the intellect and the will; is the background of our being, in which they lie,—an immensity not possessed and that cannot be possessed. From within or from behind, a light shines through us upon things, and makes us aware that we are nothing, but the light is all. A man is the façade of a temple wherein all wisdom and all good abide. What we commonly call man, the eating, drinking, planting, counting man, does not, as we know him, represent himself, but misrepresents himself. Him we do not respect, but the soul, whose organ he is, would he let it appear through his action, would make our knees bend. When it breathes through his intellect, it is genius; when it breathes through his will, it is virtue; when it flows through his affection, it is love. And the blindness of the intellect begins, when it would be something of itself. ["O," pp. 386–87]

The passage is precise in its analysis of how this power (not an organ, like Descartes's gland; not a function; not a faculty) becomes embodied by organs, by functions, by faculties. The Over-soul inhabits, vivifies, or traverses the mind, the will, the heart, but it is *not* the mind, the will, the heart. The Over-soul can be seen in those incarnations through which it "breathes": "genius," "will," "virtue," "love," and "action." Not separate from and also not equal to any particular trait, but also manifesting itself only through recognizable particularities—through actions, emotions, properties, only through what is actual and even at times visible (action would be visible, and genius, will, virtue, love might be so). In "Nature" transparency cancels being. But the Over-soul animates and makes being palpable. It is precisely this palpability that compels the personification of tribute: "would [a man] let it appear through his action, [it] would make our knees bend." In fact, it could be argued that it is the Over-soul's visibility *in* action, function, property, and person that permits us to mistake action, function, property, person for the manifestational power that animates them.

The Over-soul, then, is associated with the individual, though one can have no proprietary relation to it. (From "Illusions": "The notions, '*I am*,' and '*This is mine*,' which influence mankind, are but delusions of the mother of the world.") [13] The trouble begins when the mind falsely identifies with the powers that inhabit it. The mistake lies in associating the Over-soul with the self and particularly with the voluntary self. It is associated with the person, but not as his property, and not through his will (therefore not through "eating," "drinking," "planting," "counting"). These activities misrepresent the person not because they are palpable and also not because they are functional or social—rather, because they are limited.

In pointing to something other than the experiential world of the fragmentary (a world whose piecemeal nature he would describe most eloquently in "Experience"), Emerson is not mystically gesturing to an alien nature that he domesticates, converting the not-me into something with recognizable contour. The Over-soul always remains other, while all the time being all-accessible (see "O," p. 394). In fact it's precisely the point that we cannot relinquish our difference from it. No procedure is performed that would cancel the egotistical person, the person with interests, needs, desires, will. It is not a matter of willing to be better than we are or different than we are. It is a matter of not-willing, of seeing what we are when the will stops executing its claims. When we give ourselves up to the involuntary, "the walls are taken away. We lie open on one side to the deeps of spiritual nature, to the attributes of God" ("O," p. 387). I take Emerson's spatial image as testifying to the necessarily divided nature of our allegiance to the egotistical and the impersonal. On one side there is access, on the other there is not.

In seeing that one's true alliance is not with will or desire, not with anything piecemeal, but rather with the totality, the personal becomes impersonal. But to put it like this still implies a conventional choice, and I take Emerson to be insisting that at such a moment there is no real choice, no other way to be in *proper* relation. If what's given up by the isolate self is a deluded sense of its power, what's given back is what Emerson, silently quoting Plotinus, calls "innocen[ce]," that to which the "religious" cedes when it stops being an idea: "The soul gives itself, alone, original, and pure, to the Lonely, Original, and Pure, who, on that condition, gladly inhabits, leads, and speaks through it. Then is it glad, young, and nimble. It is not wise, but it sees through all things. It is not called religious, but it is innocent" ("O," p. 400). Thus in acceding to the impersonal, one is "beyond" emotions, beyond the idea that identity is fixed. But not beyond the social or the recognizable. We are continuously enjoined to see that we can recognize the impersonal (called "the Over-soul" or, in "Spiritual Laws," the "homogeneous" ["SL," p. 321]), though not in the familiar terms by which we customarily mistake it: not connected to sequence; not in relation to the voluntary; and not as an anomaly.

The interest of Emerson's essays lies in moments when the impersonal *emerges*. To put this in different terms: while it has frequently been noted that Emerson's essays dramatize contradiction, the *content* of the contradiction can repeatedly be specified by the process through which the personal becomes the impersonal, as in "Nominalist and Realist" where the science of universals alternates with the science of parts, and where nature (one of Emerson's ways of denominating the whole) rises up against persons, specifically against "each person, inflamed to a fury of personality" ("NR," p. 581). In the following examples, differently epitomized—by the eyes, by moods, by moral law—the impersonal is set against "the fury of personality." This contest takes the place of narrative or is the narrative of Emerson's essays.

In the essay "Behavior" allegiance to the universal is immediately articulated by a glance of the eyes. Interestingly, unlike in "Culture," where an adherence to the universal needs to be *learned*, the eyes confess the truth, from one perspective, and penetrate to it, from another, immediately and involuntarily. ("The communication by the glance is in the greatest part not subject to the control of the will. It is the bodily symbol of identity of nature.") What the eye reveals is the degree of discrepancy between the "generous and universal" and "the fury of personality":

> There are asking eyes, asserting eyes, prowling eyes; and eyes full of fate,—some of good, and some of sinister omen. The alleged power to charm down insanity, or ferocity in beasts, is a power behind the eye. 'Tis very certain that each man carries in his eye the exact indication of his rank in the immense scale of men, and we are always learning to read it. A complete man should need no auxiliaries to his personal presence. Whoever looked on him would consent to his will, being certified that his aims were generous and universal. The reason why men do not obey us, is because they see the mud at the bottom of our eye.[14]

Although the beholder reads the eye with respect to an index of behaviors (that pertain to action, to speech, to hospitality, to security), the standard for assessing each remains an alliance of the personal with the universal. The personal is the "mud at the bottom of the eye." The eyes give the lie first to what the person would *have* believed, indicating a discrepancy between what is asserted and what is true; second, they reveal when there is not in fact harmony between one person and another, hence not between the person and the universe, that the "bodily symbol of the identity of nature" (Emerson's presumptive ideal) stands degraded and betrayed. Thus the eyes reveal the personality and reveal *beyond* it. One way of understanding such a divided revelation is to see "the fury of personality" as a mere part of being that inherently also reflects something extrinsic to it. The eyes "are the great symbol" because they reveal an impersonal register of value identically legible to all.

Emerson's representation of the transience of moods further erodes the commonplace idea that mental states are personal and that we govern what occurs "within." "Circles" is a radical essay because it tells us that our moods determine us. Further, "our moods do not believe in each other.... I am God in nature; I am a weed by the wall."[15] In "Experience" life is described as a flux: "a succession of moods."[16] In "Nominalist and Realist" the very propensity to believe in universals over particulars or vice versa is a consequence of shifting moods. Thus so-called fixtures (like "truth" in "Circles," like perspective in "Nominalist and Realist," but also like temperament in "Experience") are subject to alteration. That there is no security against moods in effect calls into question the idea of any fixture legislating what is thought, believed in, felt, experienced. If every insight, like every mood, is, as Emerson implies, partial, fleeting, and mediate, then we are merely inhabited by these truly extrinsic (hence impersonal) mental states that we host without controlling. They are events in our history without being properly identified as ours. Harry Frankfurt writes: "A person is no more to be identified with everything that goes on in his mind ... than he is to be identified with everything that goes on in his body."[17] Emerson goes more than a step further, suggesting, it would seem, that there is *no* mental experience with which we are to be identified; for there is no permanence to any mood, perception, or belief ("Permanence is a word of degrees" ["Ci," p. 404]) and, further, no ability to determine when, affected by these moods, one experiences the self as "God in nature" or, oppositely, as a "weed by the wall."[18] This extrinsicality even of those determinations that most apparently define us is underscored and—from one point of view outrageously— extended in "Uses of Great Men" where Emerson asserts: "The power which [great men] communicate is not theirs. When we are exalted by ideas, we do not owe this to Plato, but to the idea, to which, also, Plato was debtor." Such erasure of identity, such a consistent dramatization (in "Circles," "Experience," "Nominalist and Realist," "Uses of Great Men") of moods as constitutive of belief and even of personality and temperament suggests that moods exist "irrespective of persons," that "moods" like the forces described in "Uses of Great Men" become "power[s] so great, that the potentate is nothing." Moods, like those forces, "destroy individualism."[19]

Thus, to say, as I did earlier, that mental states are things we "host without controlling," are "events in our history," is still to suppose a personal identity inhabited by moods extrinsic to it, just as to imply an alien physical state (like "the broken sleep" described below) is to suppose an essence to which that physical state is contrastively other. But this sense of contrast is only rhetorical (has no significant application). While it looks like such formulations presume something stable on which identity could be pinned (our body, our history), the formulations are stable only by contrast; they are something that contrast—the next formulation—shifts. Nothing is "ours" except rhetorically, or positionally. In that rhetoric a person lays claims to some elusive property which he cannot really own.

One way of understanding the impersonal then is as something that appears through *bodies* (as visible in the eyes) as a critique of the personal (also visible there), that which shows up its limits, as in the passage from "Behavior." A second way of understanding the impersonal is in terms of moods and *mental states*. The very moods that we might suppose to define our individual persons, when scrutinized in Emerson's representations, actually contradict the idea of the personal (though not necessarily the idea of the individual, since one could be individuated by mental states that were not properly one's "own"). Thus if in "Behavior" the impersonal speaks *through* the self (is visible in the eyes), in an essay like "Nominalist and Realist" the impersonal calls into question the very idea of a self as a stable or predictable entity, for the moods that define our perceptions, beliefs, and thoughts are in effect only contingent on circumstance. (In "Montaigne," even principles—opinions on right and wrong, on fate and causation—are "at the mercy of a broken sleep or an indigestion" ["M," p. 704].) In yet a third example the impersonal is associated not with the body and not with the affective life of the mind but rather with a law (alternately called "the moral sentiment") to which the "self" adheres, disregarding as it were the conditions of body and mind: "All moods may be safely tried, and their weight allowed to all objections: the moral sentiment as easily outweighs them all.... This faith avails to the whole emergency of life and objects ("M," p. 708). So much so does the ideal of law prevail against body and mind that the ideal survives the degradation of it, passionately represented in the penultimate passage from "Montaigne":

> Charles Fourier announced that "the attractions of man are proportioned to his destinies"; in other words, that every desire predicts its own satisfaction. Yet, all experience exhibits the reverse of this; the incompetency of power is the universal grief of young and ardent minds. They accuse the divine providence of a certain parsimony. It has shown the heaven and earth to every

child, and filled him with a desire for the whole; a desire raging, infinite; a hunger, as of space to be filled with planets; a cry of famine, as of devils for souls. Then for the satisfaction,—to each man is administered a single drop, a bead of dew of vital power, *per day*,—a cup as large as space, and one drop of the water of life in it. Each man woke in the morning, with an appetite that could eat the solar system like a cake; a spirit for action and passion without bounds.... but, on the first motion to prove his strength,—hands, feet, senses, gave way,... In every house ... this chasm is found,—between the largest promise of ideal power, and the shabby experience. ["M," p. 708]

Despite the hyperbolically exampled discrepancies between the ideal and the experienced, the conclusion of the essay adheres to the ideal, though without Fourier's illusions. The personal (what is experienced by the hands, the feet, the senses, and epitomized by an "appetite that could eat the solar system like a cake") is cast aside, not afforded weight, in favor of "the moral sentiment." It is cast aside not because its presence is immaterial, because it does not affect the person. From one point of view it *constitutes* the person's desire, his aspiration, his endeavor, his voraciousness and registers the thwarting of these. But if such frustration defines the *personal*, from another point of view, it does not define the *person* who rather "resist[s] the usurpation of particulars," so as to "penetrate to their catholic sense" ("M," p. 709). Here body and mind are subordinated to a manifestation of the impersonal that cannot be assigned to a will or a desiring self. And this impersonal force (called in "Montaigne" as in "The Divinity School Address" "the law") also becomes the object of our affirmation, against the evidence of the personal and, even more to the point, against the interests of the person.

2

In Emerson's writing, style functions as a validation of propositions in lieu of logic or as a supplement to logic, as I shall explain. This distrust of formal argument originates in Emerson's critique of the commonplaces of prayers and sermons. In "The Divinity School Address," against the deadliness of the formalist preacher, who substitutes "doctrine" for life, Emerson posits what is impossible to formulate:

The child amidst his baubles, is learning the action of light, motion, gravity, muscular force; and in the game of human life, love, fear, justice, appetite, man and God, interact. These [divine] laws refuse to be adequately stated. They will not be written out on paper, or spoken by the tongue. They elude our persevering thought; yet we read them hourly in each other's faces, in each other's actions, in our own remorse.... This sentiment [the perception of lawfulness] is the essence of all religion. ["DSA," p. 76]

In the passage Emerson gets his reader to accede to an important experience that only subsequently is characterized as *religious*, as "the essence of all religion." Religious experience is *integral* to ordinary experience, but because it is not separable from ordinary experience, it is not knowable in terms of easily detachable criteria. Nor can it be articulated, though it cannot help but be intuited. Moreover, arising out of concrete experience, such laws are nonetheless "out of time, out of space, and not subject to circumstance" or summary account ("DSA," p. 76). They are within and without particular experiences, embodied by experience to which they are nonetheless not reducible. Such "laws," elsewhere cumulatively called "the religious sentiment," are by definition impersonal and in "The Divinity School Address" are repeatedly juxtaposed to the person of Jesus. Such law can be analogized to a natural phenomenon ("It is a mountain air.... The silent song of the stars is it" ["DSA," p. 78]); it is knowable *in* nature, and often *as* nature. It is also knowable as *depth*. Thus Jesus' name "is not so much written as ploughed into the history of this world." That name is said to be an "infusion" ("DSA," p. 79).

In "Self-Reliance" the impersonal (which alone has depth and thus ultimate reality) is associated with "*Whim*," with the "involuntary," with "genius," and with "intuition" ("S," pp. 262, 269, 260, 271). In "The Divinity School Address" the impersonal (which alone has depth) is associated with "the soul." My point here is that, unlike a systematic thinker, Emerson makes no attempt to confer consistency on his designations, or even to establish connections among terms that occupy the same structural position in respective essays. Intuition has depth; as the soul has depth; as Jesus' name (in "The Divinity School Address"), which is "ploughed into the history of this world," has depth; but whether these are different terms for the same phenomenon remains, I believe, intentionally unaddressed. The consequence for a reader is to encounter phenomena that clearly overlap without being clearly identical. And this nonidenticality seems a purposeful block to the summarizing definition that could characterize the impersonal but that cannot do so here because the experiences in which it is shown to be situated eschew logical "comparative" relations.

If in "The Divinity School Address" Emerson preaches the soul against the religion of the person, in "The Over-soul" this entity is recognizable as what is "public and human" ("O," p. 400). Though incarnated in form, it always points inward to some identical "nature," some "centre of the world," some "influx of the Divine mind into our mind" ("O," pp. 389, 392). That "influx" is characterized sequentially in one passage as coming on condition of an "entire possession," of coming as "insight," as "serenity," and conclusively (but always nondefinitively) of coming as "grandeur" ("O," pp. 396, 397). Thus again we note the asymmetry of terms by which manifestations of the impersonal defy systemization: they are connected in this discourse, but not logically so. Their originality lies in their deliberately unexplained relations often perceptible as mere contiguity.

But if the designations for the soul keep us off balance through a nonalliance, and if we are commensurately enjoined to renounce description of the soul for habitation within it—are enjoined to reside in "that influx of the Divine mind into our mind" (called at this moment "the religious sense")—Emerson does characterize the experience of such an influx consistently as "enthusiasm," as "ecstacy," as "trance," or "inspiration," and, "in the case of remarkable persons" like Socrates, Plotinus, George Fox, and Behmen, as what he calls "ravishment" ("O," pp. 392–93). In fact "ravishment" (that proprioceptive sense of what occurs at that moment when the personal is annihilated by the influx of the impersonal) is what the essays attempt to dramatize.

What replaces philosophic logic is something like the representation of ravishment, a phenomenon all the more difficult to recognize because it occurs in relation to experiences that seem at last, as at first, categorically different from each other (the name of Jesus "ploughed into the history of this world"; the baubles of the child's play ingrained as law; innocence that results when the "soul gives itself, alone, original, and pure, to the Lonely, Original, and Pure"). There is, moreover, another reason that the representation of moments of ravishment is disorienting. In narrating such moments, Emerson assumes a stance and a voice above and beyond the personal, for his authority in these essays with respect to the "religious sentiment" (elsewhere "innocence," the "soul," "laws that refuse to be adequately stated") is the authority of one who has access to principles of organization that are conferred beyond individual experience.[20] Hence, for instance, the difficulty in attributing individuality to the voice that says, "the soul gives itself, alone, original, and pure."

This is not Emerson's voice because it is Plotinus's.[21] But it is not Plotinus's either because *in* Emerson it is legible as no one's voice at all. And that this anonymous voice, which is not a recognizable voice because not legible as a single person's voice, should tell of ravishment—ravishment being the precise moment marked in extraordinary persons at "the influx of the Divine mind into our mind"—is remarkable, given the fact that if the imperative for someone voicing the impersonal is access to experience that transcends his own, the imperative for someone voicing ravishment is to inhabit the very experience whose particularity must be owned (and experienced as such) before it is annihilated, if the experience is to register as one of ravishment. Thus the experience being described ("the Divine mind into our mind," the obliteration of the personal, call it, as Emerson does, ravishment) reveals a weird absence, the opposite of which is stylistic mimesis, since nothing counts or registers as "personal" even prior to the epiphanic moment of its proclaimed disappearance.

Emerson's voice, which is not that of a private person, is in fact public and is engaged in a performance. What is being performed is something like ravishment as a consequence of self-abandonment. In Emerson's essays the personal is most marked at the moment of its obliteration—or it would be so if it were initially iterated, as it is, rarely, in instances like the following. In the most celebrated example, from *Nature*, the self that is lost is briefly first owned: "Standing on the bare ground,—my head bathed by the blithe air, and uplifted into infinite space,—all mean egotism vanishes.... I am part or particle of God."[22] In this example the person is forfeited for "Universal Being." Whereas in "Experience" what is forfeited is something like personal affect:

> In the death of my son, now more than two years ago, I seem to have lost a beautiful estate,—no more. I cannot get it nearer to me.... This calamity ... does not touch me. ["E," p. 473]

and, ultimately, personal connection:

> the longest love or aversion has a speedy term. The great and crescive self, rooted in absolute nature, supplants all relative existence. ["E," p. 487]

In "Circles," self-abandonment is theorized as that philosophically necessary position that makes ravishment possible: "The one thing which we seek with insatiable desire is to forget ourselves, to be surprised out of our propriety, to lose our sempiternal memory, and to do something without knowing how or why; in short, to draw a new circle.... The way of life is wonderful: it is by abandonment" ("Ci," p. 414). Typically, however, while the impersonal is ostensibly represented at the moment of its emergence in Emerson, and though this emergence is ostensibly performed, there is characteristically vacancy in the place where we might expect to find a person.

Thus although the essays perform the task of ravishment—that process through which the person is annihilated by the impersonal—no sacrifice is customarily really exacted because rarely is it the case that a discrete or particularized self initially occupies the subject-position. What is great about Nature, Emerson argues in an early essay, "The Method of Nature," is "that there is ... no private will, no rebel leaf or limb, but the whole is oppressed by one superincumbent tendency, obeys that redundancy or excess of life which in conscious beings we call *ecstasy*."[23] We could say that what occupies the subject-position of Emerson's essays—how the voice we call Emerson's implicitly comes to be defined—is a rhetorical construction, the most enduring feature of which impedes or staves off any apparent individuality, any representation of a "private will." That is the sine qua non of the Emersonian "I," ostensibly styled without either point of view or idiosyncracy. (Of course voices in writing are always rhetorically constructed, but the rhetorical construction of Emerson's "I" can be characterized by its fetishized universality, its obsessively constructed anonymity.) The platitudes that often seem stunning in an Emerson essay—stunning that a writer who displays so much expertise in crafting powerful sentences could also write so vapidly—well serve this goal of voicing words whose particular source is undiscoverable. It precisely serves Emerson's purpose to rehearse commonplace remarks that could be spoken by anyone. In "Intellect," we are told that "silence is a solvent that destroys personality, and gives us leave to be great and universal."[24] In Emerson's essays contradictory propositions (along with the abstracted "I," constructed at once, as if indiscriminately out of original, vital images and empty enervated ones) are the solvent that dissolves personality.

There is a hypnotic and vertiginous momentum to the (much discussed) contradictory drift of these essays that advocate, on the one hand, self-trust and, on the other, self-abolition. Precisely because of this self contradiction, the essays implicitly promise an overall logic or an argumentative progression that would make sense of and therefore rectify the self-canceling propositions. In lieu of this context—one could say in defiance of it—the propositions, like the self who voices them, are constructed as momentary: good for the moment, but again and again cast off and re-created. The "endless seeker, with no Past at my back" ("Ci," p. 412)—one of Emerson's most wishful self-descriptions—staves off perspective, duration, and therefore questions about limit. The "person" that Emerson represents himself as being is one with no situational givens—one who, like the poet's language, is "fluxional," "vehicular," "transitive," therefore a man indifferent to needs ("P," p. 463). This Emersonian self, the "I" of the essays, can invoke the impersonal, purporting to be embodied by or fed to it (and this without sacrifice, or with "nothing ... that seems much"), the celebration of which process is said to produce excess, ecstacy, and, alternately, ravishment, because his own being is so spectacularly unconstituted by anything physical. The Emersonian speaker who celebrates the impersonal is something like the "soul" he frequently catechizes. Or if not a soul, then "a method, a progressive arrangement; a selecting principle" (in "Spiritual Laws," these explicitly constitute the definition of "a man" ["SL," p. 311]). Or he is an intellect ("intellect goes out of the individual, floats over its own personality" ["I," p. 417]). Or a force like love, which we are told "must become more impersonal every day."[25]

In view of these peculiarities—speech that is unsituated, unreferenced to a body; constituted by contradiction and by nonsummatory arguments; conciliatory with respect to loss ("nothing that can be taken from us seems much"); and delegating away various properties like love, like intellect—I wish to ask: what is the appeal of the impersonal; what makes it attractive?

The context that might explain the enticement of the impersonal above what Henry Ware, Jr., in 1838, writing against Emerson, called "the happiness of human life" is the heroic—a model, or an ideal, that, it could be argued, Emerson shares with Kant.[26] Thus for example when Emerson advocates dismissing "the eating, drinking, planting, counting man" for the Over-soul, what is being distinguished is personal interest in an entity aspiring to be "something of itself" for the sake of interest in "an immensity not possessed and that cannot be possessed" ("O," p. 387).[27]

When Kant distinguishes the categorical from the hypothetical by saying that in the case of the former "all interest is renounced, which is the specific criterion of categorical as distinguished from hypothetical imperatives,"[28] this self-abnegation sounds peculiarly like Emerson, although Kant is talking about what constitutes the basis of proper (ethical) action and Emerson is talking about what constitutes the basis of proper identification (since the interested or partial man "does not ... represent himself, but misrepresents himself"). For Kant—at least in regard to ethical action—the worth of rational beings lies in their capacity to adhere to "a mere idea" that serves as "an inflexible precept of the will" (in other words, dignity is the result of the autonomy of man's will from "the physical law of [the self's] wants") (FP, p. 68). I call this heroic because it presupposes a contact with the real that is not contingent on this or that condition. For Kant "personal worth" consists in adhering to the requirements of pure practical reason independently of inclination (FP, p. 81). Hence, what is involved is choice of nobility. According to the Fundamental Principles of the Metaphysics of Morals only in the moral world "is [a person] his proper self (being as a man only the appearance of himself)" (*FP*, p. 91). For Emerson, as for Kant, a higher interest and identification with something higher presupposes a person's access to the real stripped of inessentials. Thus in "Worship": "We are never without a hint that these powers [of sense and understanding] are mediate and servile, and that we are one day to deal with real being,—essences with essences."[29] The promise of the essays is access to "real being," to being further irreducible (at the end of "Worship" called "the superpersonal Heart," the "nameless Power"),[30] to contact with the real—a sudden often apocalyptic encounter with it ("I am nothing; I see all" ["N," p. 10]) in comparison with which contingent or personal identity not only misrepresents the self but is in effect trivial. Emerson dismisses the eucharist—the conventional trope for figuring such an encounter—in order to reinvent the necessity of some way of representing unmediated, face-to-face contact with this reality ("real being,—essences with essences") whose fundamental nature must each time be gleaned anew.

It is an unmediated "face to face" that the essays again and again retrieve. They can do this "again and again" precisely because there is no rite, no symbol or authorized entity—not Christ, not the moral sentiment, not the Over-soul—nothing *repeatable* to be apprehended in these essays. It is precisely Emerson's point that an encounter with the real cannot be repeated. Hence there is no single name for it and, often, only negative attributes. Contact is mystified because it is irreducible to anything but style and to the idiosyncracies of style. What is performed is idiosyncracy. At the emergence of the idiosyncratic formulation, conventional features of the prose—the sententious exhortation ("Trust thyself" ["S," p. 260]); the apostrophe ("O my brothers, God exists" ["SL," p. 309]); the aphoristic and pedantic formulation ("The soul's emphasis is always right" ["SL," p. 312]); the propositional banality ("We must go alone" ["S," p. 272])—drop away. The point about the revelatory language that replaces such banal formulations is to dramatize the heuristic often in arcane images that thwart *understanding* of the exact relation ostensibly being adduced.

One could argue that the ultimate prestige in an Emerson essay depends upon the direct discrepancy between a straightforward claim and the eccentric, sometimes grotesque, and often mysteriously physical trope in which it is enveloped—as in the following passage where at one level the experience is recognizable, and at another level it cannot be recognized. The "surprise" part of the following passage from the second essay "Nature," and the climactic finish in which it is couched, is key to the Emersonian formula. Such a moment cancels the person's servitude to particulars, in effect by illuminating that everything outside of the self is comprised of the same elements:

Man imprisoned, man crystallized, man vegetative, speaks to man impersonated. That power which does not respect quantity, which makes the whole and the particle its equal channel, delegates its smile to the morning, and distills its essence into every drop of rain. Every moment instructs, and every object: for wisdom is infused into every form. It has been poured into us as blood; it convulsed us as pain; it slid into us as pleasure; it enveloped us in dull, melancholy days, or in days of cheerful labor; we did not guess its essence, until after a long time. ["N," p. 555]

This is a signature Emersonian paragraph; it has all the recognizable components I have been considering. At issue is "essence," in the Emersonian world not only startling when ascertained but also violent, as the verbs imply, a power that affects physical being through pain (as the word "convulsed" reiterates), but also through pleasure (as the word "slid" reiterates), raising an irrelevant question about a potentially confused relation between pleasure and pain, and about conferred physicality in general ("is infused.... has been poured"). It is easy to forget the subject of such a passage. (What is difficult about the passage is the constant drifting of reference and a syntax that can't be sustained because this would keep persons in their place.) Most immediately, that subject is "wisdom," the antecedent of "it." But it is wisdom about "Power," and if we read back further still, it is wisdom about the power of the general—the ability to see that what is said to "exist in the mind as [an] idea" in nature is forever embodied ("N," p. 554). The ultimate discovery, then, concerns a perceived identity among animal, vegetable, mineral, between mind and nature. And the specific gesture accomplished by style here (as well as by the asymmetry of terms such as "moments" and "objects," which are given syntactical equality, both being subjects of "instructs") is to make such identity unmistakable. There would be a discrepancy between container (the human body) and thing contained (the blood) because of the latter's source in the world, which we could assume to be substantial, were it not the case that all aspects of the passage are at work to critique a term like *discrepancy* to refer to a phenomenon the confrontation of which—the seeing it face to face— cancels any distinction between "the whole and the particle." Therefore essence can be spoken of in terms of "drops of rain" *and* essence can be spoken of in terms of human "blood." Nature is not outside of us. If we can't oversee nature, that's not because it's alien but is rather because it is internal. These half-implicit propositions are enacted by style. They could never be made in logical form because such terms would subvert the "originary" impulse of these essays that generate endless text in order to dramatize the essayist's encounter with "the catholic sense" of things, a sense that is best discoverable again and again at the core of one's own being.[31] The tenor of such a passage and its denotative meaning, being in all cases what the essays have worked towards (often in explicit and trite formulation), is all but unmistakable—it is never in doubt—while the vehicle, as well as the statement's residue, characteristically prohibits easy, or even intelligible, formulation (as in the indecipherable relation between "man impersonated" and "man imprisoned").

Thus, oddly enough, although the goal of these essays is generality (however it is called) and although the style is often inimitably general—Emerson writing in no man's voice—the point of the essays' climactic figures is the representation of an encounter whose truth is somehow tied to its stylistic or rhetorical singularity. The untransmissible trope, irreducible to symbol or rite and buried in unmistakable, often clichéd figuration, counts as evidence in lieu of evidence that the author of the essay—in distinction to the reader whose tutelage the author implicitly takes on—has knowledge of an encounter with ultimate reality. In this way Emerson's banal assertions combine with his solecisms to produce a style whose inimitability serves a logical function.

I have argued that in Emerson's essays what is dramatized is the fact that the impersonal speaks despite us, though *through* us (it is visible in the eyes), even as it perpetually (in the transformation of moods) calls the idea of a fixed self into question; or it is otherwise seen as an alternative to moods (in the fixture of the "moral sentiment"), something having a stability no experienced self could have. But this impersonality is not, for Emerson, abstractly dissociated from the idea of self. It is viscerally represented as what must be "owned" by the very self with which it is understood not to be identical.[32]

When Emerson recommends "own[ing]" what is other, this endorses a logic equivalent to Hegel's idea that the single individual is incomplete Spirit. But, readers commonly object, while Emerson has the right to sacrifice his personal interest—the interest of *his* person—to that universal spirit, he does not have the right to sacrifice another's personal interest to or for something higher. He can neither ethically approve such a sacrifice for others nor ethically recommend it to them. Nor can he define interest (whether higher or lower) for another. Moreover, he cannot define *his* interest as equivalent to another's. He cannot assume that *his* higher interest is precisely *theirs*. He has no authority to do so. Although this complaint is posed by readers who object to Emerson's social conservatism (as discussed below), such a question about authority is in my view also raised by a more theoretical question about what kind of alliance to, and difference from, other persons a speaker must acknowledge or prove to speak on their behalf. The subject of authority and legitimacy with respect to another's interest raises the odd question of whether Emerson speaks on his own behalf.

3

The subject of authority might be usefully examined in relation to William Ellery Channing. When Channing writes, "We conceive that the true love of God is a moral sentiment" and "we see God around us be cause he dwells within us," such sentences sound like Emerson's. But they are not in fact comparable, for what authorizes Channing's assertions is his position as a minister; specifically, as a minister he has authority to create analogies between the human and the divine and to show they are *only* analogies. For Channing the source of divinity is not the impersonal but is rather the *person* of "God as the Father and quickener of the human mind."[33]

To make statements about the divinity of the soul without authority is to make them *casually*, to construct or imagine them. No tradition is being explained in such statements; rather, something is being composed and invented against tradition. But why trust this invention about a universal that demands the same sacrifice as conventional religion without any of its compensations? Moreover, although Emerson proclaims a nonsectarian universal we have only to look at Emerson's distinctions—and his dismissal of those distinctions—to see that persons are not always the undifferentiated beings constructed by the prose. The great shame of Emerson, as his detractors observe, is his callous indifference to the very social distinctions he occasionally recognizes.

"Compensation" of course *denies* social distinction by immediately trivializing it: "In the nature of the soul is the compensation for the inequalities of condition.... The heart and soul of all men being one, this bitterness of *His* and *Mine* ceases. His is mine" ("C," p. 301). But except in the verbal world of the essay there is no impersonality of ownership. *His* is not *mine.* Nor do "we all take turns at the top" as "Nominalist and Realist" would have it ("NR," p. 582). This barbarous idealism infects all of the writing. Emerson's capitalist economic theory, his proprietary individualism, sanctions the drama of social injustice by denying its existence (as in the citations above), or by *justifying* its existence as in the following from *Nature*:[34] "Debt, grinding debt, whose iron face the widow, the orphan, and the sons of genius fear and hate;—debt, which consumes so much time, which so cripples and disheartens a great spirit with cares that seem so base, is a preceptor whose lessons cannot be foregone, and is needed most by those who suffer from it most" ("N," pp. 26–27). In writing that *denies* the differences of persons, that *justifies* those differences, or that *deprecates* the acknowledgement of difference as petulant, finally, in writing that, as above, sees "grinding debt" as moral and as imposing a moral that some require and others, differently, do not—how, but as barbarous, shall we read "all loss, all pain is particular. The universe remains to the heart unhurt"? For it looks suspiciously as if what is being made light of is someone else's pain. What one wants, given the dissonance in Emerson's writing between an impersonality that enables by providing access beyond one's own limited self-interest and an impersonality that imperiously dismisses others' interest, is something like the Kantian acknowledgment of happiness. For Kant does not deny the legitimacy of either happiness or interest; he merely specifies that neither may be consulted as motivations for moral action. And while the categorical imperative is the same for all—unlike things, all beings have unconditional value and must be treated as ends in themselves—one function of that imperative is to prescribe certain duties, among them beneficence. But if one has a duty to promote another's happiness, this involves the recognition that there are different specifications of that general end. In other words, the Kantian universal or categorical imperative does not preclude the idea of individuals at variance with each other; in fact, it presupposes that difference. The Kantian universal does not presuppose impersonality. What one wants in Emerson is the acknowledgment of the legitimacy of material self-interest. In addition, one wants something to separate those statements that enlarge the idea of (one's own) interest from those that annihilate the idea of (another's) interest.

It is in the context of Emerson's failed acknowledgment of material difference in a social world that I return to the subject of the heroic, for the acknowledgement of singularity, and so of difference, is conceptually central to the idea of the heroic and therefore to the Emersonian impersonal, from which it may seem so dissociated. I refer here to something like a reinvented American heroic (reinvented in the sense that its emphasis on the face-to-face confrontation with the divine is originally Homeric as well as Old Testament), a heroic as it is reimagined by Whitman, Dickinson, Melville, and Thoreau. When Whitman, in "Crossing Brooklyn Ferry" says, "Floodtide below me! I see you face to face! ... you furnish your parts toward the soul";[35] when Dickinson's speaker is stopped dead in "Our journey had advanced—" by "Eternity's White Flag Before— / And God—at every Gate—";[36] and, finally, when Melville in *Moby-Dick* constructs tragedy and in *Pierre* and *The Confidence Man* the parody of tragedy upon the *masking* of a face, these pivotal moments recall exactly the logic of Emerson's impersonal. In so doing, they also, indirectly by counterexample, reveal the source of its deficiency.

What deprives Emerson of the authority to speak of the soul's manifestations of divinity is not after all—or, precisely, not *at* all—that his pronouncements are personal rather than ministerial. Conversely, what deprives Emerson's voice of authority is that his statements are *insufficiently* personal, except in the passages I have discussed, and there only by inference. That is, their authority is neither functional *nor* personal. The *content* of Emerson's impersonal implies a heroic *context*: an encounter with the real, however indecipherable its name, the "owning" of that encounter, as well as an acknowledgment of the real or, in the language of "Character," the "*know[ing of] its face.*" But the heroic implies a *person's* contact with the real. This source and this source alone gives it authority, as Dickinson, Whitman, Melville, and, of course, Thoreau knew. Emerson, strangely, *doesn't* know this. He invents a mode of discourse dissociated from the institutionally religious. He produces a discourse that has access to the real prior to the mediating symbol or rite whose necessity it obviates. The legitimacy of that discourse therefore depends on the visibility of the person speaking. It depends on the fact that an epiphanic encounter occurs to someone *in particular* who, by virtue of that particularity, is in a position to describe it. But except in the essay's climactic moments—moments that, as I've argued, are typified by their idiosyncrasy—Emerson then erodes the representation of any self-articulated distinction that would make his discourse legible and meaningful. Not able to countenance or represent what makes him different, he similarly betrays the differences of others, which he either denies or denigrates. Thus Emerson is unable to represent the encounter for the sake of which his discourse exists, for there is ultimately no one to whom that encounter happens. The deficiency in Emerson's representation of the impersonal lies peculiarly in the missing sense of the person. The power of such an encounter could therefore only be rhetorical. The "person" of Emerson—by which I mean something like the invented persona, Foucault's author-function—is not visible, except through style, and except perhaps in "The Poet," one essay where a person comes frontally into view.

In "The Poet," we are offered serial descriptions of what imprisons us ("the custody of that body in which [we are] pent up" ["P," p. 460]); of "the inaccessibleness of every thought but that we are in" ("P," p. 463); of our phlegmatic nature, and of how the poet—"a beholder of ideas, and an utterer of the necessary and causal" ("P," p. 450)—can liberate us. Among his many skills, he invites us "into the science of the real" ("P," p. 452). In other words, the poet makes our birthright discoverable to us. Significantly, he can do this because beside "his privacy of power as an individual man, there is a great public power, on which he can draw, by unlocking, at all risks, his human doors" ("P," p. 459). ("Public" here means something like "universal.") The poet is, therefore, a transformer: he is free and he makes us free (see "P," p. 462). The mechanism for escape, called here "true nectar," is "the ravishment of the intellect by coming nearer to the fact" ("P," p. 460). (Such immanence is marked by a talismanic naming precisely coincident with the poet's liberation "from the custody of that body" and from "the jailyard of individual relations in which he is enclosed.") "Ravishment" is a word we encountered before—in the context of "the influx of the Divine mind into our mind." In "The Poet" the "fact" occasioning ravishment is a man's "passage out into free space" ("P," p. 460). As elsewhere, ravishment signals the transformation whereby the person vanishes into what is "owned" as other. But one difference between this and the other essays is the fixture of "The Poet" at the nexus of transformation, the act and iteration of which is, as it were, diffused throughout the essay. There is no climactic moment at which the transformation could be said to be performed.

Power, a "dream-power ... transcending all limit and privacy" "intoxicates" the poet ("P," pp. 467, 461). But it does not intoxicate thoroughly enough. For though the essay tirelessly dramatizes the poet in relation to his liberating task, this very repetition produces a felt sense of *what* is being transformed, specifically of the person prior to his emergence from the private and the individual, therefore of a person locked in his thought, limited by self-identification and excluded from full expressiveness. In "The Poet" the transformation from the personal to the impersonal does not occur. The essay ends by resorting to a promissory note on what will be performed but is *not yet* performed ("I look in vain for the poet whom I describe" ["P," p. 465]). While the poet is not visible, the one who calls him into being is precisely visible as a presence whose rhetoric fails. If we ask, with Foucault, What are the modes of existence of this discourse? Who can assume these various subject functions? a response would gesture toward the crossed viewpoints that the essay inevitably expresses. For, on the one hand, the reference for the speaking voice is the unemancipated person who anticipates the poet. But, on the other, the poet being evoked also seems referenced to the subject-position we call Emerson. The one who calls for the poet, who calls the poet forth, is the one who knows enough of bondage not to be wholly or even mainly defined by freedom. Thus the essay charts two positions and has a double voice. The all-consuming frenzy ("ravishment") epitomized at the essay's end by the figure of "transparent boundaries" ("P," p. 468) is repeatedly contested by the essay's enumerated impediments (caves, cellars, prisons, drifts, chains, pans and barrows, stuttering and stammering, jail yards) that the frenzy can't vanquish. These movements, or subject-positions, are inseparable in Emerson's "The Poet."

In the space of their negotiation a person is almost legible, making credible, as well as meaningful, an idea of the impersonal again and again in the space of this essay incompletely realized.

Modern criticism shows the point at which the idea of the impersonal is completely detached from religion, which initially gave it life (either traditionally defined—as sourced by God or Law, or alternatively defined as Whitman, Dickinson, and Melville define it—as sourced by a spectacle of the real apprehended by a person). Emerson proleptically marks the moment when the idea of the person is evacuated from the scene of the impersonal. The discourse that remains exhibits an apparently unrecognized nostalgia for the idea of the person on whom the impersonal is imagined to register. This is how I understand the odd pathos of the summary accounts that make a gesture of dramatizing the impersonal even as they retreat from actualizing such a confrontation in the climactic or figural moments whose style I discussed in the passage about "man impersonated."[37] Yet, as I have suggested, something is deficient in Emerson's representations, and this deficiency directly pertains to the understood relation between impersonality and individuation. I conclude by elaborating the contours of this relation as it is made visible by two sets of reflections upon it.

In *Time and the Other* Levinas posits a state of impersonality that *precedes* individuation; in *Reasons and Persons* Parfit posits a state of impersonality that *constitutes* individuation. I want briefly to consider these two notions for the light that, albeit differently, they shed on Emerson's relation to his central construct of impersonality. Levinas distinguishes between existing and an existent, between an anonymous and impersonal "there is" and a state of consciousness "where an existent is put in touch with his existing," hence with his materiality and solitude. In Levinas's account the anonymous, impersonal state precedes the formation of a material "I" for whom suffering is a direct consequence of being imprisoned in the experience of personal identity. Thus, "solitude is not tragic because it is the privation of the other, but because [the self] is shut up within the captivity of its identity, because it is matter." The experience of the "I am" is, therefore, what Levinas calls "enchainment."[38] Parfit also argues that the idea of personal identity enchains. But for Parfit, in a passage I cited earlier, that idea is understood to be *false*:

> We are not separately existing entities, apart from our brains and bodies, and various interrelated physical and mental events. Our existence just involves the existence of our brains and bodies, and

the doing of our deeds, and the thinking of our thoughts, and the
occurrence of certain other physical and mental events. Our
identity over time just involves ... psychological connectedness
and/or psychological continuity. [RP, p. 216]

In this Reductionist View there is no deeper fact—no spiritual substance (or
soul), no purely mental construct (a Cartesian pure ego), no separate physical
entity, "of a kind that is not yet recognised in the theories of contemporary
physics," nor any other ineffable essence—to which we can ascribe identity
[RP, p. 210]. (The consequence of this, Parfit argues, is that there is no
distinct entity that constitutes identity; that the unity of consciousness and
the unity over time need not be accounted for by the claim that "the
experiences in this person's life are had by this person" who is a separately
existing entity [RP, p. 210]. Such unities can rather be explained by the
relations of psychological connection and continuity; we can therefore
understand our life in an impersonal way; and the Reductionist View has
radical moral consequences.)[39]

What strikes me, it might seem randomly, is the subject of resistance,
even "suffering" (Levinas's term) that attends both discussions of
impersonality. For Levinas personal identity is the *cause* of suffering, while
for Parfit, at least initially, the absence of personal identity has central
afflictive power. (Ultimately Parfit will claim that the impersonal view is not
only the more beneficial but is also personally consoling: "It makes me less
concerned about my own future, and my death" [RP, p. 347].) There is,
however, a compelling moment in a chapter entitled "Is the True View
Believable?" in which Parfit, who has been arguing against the absence of
some deep fact beyond physical and psychological continuity—no soul, no
pure ego, no extrapolated physical presence that would testify to a person's
unique, unreplicable identity—exemplifies, shockingly, the practical
implications of his austere theory. In relation to a science fiction fable that
Parfit invents to preface his analysis of the *absence* of any extra identificatory
essence on which discrete personhood could be founded, he asks whether the
idea of being replicated (physically and psychologically) and teletransported
to Mars produces someone who "*would* be *me*" or "someone else, who has
been made to be exactly *like* me" (RP, pp. 200, 201; italics mine). The
question here is whether, if the Replica is qualitatively identical with me but
not numerically identical with me, the Replica is the same person as I am (see
RP, p. 201). Parfit concludes his discussion by arguing that there is nothing
extra that would define me (like a soul or a cogito) that could make such a
question intelligible:

When I fear that, in Teletransportation, I shall not get to Mars, my fear is that the abnormal cause may fail to produce this further fact. As I have argued, there is no such fact. What I fear will not happen, *never* happens. I want the person on Mars to be me in a specially intimate way in which no future person will ever be me. My continued existence never involves this deep further fact. What I fear will be missing is *always* missing. Even a spaceship journey would not produce the further fact in which I am inclined to believe.

When I come to see that my continued existence does not involve this further fact, I lose my reason for preferring a spaceship journey. But, judged from the standpoint of my earlier belief, this is not because Teletransportation is *about as good as* ordinary survival. It is because ordinary survival is *about as bad as*, or little better than, Teletransportation. *Ordinary survival is about as bad as being destroyed and having a Replica.* [*RP*, pp. 279–80]

Ordinary survival is as bad as being destroyed and replicated because ordinary survival does not presuppose anything that would distinguish a self as a discrete separate entity whose personal identity matters. What the truth about ordinary survival destroys is the idea of the person and the personal.

I mark these moments in Levinas and Parfit because, albeit to different ends, they represent a *person's* resistance to the idea of impersonality nonetheless being expounded.[40] Suffering is occasioned by the friction of *feeling* oneself a person (Levinas's "I am") where such a feeling is shown to be unfounded. There cannot help but be resistance to the idea of the impersonal since the consequences of the impersonal destroy being the only way we think we know it.

But Emerson's accounts of the impersonal exist without such acknowledgment, uncontaminated by resistance and free of any hint of the registration of suffering whose expression might taint them. It is as if the perspective from which Emerson's words are voiced is an imaginary perspective, purified of unideal motivation. Emerson's perspective does not take into account what thwarts the ideal or how it might affect the voice that is propounding it. The plea for impersonality has been evacuated of religious content. Yet there is something evasive, incomplete, and empty about the fact that Emerson does not acknowledge what replaces the idea of a God, as if the idea of God had not actually been dismissed but had rather been transferred to the omniscient speaking voice (hence Nietzsche's valorization of Emerson). That is, Emerson does not take the responsibility a person should take for his words and therefore betrays the complexity of a person's response to their desirability. But can there be real knowledge of the impersonal if its consequences, and even its constitutive terms, remain unintelligible? If one tries to answer the question, What is a person? no answer with any coherent substance can be produced with reference to Emerson's writing.

One of the reasons Emerson fails to acknowledge others' suffering, which is never very real to him, is that he fails to acknowledge his own suffering, which is never very real to him. I don't mean to suggest that suffering, or any other displayed affect, is a criterion for successful theorization. But I do mean to repeat one last time that Emerson's words are iterated in a register unmarked by the ambivalence that, one might suppose, would challenge a wholehearted endorsement of a machine as undiscriminated as a Superpersonal Heart, an immeasurable mind, or an Over-soul. For ambivalence to the impersonal is the one contradiction Emerson successfully resists. Yet, as Parfit makes clear, if we assume the truth of the impersonal, "ordinary survival is about as bad as being destroyed and having a Replica." Thus Emerson does not become accountable to the implication of his words that are voiced without penetrating. It is as if, in his sentences, his life failed to be experienced as his own. If this is a supreme fulfillment of the imperative of impersonality—to speak without the registration of any affect that would contest the *construct* of impersonality— it nonetheless leaves undisclosed the *experience* of impersonality (ravishment), to which the essays, from first to last, seductively promise access.

NOTES

1. Derek Parfit, *Reasons and Persons* (Oxford, 1984), p. ix; hereafter abbreviated *RP*.

2. Parfit's argument contains two strands that I find productive for thinking about Emerson's "impersonal." The first strand involves Parfit's claim that there is no substantial entity in virtue of which it is true to say of a person that he is the "same" person over time. (Selfhood, or what Parfit calls "the unity of our lives" [*RP*, p. 446], is a complex relation among psychological states capable of degrees we can affect.) The second strand is more specifically ethical and pertains to the relation between self-interest and concern for other persons. Parfit links these two strands through the suggestion that a change in our view of the conditions of personal identity can rationally lead us to a more impersonal concern for the quality of human experiences, regardless of *whose* experiences they are.

3. Ralph Waldo Emerson, "Nominalist and Realist," *Essays and Lectures*, ed. Joel Porte (New York, 1983), p. 580; hereafter abbreviated "NR."

4. Emerson, "Montaigne," *Essays and Lectures*, p. 709; hereafter abbreviated "M."

5. Emerson, "The Over-soul," *Essays and Lectures*, p. 390; hereafter abbreviated "O:, Emerson's primary understanding of the meaning of *person* and of *personality* (hence of *impersonality*) originated with the sense *of* the three-personed God. Despite the fact that Webster, following Johnson, in 1828 never mentions that there's a millennial idea of person bound up with the idea of Christ, Emerson certainly would have known this from Patristic sources.

Thus although Emerson uses the idea of the impersonal as if its divinity is part of his intuitive sense of the word, rather than part of its etymology, when he brings in the idea of God what he is bringing in is the long history of *person* associated with the theology of the Trinity.

In fact what Emerson inherits is a misunderstanding. For the word *person* when it pertains to God was not originally meant to indicate an individual, but rather to denote a way of subsisting, a way of being, a hypostasis. Not pertaining to aspects of God, nor to mythological intermediaries for God, and certainly not to any modern sense of individual, the Trinity originally implied a sameness of divine essence through three modes that belied the idea of person-as-individual that Emerson found so abhorrent. See the entry by M. J. Dorenkemper, "Person (in Theology)," in *New Catholic Encyclopedia*, ed. Catholic University of America, 18 vols. (New York, 1967), 11:168–70, for the sense of *person* as Emerson would have inherited it. For the more modern, philosophical sense of person as self, as in *personality*, see J. Ellis McTaggert on "Personality," in *Encyclopedia of Religion and Ethics*, ed. James Hastings, 13 vols. (New York, 1908), 11:773–81.

For a historically nuanced account of Emerson's complex relation to individuality, see Sacvan Bercovitch's clarifying discussion of the understanding of *individualism* Emerson inherited from the socialists, of his reconception of this idea in the 1840s as a "vision of cosmic subjectivity" (opposed to socialism), and of his ultimate understanding in the 1850s of individuality as allied with industrial-capitalist "Wealth" and "Power". (Sacvan Bercovitch, "Emerson, Individualism, and Liberal Dissent," *The Rites of Assent: Transformations in the Symbolic Construction of America* [New York, 1993], pp. 310, 323, 330, 340). Bercovitch charts the shifts in Emerson's understanding of individualism as it moves from the utopian to the ideological, but in doing so he fascinatingly demonstrates the dynamic relation between these impulses throughout Emerson's thought and writing.

6. Emerson, "History," *Essays and Lectures*, p. 237, and "Spiritual Laws," *Essays and Lectures*, p. 322; hereafter abbreviated "SL."

7. Emerson, "The Poet," *Essays and Lectures*, pp. 460, 459; hereafter abbreviated "P."

8. Emerson, "The Divinity School Address," *Essays and Lectures*, p. 89; hereafter abbreviated "DSA."

9. Emerson, "The American Scholar," *Essays and Lectures*, pp. 64, 67.

10. All major critics of Emerson have understood that if one threat to self-reliance is conformity, the other is petty self-interest or self-cherishing. See, for instance, Barbara Packer's discussion of self-reliance and self-abandonment (self-reliance, in Packer's account, rests not on "persons but powers") (B. L. Packer, *Emerson's Fall: A New Interpretation of the Major Essays* [New York, 1982], p. 143); Harold Bloom's analysis of the dialectical relation between an "Apollonian Self-Reliance" and a "Dionysian influx," the latter often perceptible as ecstatic energy that transforms mere individualism (Harold Bloom, "Emerson and Influence," *A Map of Misreading* [New York, 1975], p. 166); and Richard Poirier's discussion of genius, as countering the self as a conventionally defined entity, genius being what is not psychological, not moral or political, not stable, indeed not recognizable—rather, to be seen as something "vehicular, transitive, mobile," something performed in writing (Richard Poirier, "The Question of Genius," *The Renewal of Literature: Emersonian Reflections* [New York, 1987], pp. 89–90). I understand Emerson's impersonality to be *related* to, but not identical with, Poirier's genius, Bloom's energy, Packer's powers, as his corrective to the deformation of personal identity. These terms rely on a Neoplatonic, upward, sublimatory movement away from material particularity, whereas Emerson's impersonal moves in the opposite direction. For in impersonality

Emerson is elaborating a paradox that truth to the self involves the discovery of its radical commonness.

A recent, important contribution to this debate is George Kateb's *Emerson and Self-Reliance* ([Thousand Oaks, Calif., 1995]; hereafter abbreviated *ES*), a book notable on a number of counts. First, he has an excellent discussion of how antagonism and contrast lie at the heart of Emerson's notion of identity. Specifically, Kateb claims that Emerson's self-reliance depends upon an acknowledgment of the otherness and impersonality one might suppose antithetical to it; see *ES*, p. 17. "Impersonality registers an individual's universality or infinitude" (*ES*, p. 31). In this registration what is reduced is the "'biographical ego'" and one acts "at the behest of 'the grand spiritual Ego,' at the behest, that is, of one's impersonal reception of the world" (*ES*, p. 33). Second, Kateb then correctly associates Emerson's impersonality with the religious ("Emerson is ravenously religious. Anything in the world ... matters and is beautiful or sublime only if seen and thought of as part of a designed, intentionally coherent totality; indeed as an emanation of divinity" [*ES*, p. 65]). But, third, Kateb then tries to divorce the idea of the impersonal from the religious (because its piety embarrasses him and because it appears to him that the driving thrust for unity, at the heart of the religious, betrays Emerson's commitment to antagonism). Kateb approves of Emerson's sense of the "interconnectedness" of things; he likes the idea of affinity, but not the idea of an all or a one with which interconnectedness is integral in Emerson's thought. But the very impersonality so crucial to Kateb's explanation of self-reliance is also, I argue below, inseparable from the religiousness from which Kateb would sever it. The radicalness Kateb admires depends upon the "religiousness" that he fears trivializes it. Also central in this context is Stanley Cavell's "Aversive Thinking: Emersonian Representations in Heidegger and Nietzsche," *Conditions Handsome and Unhandsome: The Constitution of American Perfectionism* (Chicago, 1990), pp. 33–63, an earlier, important reading of "Self-Reliance," antagonism, and transfiguration. Cavell understands Emerson's "moral perfectionism" as specifying a structure within the self that requires constant "martyrdom" (p. 56). In other words, in Cavell's analysis of Emerson, as in his reading of Nietzsche, the "higher" self is not elsewhere or other, but is located "within." In this idea of perfectionism the self is not fixed, but neither is it absent. Perfectionism, so defined, supposes a structure essentially more conservative than that of impersonality.

11. Emerson, "Compensation," *Essays and Lectures*, pp. 287, 291; hereafter abbreviated "C."

12. Emerson, "Self-Reliance," *Essays and Lectures*, p. 271; hereafter abbreviated "S."

13. Emerson, "Illusions," *Essays and Lectures*, p. 1123.

14. Emerson, "Behavior," *Essays and Lectures*, pp. 1042, 1043.

15. Emerson, "Circles," *Essays and Lectures*, p. 406; hereafter abbreviated "Ci."

16. Emerson, "Experience," *Essays and Lectures*, p. 476; hereafter abbreviated "E."

17. Harry Frankfurt, "Identification and Externality," in *The Identities of Persons*, ed. Amélie Oksenberg Rorty (Berkeley, 1969), p. 242. Frankfurt's preliminary distinction between desires that are external to a self and those that are identified with it revolves around a decision made with respect to these desires (a decision rather than an attitude, for a decision, unlike an attitude, cannot be disowned). See pp. 243–50 for what kind of decision qualifies a desire for being situated outside the person.

18. In this connection, see also this passage in "Montaigne": "There is the power of moods, each setting at naught all but its own tissue of facts and beliefs" ("M," p. 704). This passage, and the essay as a whole, are brilliant for the way in which they ventriloquize the absoluteness of point of view conferred by a mood that another mood undermines.

Understood in terms of the "machinery" of moods registered in the essay there is only "rotation" of all "the states of mind" ("M," p. 704).

19. Emerson, "Uses of Great Men," *Essays and Lectures*, pp. 623, 625.

20. In Emerson's "Experience," such moments of impersonality are dispersed across that essay after its initial pages, which acknowledge loss as personal: "the death of my son…the dearest events…the costly price of sons and lovers." "Experience," therefore, atypically makes visible a person's relation to impersonality. See "Representing Grief: Emerson's 'Experience'" in my *Impersonality: Seven Essays* (Chicago, 2006). In essays discussed in "Emerson's Impersonal," however, Emerson blocks such a relation.

21. Emerson echoes a line from *The Enneads* (1.6.7) but not an idea, in the sense that for Plotinus impersonality is the result of an ontological change: in Plotinus the self or personality is there to be relinquished. In distinction, Emerson's text is more radical since, however oddly, as I argue below, impersonality characterizes both sides of the conversion marked by the passages discussed. See Pierre Hadot's discussion of the "levels" of self in *Plotinus, or The Simplicity of Vision*, trans. Michael Chase (Chicago, 1993), pp. 23–24, as well as Arnold I. Davidson's introduction to that volume, "Reading Hadot Reading Plotinus," pp. 1–15.

Emerson's Plotinus was most likely from Thomas Taylor's 1817 *Selected Works*. See Walter Harding, *Emerson's Library* (Charlottesville, Va., 1967), p. 217.

22. Emerson, "Nature," *Essays and Lectures*, p. 10; hereafter abbreviated "N."

23. Emerson, "The Method of Nature," *Essays and Lectures*, p. 121.

24. Emerson, "Intellect," *Essays and Lectures*, p. 426; hereafter abbreviated "I."

25. Emerson, "Love," *Essays and Lectures*, p. 335.

26. Henry Ware, Jr., *Personality of the Deity* (Boston, 1838), p. 12. In Ware's reply to Emerson's "Divinity School Address," this happiness is directly attributable to "the interest which the soul takes in persons" (ibid.). For Ware, to destroy personality is effectively to annihilate everything recognizable, including divinity.

27. In using the word *heroic* here I have in mind what Gregory Nagy identifies as that nobility or honor which in Homer and the Bible are a direct consequence of a face-to-face encounter with God or with another heroic human. See Gregory Nagy, *The Best of the Achaeans: Concepts of the Hero in Archaic Greek Poetry* (Baltimore, 1979). Emerson reimagines something like the idea of the heroic in the presumption of a direct confrontation with the Over-soul, the Superpersonal Heart, the Immeasurable Mind, while in Kant this direct access to something ultimate is epitomized by moral law, possible to realize if all empirical interest is subordinated to it. It's the direct apprehension of something supreme or ultimate that in both cases suggests what might appear a bizarre analogy to the heroic. For an analogous contemporary reimagining of the heroic as defined by the immediacy of encounter with the divine or with an ultimate reality in the human, see Thomas Carlyle, *On Heroes, Hero-Worship, and the Heroic in History*, ed. Carl Niemeyer (1841; Lincoln, Nebr., 1966).

28. Immanuel Kant, *Fundamental Principles of the Metaphysic of Morals*, trans. T. K. Abbott (Amherst, N.Y, 1988), p. 60; hereafter abbreviated *FP*.

29. Emerson, "Worship," *Essays and Lectures*, p. 1062.

30. Ibid., p. 1076.

31. Such an erasure of distinction between container and thing contained, between self and universe is repeatedly enacted in Emerson's off scale representations of the human, as in this formulation from "Character": "a man should be so large and columnar in the landscape, that it should deserve to be recorded, that he arose, and girded up his loins, and departed to such a place" (Emerson, "Character," *Essays and Lectures*, p. 505). Or as in this one from

"Montaigne": The universe "has shown the heaven and earth to every child, and filled him with a desire for the whole; a desire raging, infinite; a hunger, as of space to be filled with planets" ("M," p. 708). In the first example, what is human and personal is matched to the landscape, is given its dimensions, as in the second example where desire is matched to the stratosphere. These reconstructed propositions of the human, the human made gargantuan, are a reciprocal gesture, an accommodation in scale to the "catholic sense of things."

32. See, for instance, the last paragraph of "Character" where the language of ownership for what is alien is explicit. Here *identifying* (in the sense of detecting) "the holy sentiment we cherish" quickly turns into *identification with* it ("only the pure and aspiring can know its face, and the only compliment they can pay it, is to own it") (Emerson, "Character," pp. 508, 509). Such ownership is understood in terms of a religious discovery.

33. William Ellery Channing, "Unitarian Christianity," *"Unitarian Christianity" and Other Essays*, ed. Irving H. Bartlett (Indianapolis, 1957), pp. 31, 92, 108.

34. Examples of both types of statement appear frequently in the essays. Of the first type, see, for instance, all of "Compensation" and the philosophy of "Gifts," which presumes that all have enough; for the second kind of statement, see "Nature" for an implicit critique of "the private poor man" ("N," p. 13); "Intellect," which critiques "he who is immersed in what concerns person or place" ("I," p. 417); and "Prudence" for a dismissal of that class which needs to be concerned with health and wealth. Finally there is a third category of statement that deserves mention in this context—those statements that dismiss the idea of social reform because you can't reform society if you don't first reform the self (the argument of "New England Reformers"). If suffering is one's own fault, or the fault of one's too limited identification (the argument of "Spiritual Laws"), one can, according to "Fate," rectify it accordingly: "So far as a man thinks, he is free" (Emerson, "Fate," *Essays and Lectures*, p. 953).

35. Walt Whitman, "Crossing Brooklyn Ferry," *Leaves of Grass* (1856; New York, 1980), pp. 144, 149, secs. 1, 9.

36. Emily Dickinson, "Our journey had advanced" (no. 615), *Final Harvest: Emily Dickinson's Poems*, ed. Thomas H. Johnson (New York, 1961), p. 157, 11. 1, 11–12.

37. Both nostalgia and rhetorically heightened summary equally testify to an eviscerated religious sense and, I have argued, to a deficient sense of the individual. They testify to a religious sense that is dismissed incompletely, that is absent but not forgotten. In the space of that absence autobiography will ultimately link up with philosophy as a newly constructed subject. This is epitomized by Friedrich Nietzsche, *Ecce Homo*, trans. Walter Kaufman (New York, 1969), and differently attested to by Jacques Derrida, *The Ear of the Other: Otobiography, Transference, Translation*, trans. Peggy Kamuf and Avital Ronell, ed. Christie McDonald (Lincoln, Nebr., 1988), on the one hand, and Cavell, *A Pitch of Philosophy. Autobiographical Exercises* (Cambridge, Mass., 1994), on the other.

Nietzsche presumes a separation of autobiography and philosophy that *Ecce Homo* will rectify. The exceptionalism of his position is continuously reiterated there. For instance: "I only attack causes against which I would not find allies, so that I stand alone—so that I compromise myself alone" (Nietzsche, *Ecce Homo*, p. 232). Derrida, writing about *Ecce Homo* asserts, "Let it be said that I shall not read Nietzsche as a philosopher (of being, of life, or of death) or as a scholar or scientist, if these three types can be said to share the abstraction of the biographical and the claim to leave their lives and names out of their writings" (Derrida, *The Ear of the Other*, p. 7). Cavell argues that "philosophy's arrogance is linked to its ambivalence toward the autobiographical" and that, following Austin and Wittgenstein whose methods demand an engagement of the philosophical with the autobiographical, he will "think about an autobiographical dimension of philosophy, together with a philosophical dimension of the autobiographical" (Cavell, *The Pitch of Philosophy*, pp. 3, 6). The point I want to make here is that the attempt to fashion anew a connection between autobiography and philosophy occurs in just that space where, as in Augustine's *Confessions*, impersonality once *assumed* the centrality of a personal existence to a discourse of the impersonal.

These three endeavors to join the autobiographical with the philosophical raise questions about a related conjunction, the personal and the impersonal, namely, the question of how the two were ever separated.

38. Emmanuel Levinas, *Time and the Other*, trans. Richard A. Cohen (Pittsburgh, 1987), pp. 51, 57. The project in this book is to show the trajectory from "anonymous" existing to subjectivity to the alterity of the other person, an alterity with which time is associated. What interests me about this early work of Levinas is where he locates suffering (as produced by the experience of personal identity) as opposed to where Parfit locates suffering (as produced by relinquishing the idea of personal identity).

39. Of course it could be argued that to say there is no entity that would distinguish what makes persons separate is to invent an absence. For if Parfit's point is that we can't make sense of the thought that there is such an entity, why should we expect the negation of this thought—expressed in the assertion that there is no such entity—to be any more intelligible? That is to say, someone might feel that Parfit's discussion does not adequately distinguish between what is true and false and what makes sense.

40. Such resistance is not the point of Parfit's argument; indeed, on the contrary, Parfit's "point" is the moral and personal freedom of the impersonal view he espouses. But his resistance surfaces despite the point: "I would never completely lose my intuitive belief in the Non-Reductionist View [of identity]. It is hard to be serenely confident in my Reductionist conclusions. It is hard to believe that personal identity is not what matters" (*RP*, p. 280). This perseverative intuitive view enables Parfit to speak of a "person's" response to the nonexistence of personal identity.

For a fascinating discussion of how "personality" and "persons" are differently constructed by Bloom, Lévi-Strauss, and Bentham, see Frances Ferguson, "Canons, Poetics, and Social Value: Jeremy Bentham and How to Do Things with People," *MLN* 110 [Dec. 1995]: 1149–64. I am particularly interested in Ferguson's discussion of how for Bentham persons are "reciprocal" constructions, "produced" by groups (p. 1161). No sense of this reciprocity characterizes Emerson's essays; what is missing from Emerson's account of impersonality is any sense of the persons who constitute it.

GEORGE KATEB

Self-Reliance and the Life of the Mind

In Emerson's thought about individualism, the idea of self-reliance occupies the central place. The essay "Self-Reliance" (*Essays: First Series,* 1841) is perhaps his most famous statement of it. Many sentences and passages in this essay are commonly quoted. Indeed, some have lent themselves to ideological exploitation and have even been used in advertisements and commercials. The essay has fame and notoriety, both. Thanks to the essay, the very phrase "self-reliance" has become a common synonym for individualism. Yet the idea of self-reliance is everywhere present in Emerson's thought, not only in the essay named "Self-Reliance." For all its familiarity, the idea is certainly difficult and elusive, just as Emerson's thought usually is. Though much has been written on Emersonian self-reliance, and though Stanley Cavell has recently written about it in three powerful books, perhaps something is left to say about it. By trying to work through some of the meanings and suggestions of self-reliance we can add, I believe, to our own thought about individualism—especially the sort of individualism that I have been calling democratic individuality.

It is well to emphasize at the start Emerson's difficulty and elusiveness. He is full of assertive sentences that may seem unconditional. Every sentence seems a declaration of faith. He seems to stand behind every utterance with his whole being, and risks his being by the completeness of his candor. His

From *Emerson and Self-Reliance.* © 2002 by Rowman and Littlefield Publishers, Inc.

variety of declarations tempts us to say that he contradicts himself, but even if we resist the temptation, we are still not sure where he finally stands. We can admit the force of his impeachment of consistency in "Self-Reliance" (p. 265), but may still wish that his assertions did not so frequently collide and perhaps qualify one another to the point of damaging all of them, leaving us suspended and uncertain.

Let us say, however, that he intends to qualify his assertions. In fact, many of the assertions are not assertions at all. He does not stand behind most of his utterances, even though he expends his full virtue in them. In his experiments, he is more like Plato than even Nietzsche is. Emerson is not Thoreau. As he says in one of his numerous programmatic formulations, an intellectual person must have "no engagement in any thought or feeling which can hinder him from looking at it as somewhat foreign." (Emerson usually means "something" when he says "somewhat.") He adds that "the true scholar is one who has the power to stand beside his thoughts or to hold off his thoughts at arm's length and give them perspective" ("Natural History of Intellect," *Natural History*, pp. 39–40).

An almost exasperated Walt Whitman can therefore say of Emerson:

> He does not see or take one side, one presentation only or mainly, (as all the poets, or most of the fine writers anyhow,)—he sees all sides. His final influence is to make his students cease to worship anything—almost cease to believe in anything, outside of themselves. ("Emerson's Books, (The Shadows of Them)," *Whitman, Complete Poetry and Collected Prose*, p. 1052)

A genuinely exasperated Henry James says that Emerson "was never the man anyone took him for" (*Literary Criticism*, p. 266). assume that James's formulation applies to Emerson's thought, and if it does, it is most apt. The key is found when we see that Emerson makes Plato—whom he regarded as the world's greater thinker and as indispensable to all creative thought—sit for the portrait of Emerson. In *Representative Men*, he says of Plato:

> He has not a system. The dearest defenders and disciples are at fault. He attempted a theory of the universe, and his theory is not complete or self-evident. One man thinks he means this, and another that; he has said one thing in one place, and the reverse of it in another place. (p. 652)

Emerson means these words as praise: in turn, we praise Emerson by transferring them to him. His purpose is to have no system, but a theory instead—a theory of the need not to have a system in any usual sense. "At bottom he had no doctrine at all," said Santayana ("Emerson," *Interpretations of Poetry and Religion*, p. 131).

Emerson *aims* at making his philosophy difficult and elusive. He means to disappoint the expectation that he will supply doctrinal conclusions. His belief in the possibility of truth requires him, he thinks, to commit himself only for a time to a particular value, principle or idea (or to any practice or institution derivative from them), and then to a contrasting one for a time, trying at the same time to withhold a final judgment, a definite assent, whenever possible. We may finally observe in him an unreserved commitment, but it is a commitment to a method of intellect. A commitment to method enables him to withhold lesser, substantive commitments. (I use the ascetic or Cartesian word "method" because Emerson favors it.) Hence we must be as careful as possible in assigning beliefs to Emerson. It is not skepticism but his understanding of truth that makes him so sparing in acquiring commitments. The matter does not stop here: the core of self-reliance is a proper engagement with truth, requiring as much substantive withholding as possible.

> Truth is our element of life, yet if a man fasten his attention on a single aspect of truth, and apply himself to that alone for a long time, the truth becomes distorted and not itself, but falsehood. ("Intellect," p. 424).

It should always be difficult to attribute commitments to a self-reliant person—whether it is Emerson himself or anyone who conceives of self-reliance as he does. Why? What are the connections between self-reliance, truth-seeking, and substantive withholding?

Emerson thinks that every important value, principle, idea (or derivative practice or institution) is permanently indispensable for life, even though any may be at odds with any other. Taken together, they are forces "by whose antagonism we exist" ("Fugitive Slave Law," 1854, *Miscellanies*, p. 231). Man himself, Emerson says, is a "stupendous antagonism," the cause and effect of the world's constitutive antagonisms ("Fate," *The Conduct of Life*, p. 953). Life is a "gale of warring elements" ("Works and Days," *Society and Solitude*, p. 172). When there are two "metaphysical antagonists," he says, "each is a good half, but an impossible whole" ("The Conservative," p. 175). If "the world stands by balanced antagonisms" the thinker must temporarily stand by each antagonistic element in turn ("Natural History of Intellect," *Natural History*, p. 53). Emerson is a sustained practitioner of a multiple perspectivism. He tries to make each element believable, giving it its own essay or passage, or he dwells on its different facets in several essays, while his whole work sets an example of abundant but also sympathetic withholding. But he withholds nothing, it would seem, from the principle of self-reliance, which is the method of sympathetic withholding. It earns Emerson's true loyalty. The principle is Emerson. In the main respects, therefore, self-reliance is not one particular substantive or doctrinal principle like other ones. At its best, self-reliance is nothing but an intellectual method, a method of truth. Emerson's whole work illustrates it, and it may very well define any person's self-reliance as such. This will be my main emphasis, but other meanings of self-reliance will also be examined.

Mental or philosophical self-reliance means, precisely, the readiness to treat with sympathetic understanding ideas and values that have no sympathy for one another. In order to develop such understanding, one must try to remain not free of substantive commitments, but sparing of them. This is the highest aspiration of self-reliance. Emerson acknowledges the temptation to selectivity when he says in "Spiritual Laws" that:

> A man is a method, a progressive arrangement; a selecting principle, gathering his like to him wherever he goes. He takes only his own out of the multiplicity that sweeps and circles round him. (pp. 311–312)

Despite these words, Emerson's work shows the effort of achieving a method that refuses any "selecting principle" which derives from something as narrow as one's "own" personality, and which has so limited an aim as to gather one's like wherever one goes. Emerson's method aims to embrace as much as he finds possible. That is the example he would set. His practice is faithful to most of the formulated precepts of his method that recurrently appear in his writings, but not the one just quoted. Self-reliance as a method of thinking with its own intrinsic value means more than any substantive commitment to a particular value, principle or idea, or to any practice or institution that embodies or derives from them. (But I do not deny that self-reliance has institutional preconditions and effects, as we shall see.)

One relies on oneself rather than seeking support in external commitments. One stays within oneself in order to enter imaginatively into all the commitments that social life displays, and must display. One increases, the amount of value in the world by keeping oneself from embracing favorite ideas and works exclusively.

Emerson is persuaded of two things: every position is held for at least plausible reasons and perhaps for necessary ones; and every position is inevitably accompanied by or engenders an opposition that is also (though not always equally) plausible or necessary and also narrow. Opposition appears,

> because something has been overstated or omitted by the antecedent sect and the human mind feels itself wronged and overstates on the other side as in this. Each of our sects is an extreme statement and therefore obnoxious to contradiction and reproof. But each rests on this strong but obscure instinct of an outraged truth. Each is, as it were, a cry of pain from the violated soul. ("Society," *Early Lectures*, 2, p. 108)

That antagonists need each other for the sake of their own sanity is shown, Emerson thinks, in the political sphere where parties goad, check, and define each other. But antagonism—not just in politics—is the health of the whole world: its value is perpetual and to be preferred over synthesis or diluted compromise. No position is arbitrary or accidental. The self-reliant thinker will try to disclose, in every case, why a partisan must say what he says and what "insurmountable fact binds him to that side" ("The Conservative," p. 176). As one example, Emerson thinks that "No Burke, no Metternich has yet done full justice to the side of conservatism" ("Lecture on the Times," p. 158). The steady message from Emerson is that no side—no principle or value or practice—has yet been done full justice. But he will try to make amends. He says, "The finer the sense of justice, the better poet" ("Sovereignty of Ethics," *Lectures and Sketches*, p. 185).

In the work he does, he displays and inspires what we may call the democracy of intellect; he gives an example of the spirit of democracy at its best. That is self-reliance. It is sometimes overt in Emerson's work, more often unspoken, that he is presenting and defending the aspirations of the mind of democratic culture, nothing less. It is a mind needed to understand the culture in which it grows, but that can also extend its receptivity to other cultures and also to nature. Henry James said in a review (1883) of the Carlyle-Emerson correspondence:

> In a genuine democracy all things are democratic; and this spirit of general deference, on the part of a beautiful poet who might have availed himself of the poetic license to be fastidious, was the natural product of a society in which it was held that every one was equal to every one else. (*Literary Criticism*, p. 245)

I am not sure that Emerson's spirit is "a natural product" of anything. He is more like one who reveals a secret obscured by its obviousness and kept obscure because it is too radical in its perfect appropriateness. He is revealing democracy. But James is right to insist on Emerson's democracy: his receptivity, his power of uncommitted sympathy, is democracy. Receptivity is the highest form of self-reliance.

Emerson's method of apprehending general ideas and practices—the kinds whose names provide titles for many of his essays—is the heart of his self-reliant intellectuality. But he sometimes devotes his attentive powers to human and natural particulars, on the one hand, and he aspires to a transcendent vision of the totality of things, on the other hand. For a while, however, I will concentrate on his methodical treatment of general ideas and practices. Later, I will say something about Emerson's reception of particulars and his sense of totality.

One of the most compressed statements of his self-reliant method is found at the beginning of "Fate," the first of nine essays in *The Conduct of Life* (1860). He says:

> If we must accept Fate, we are not less compelled to affirm liberty, the significance of the individual, the grandeur of duty, the power of character. This is true, and that other is true. But our geometry cannot span these extreme points, and reconcile them. What to do? By obeying each thought frankly, by harping, or, if you will, pounding on each string, we learn at last its power. By the same obedience to other thoughts, we learn theirs, and then comes some reasonable hope of harmonizing them. We are sure, that, though we know not how, necessity does comport with liberty, the individual with the world, my polarity with the spirit of the times. The riddle of the age has for each a private solution. If one would study his own time, it must be by this method of taking up in turn each of the leading topics which belong to our scheme of human life, and, by firmly stating all that is agreeable to experience on one, and doing the same justice to the opposing facts in the others, the true limitations will appear. Any excess of emphasis, on one part, would be corrected, and a just balance would be made. (pp. 943–944)

"Excess of emphasis" characterizes all of Emerson's writing.

The excess is meant to compensate for the reserve that Emerson feels in the face of the way people esteem the things they do. Their estimation tends to be blindly or insanely excessive—it is too partial and unduly favors a few worthy things to the exclusion of others that have equal or comparable claims. Commonly, exaggeration makes every thought a prison and hence is "incipient insanity" ("Intellect," p. 424). However, Emerson can say a good word even about one-sidedness:

> Exaggeration is in the course of things ... to every creature nature added a little violence of direction in its proper path, a shove to put it on its way; in every instance, a slight generosity, a drop too much ... without a spice of bigot and fanatic, no excitement, no efficiency. ("Nature," p. 549)

A person "can't make any paint stick but his own." Nevertheless, insofar, as one is a self-reliant thinker, one cannot be a partisan either for oneself or one's cause. A person of one idea is a monotone and must be treated as if a little deranged ("Natural History of Intellect, *Natural History*, p. 50). Only the mediocre, he says, take sides (Notes to "Self-Reliance," *Works*, 2, p. 391).

For Emerson to give everything its due requires that he overcome his characteristic revulsion to unconscious idolatry. In contrast, his own idolatry is deliberate: he will write about something as if it were the best or only thing, but then go on to another. He as it were impersonates ideas and principles, practices and institutions. His impersonations explore actualities and their latencies, and are thus sources of endlessly fertile suggestion. Emerson shows a different power from that of writers who create fictional characters, which are explorations of invented possibilities, or pictures of unrealizable personal roundedness. These interest him less. Following Nietzsche, however, I must not make absolute the difference between the power of conceptual impersonation and the power to create characters. The basic link between the two powers, Nietzsche says, is found in a common "self-possession": "a way of viewing himself as a mirror of the world" (*Philosophy in the Tragic Age of the Greeks* [M. Cowan, Trans.], p. 44). I do still think the difference is substantial.

"I should think water the best invention if I were not acquainted with fire and earth and air" ("Religion," *Early Lectures*, 3, p. 284). He also has to say, "I should think fire the best thing in the world if I were not acquainted with air, and water, and earth" ("Art," p. 433). He approvingly allows that it is the

> habit of certain minds to give an all-excluding fullness to the object, the thought, the word they alight upon, and to make that for a time the deputy of the world ... The power to detach and to magnify by detaching is the essence of rhetoric. ("Art," p. 433)

This rhetoric is a power "to fix the momentary eminency of an object" ("Art," p. 433). The true benefit of rhetoric, however, comes only when we see it bestowed on contrasting or antagonistic ideas and objects, one after another.

Therefore when the self-reliant individual receives instruction, as he or she must, from the "rhetoric" of others as it is contained in great or good writings, variety must be the rule. Great writers, Emerson says, "are antidotes to each other's influence." After one great writer has been studied,

> then comes by another luminary ... and with equal claims on our wonder, and affords us at once the power of self-recovery, and that of comparing system with system, influence with influence, and, at last, man with man. ("Lord Bacon," *Early Lectures, 1*, p. 321)

Yet because Emerson is so little partisan, it is hard to know which writers could serve as antidotes to him. He is an antidote to many others.

Emerson means to persuade us to a *happy* responsiveness to contrasting or antagonistic thoughts and phenomena, and he makes it the salient quality of his method. He does not necessarily want us to agree with his insights or judgments, or even to go on discussing all his subjects. He only wants us to feel delight with him in the spectacle of contrariety that the world offers and that he tries to capture in his work. His great lesson is that some large part of the interest or fascination in the world comes from the fact that meaning or beauty or truth can be found in conflicting or incompatible ideas, principles, forces, and practices. The common tendency is to escape such clamor and seek clarification, or to come to the world fully armed with dogma and preconceptions. Rather than feeling dismay from opposition to oneself or from the very abundance of seemingly irreconcilable antagonisms, one can strive for a self-mastery that rides above one's likes and dislikes, and one's cravings for simple clarity.

One can profess what Emerson calls "the joyous science" ("The Scholar," *Lectures and Sketches*, p. 262), and do so by looking at one's mutable opinions "as a bird that flieth" and thus "put himself out of the reach of skepticism" ("Prospects," *Early Lectures, 3*, p. 379). Only the self-reliant person can aspire to the joyous science. Each of the things in contention can be seen separately as worthy or beautiful, but so can the contending things when juxtaposed and held together. What is involved in Emerson's joyous science is something less like seeing all sides of a disputed issue, and more like admiring all sides in an unstoppable struggle. Emerson is eager to present the struggle. I do not think that Emerson typically seeks to create, say, a third thing better than the two seen in contention or held in contrast; nor does he want to "harmonize" them, despite what he says in "Fate." He does not aspire, as John Stuart Mill does, to combine the best elements from contrasting ideas into a new idea better than those from which it selects. Nor is he very eager to compare, because comparison necessarily deprives anything of its "munificence" and makes it "look less" (Notes to "Character," *Lectures and Sketches*, p. 532). He may theorize harmonization, but fortunately, he does not practice it. Rather he seeks to keep each thing alive by giving it good words, considering it "as if it existed for itself alone" and not as if it were to be judged by its conformity to one's wishes ("The Head," *Early Lectures*, 2, p. 17). Each idea or value, practice or movement, has an equal right to exist, even if it does not have a right to an equal influence. The world is full of gods, joined in enmity and kinship. Self-reliance embraces this condition. It seeks to guard the world's complexity and search out the necessity of its turmoil.

In the following pages I will often quote Emerson in support of one idea (or practice) or another. But I know that his statements often stand in a relation of mutual qualification, or are offered exaggeratedly because they are tentative. I do not deny that he favors some outlooks, conceptions or attitudes as well as some institutions and tendencies more than others. He had views, after all: loyalties and inclinations, apart from or in spite of his philosophy. But he deems it essential to struggle against his own mere preferences in order to make almost everything valuable. "A man should be a guest in his own house, and a guest in his own thought" ("The Sovereignty of Ethics," *Lectures and Sketches*, p. 194). Feeling too much at home in one's inclinations, one refuses accommodation to what is different. In reading Emerson, one runs the risk of arbitrarily deciding which statements more nearly represent Emerson's views, and which statements he is only trying out. I am sure that I have not avoided that danger while I persistently go about attributing views to him. Alternatively, one can say that he means everything he says, but that must mean that he moves beyond belief into undiscriminating acceptance. In either case, when we quote him we must believe him, but we should do so with (Emersonian) reservation.

I am sure, however, that whenever self-reliance (in any of its several forms) is at stake, Emerson is always finally on the side of any idea or practice that creates or sustains or favors it. In the form of intellectual method, self-reliance does itself necessitate that Emerson be attentive to and appreciative of the opposition to self-reliance and also be aware of its inherent difficulties and uncertainties. But despite all the indeterminacy that Emerson's work fosters, he is unwaveringly committed to self-reliance. The result is that I have tended to treat his words as expressing his unreserved beliefs when they contribute to the elaboration and defense of the idea of self-reliance and of its institutional preconditions and effects. Of course, not everything in the world is causally or directly related to self-reliance; not everything favors or threatens it. There were almost no democratic societies in the past and therefore self-reliance in its democratic manifestation was not a possibility. Yet the self-reliant mind must absorb the past hospitably. On the other hand, the safety of the ideal of self-reliance is not always at stake amid the disagreements and struggles of democratic life. All the parties, factions, and sects cry for sympathy. These facts leave him a large field for the play of his sympathetically disengaged intellect. That is to say, these facts leave him a large field for the display of mental self-reliance, understood as a method of intellect. Where does Emerson's greater power show itself? In formulating the meanings and implications of self-reliance or in practicing mental self-reliance by engaging with the vastness of life and the world in the manner of sympathetic disengagement? It is not necessary to decide.

Emerson does not lie. He makes sure that he will not have to lie by not dwelling on what repels him. In fact, he engages only with what attracts or tempts him. He thus limits the scope of his method. He can say of the hospitable soul that it "entertains in its spirit all travellers, tongues, kindreds, all employments, all eccentricities, all crimes even, in its vast charity and overcoming hope" ("The Poet," *Early Lectures, 3*, p. 356). But Emerson is no friend of crimes. Some readers may think his digestive powers too narrow or selective or driven by a metaphysical bias. His range is not, in any case, as synoptically or historically wide as Hegel's in *The Phenomenology of Spirit* or *The Philosophy of History*, to mention a remotely analogous enterprise. In compensation, he has only a subdued disposition to believe in teleological historical (as distinct from bio-evolutionary) advance, and hence in the chance that obsolescence can overtake most ideas or many practices. He tends to see, I think, permanence, not eventual supersession, in the phenomena he interprets. He says:

> Without hurry, without rest, the human spirit goes forth from the beginning to embody every faculty, every thought, every emotion which belongs to it, in appropriate events. But always the thought is prior to the fact. All the facts of history preexist in the mind as laws. Each law in turn is made by circumstances predominant, and the limits of nature give power to but one at a time. Therefore there is no progress to the race. Progress belongs to individuals and consists in becoming universal. ("Introductory," *The Philosophy of History, Early Lectures, 2*, pp. 13–14)

He therefore does really lend himself to many and diverse phenomena, while nevertheless *giving* himself only to his self-reliant method of encompassing these phenomena.

His exaggerated defense of some phenomena is better than arguments that exclusive partisans could mount, and at the same time, it is a defense that is qualified (explicitly or implicitly) by exaggeration in support of competing objects of idolatry. The qualification may come immediately or be deferred; it may be stark or sly. He sees worth everywhere. Yet it is also true that he sees more worth than he instinctively feels. "I love everything by turns, and nothing long" ("Nominalist and Realist," p. 587). His mind is always desirous because it is only briefly and incompletely appeasable. The self-reliant mind must grow voyeurist and promiscuous, to use opprobrious terms favorably—terms that he of course does not use. Indeed he sometimes criticizes his own tendency. In the first edition of "History" (1841) he can praise "intellectual nomadism" without qualification: "eyes which everywhere feed themselves" (Notes to "Self-Reliance," *Works*, 2, p. 384). But in the second edition (1847) he says that in its excess, intellectual nomadism "bankrupts the mind, through the dissipation of power on a miscellany of objects" (p. 247). The first edition is truer to Emerson than the second.

Henry James said of Emerson that "He liked to taste but not to drink—least of all to become intoxicated" (*Literary Criticism*, p. 265). That is a good description of Emerson's aspiration. To condemn it is to condemn Emerson. This aspiration does not make him playful or merely ironic. His inexhaustible impersonations are not exhibitions. No, his writings as a whole are a battleground; often, any single essay is, too. That is why he tastes, not drinks. He is a battleground and therefore ends up appearing above the battle.

Exactness cannot be reached directly, undialectically. Impersonation requires close attention to the impersonated, but it is more than close attention. In the face of complex and contending phenomena, honesty compels extravagance. Present exaggeration may turn into future accuracy because it discloses unsuspected but latent virtues. Present exaggeration may also be good because it can delineate and detect "occult symmetries and unpublished beauties" ("The Scholar," *Lectures and Sketches*, p. 262).

One other purpose is served by present exaggeration in Emerson. It contributes to recovering the original "inspiration" of any long-standing precept or permanent human tendency. Emerson sometimes practices a benign genealogy. In a lecture, "Religion" (1837), he says:

As I have said, the invariable badge of virtue is usefulness. It serves the temporal need of the human race. The law which it gives to the listening enthusiast, "Be just," comes to serve for the protection of all the society in the form of "Thou shalt not steal."

> The law which he heard in his heart, "Serve no furious passion," comes to serve for the police of society in the form of "Thou shalt not kill," "Thou shalt not commit adultery." Meantime when, at intervals, to each heart the Supreme Reason reveals itself it perceives the deep truth of these prior commandments and adds to them new titles and rules of veneration to secure the precious palladium to mankind. (*Early Lectures*, 2, p. 93)

Exaggeration can therefore reinflate something to its real size and show how large or great it really is, more so than is commonly thought. Exaggeration wars against the shrinkage that time indefatigably inflicts. An idea or practice can be better than its own faithful adherents know, better than its own most favored perspective on itself suggests that it is.

Is exaggeration permanently necessary to any mind seeking to communicate its self-reliance? Probably. There may have been greater pressures in Emerson's time to refuse receptivity than we currently feel, and his fight may have been a good deal harder than ours today. But the fight has to be fought always. He exaggerates in order to get his audience to attend to what it unjustly feared, despised, ignored or depreciated. A self-reliant mind today will also feel the need to rescue many things and encourage receptivity to them, despite supposedly greater openness. Exaggeration or extravagance can awaken generosity, which always tends to be in short supply.

The truth is got, then, not when one adheres to the precept of moderation, but when one pursues conflicting excesses that qualify each other. The qualifications are meant to deepen our responses, not to impoverish them. In "Circles," he says, "Our moods do not believe in each other" (p. 406). But his steady suggestion is that we must believe in them, provided that we believe in all of them, excluding none and letting none exclude any other or all the others. Knowing that the full power of a mood is discernible only after the mood passes, we must be wary of thinking that we can ever rest in a present certainty. Mobility is the check on mood. "I am always insincere, as always knowing there are other moods" ("Nominalist and Realist," p. 587). But though "insincere," Emerson surrenders to every mood and utters its message without letting his awareness that he will later speak in and for a different mood inhibit his utterance or make it less one-sided. He carries out the program he urges for all of us:

> The commonest remark, if the man could only extend it a little, would make him a genius; but the thought is prematurely checked, and grows no more. All great masters are chiefly distinguished by the power of adding a second, a third, and

perhaps a fourth step in a continuous line. Many a man had taken the first step. With every additional step you enhance immensely the value of your first. ("Natural History of Intellect," Natural History, p. 25)

To be sure, each of Emerson's essays is more than the statement of a mood, but its core is a mood—if not a present mood, then a remembered or expected or imagined one.

A mood may attune itself to the matter under consideration and therefore provide greater receptivity; or, contrastingly, it may qualify what one said earlier on the same matter, in a different mood. Thus different moods are many eyes for looking at the diversity of the same thing or looking sympathetically at many contending things.

What claim is Emerson making for his impersonations? To speak truthfully. But is that to grasp essences? I think not: his tone is not that of one who presumes to say the last word. A profound idea or a durable practice can inexhaustibly engender interpretations. Analysis of it is interminable; it is richer than any one mind can know, no matter how many perspectives on it that the same mind, in various moods, is able to take, and no matter how hard that mind tries to befriend it and make the best case for it. But it is also true that Emerson is not a pure perspectivist. Although he lets his moods speak, and although he goes to the limit of the perspective that a mood opens up, he appeals to others, if not for their agreement, then for their provisional assent. He is not speaking only on his own behalf, or simply adding just one more perspective. He takes a broad view. What he sees we can see, and not just because he has instructed us, but mostly because our own resources permit us to understand him and perhaps confirm him, even as they should sustain us in the effort to amend or abandon him. But on the most important matter anyone's self-reliant mind will not amend or abandon Emerson, but be like him: receptive to contrast and antagonism as such and to each element that takes a part in the play of life and the world.

As I will try to show later at some length, Emerson's principal tactic of receptivity and response is to see beauty where others do not. "Beauty," he says, "is the form under which the intellect prefers to study the world." He is faithful to the office of the poet as he defines it in "The Poet": it is "announcement and affirming" (p. 452). His whole work teaches that "Thought makes every thing fit for use ... What would be base, or even obscene, to the obscene, becomes illustrious, spoken in a new connection of thought" (p. 454).

What is it that can dispose a person to receptivity and response? I believe that the most sustained answer Emerson gives is found in "History," the first essay of *Essays: First Series*. In this piece, Emerson asks us, as Whitman does later on, to see the human world's historical mutability and diversity as either a projection of elements in every soul or an enactment, on a large scale, of private events in any person's life. History could not be understood if all people were not similarly manifold and equally experienced. "This human mind wrote history, and this must read it. The Sphinx must solve her own riddle" (p. 237). The aim of the study of history is to demonstrate that all history is the work of the generic human being and that it is nothing more than the display of powers lodged in any human soul. The study of history

> will pierce into the subtile streams of influence that pass from man to man, from society to society and uncover the outer and inner bands by which neighborhoods, societies, nations, and the whole race are knit up into a common hope and fear, a common aim and nature, into one man. ("Introductory," *The Philosophy of History, Early Lectures*, 2, p. 10)

(This thought is distinct from Emerson's contention that the processes of nature are projections of a divine mind that is not totally separated from the human mind, and hence are rational and ultimately moral.) The benefit of a greater self-acquaintance is a greater sympathetic understanding of the world's past and present cultures, and of their deeds and achievements. Emerson speaks of "the knowledge of all men which belongs to self-knowledge" (Notes to "Works and Days," *Society and Solitude*, p. 394). Knowledge of the world leads in turn to deeper self-knowledge.

"Man is explicable by nothing less than all his history" ("History," p. 237). One will find in oneself the raw material of every configuration or position or tendency; or one will find in one's life "quite parallel miniature experiences of his own" (p. 249). Nothing human should count as inhuman:

> There is nothing but is related to me; no mode of life so alien and grotesque but by careful comparison I can soon find my place in it; find a strict analogy between my experiences and whatever is real in those of any man. ("Introductory," *The Philosophy of History, Early Lectures*, 2, p. 19)

Let us notice that Emerson is willing to include the "alien and grotesque" in the scope of his sympathetic understanding.

To be sure, Emerson allows for distorted and therefore unrecognized resemblances:

> As in dreams, so in the scarcely less fluid events of the world, every man sees himself in colossal, without knowing that is himself ... Every quality of his mind is magnified in some one acquaintance, and every emotion of his heart in some one. ("Spiritual Laws," p. 314)

But howsoever remote and seemingly unlike, any given part of history is potentially stored in every soul.

> Every thing the individual sees without him corresponds to his states of mind, and every thing is in turn intelligible to him, as his onward thinking leads him into the truth to which that fact or series belongs. ("History," p. 247)

It is worth noticing that in this essay Emerson refuses to absorb animal and vegetable nature because they are not made by human beings, as history is:

> What is the use of pretending to know what we know not? ... I hold our actual knowledge very cheap. Hear the rats in the wall, see the lizard on the fence, the fungus under foot, the lichen on the log. What do I know sympathetically, morally, of either of these worlds of life? (pp. 255–256)

Nevertheless, within the human realm, every fact is available to the self-reliant mind, the mind willing to search itself and face what it finds without orthodox or conformist narrowness or fear.

* * *

To repeat: we must not expect anything simple when we take up Emerson on self-reliance. The point put in academic language is that democratic individuality is nothing simple. What, then, more explicitly, is self-reliance? What is reliance on oneself, what does it come to? Though I believe that self-reliance in its highest Emersonian form is a method of intellect, it presents itself memorably as a principle for the conduct of a whole life. In the essay, "Self-Reliance," Emerson mingles reflections on mental self-reliance and active self-reliance. In passing, he does distinguishes between "actual" and "intellectual" life, but appears to suggest that they are inextricably copresent, or indeed, that if a distinction can be made, mental self-reliance is merely preliminary and instrumental to active self-reliance (p. 263). Let us therefore stay awhile with the idea of self-reliance as a way for the self to be and to act in the world. Eventually I will try to force a sharp distinction between mental self-reliance and active self-reliance, a distinction that not only ranks mental higher than active self-reliance, but actually severs them and places them in nearly untouching spheres of life. I think Emerson himself intends such a distinction. Let us for a time, however, work with an unsorted idea of self-reliance.

I have said that Emerson develops the idea in numerous places besides "Self-Reliance." An invaluable concentration is found in this essay; it is, all in all, one of his greatest performances of impersonation. But other writings, before and after, contribute to our understanding of the idea. A way into the idea is to suggest what Emerson thinks is opposed to self-reliance. The most general negative conception is that self-reliance is a refusal to rely on church religions. To be self-reliant is to be free of attachment to church doctrine, church worship, church ritual, and church prayer. Implicit in Emerson's work is the assumption that when church religions are weakened in (and, in part, because of) democratic society, self-reliance will appear, not the nihilism of despair or of frivolity. I do not say that self-reliance is independence from religiousness. To the contrary, Emerson's ultimate meaning of self-reliance is to be properly religious; "self-reliance, the height and perfection of man is reliance on God" ("The Fugitive Slave Law," 1854, *Miscellanies*, p. 236). We will come to Emerson's religiousness later. For now, let us see that Emerson's war, especially vivid in his writings throughout *Essays: Second Series*, is against the effects of church religions on their adherents and communicants. That he resigned his ministry in the Unitarian church in 1832 is a great emblematic fact. Emerson thinks that not only in his time, but also throughout time, church religions take, for the most part, the side of the social given and thus strengthen, its hold. Acceptance of society is the normal posture of church religions, what they eventually come to, no matter how disruptive their beginnings may be. Church-faithful minds are dependent minds, and dependent minds produce expected and conformist behavior, even when such behavior seems at odds with church doctrine.

Another rough way of indicating what is opposed to self-reliance is to emphasize the continuous antipathy that Emerson shows toward the social given. Not only does he find the prevailing aims of action and some of the arrangements of life questionable and probably unsatisfactory to those who uphold them, he also, I think, is temperamentally given to shuddering at the thought of clustered humanity, lost together because each is lost to himself or herself. This shudder is part of what it means to be a principled individualist. He exceeds Nietzsche in queasiness. But his reproaches of the herd-spirit, in the name of self-reliance, usually proceed without malice or vanity. One vivid exception to his generosity occurs when, apparently speaking in his own voice, he says that "enormous populations, if they be beggars, are disgusting, like moving cheese, like hills of ants, or of fleas—the more, the worse" ("Uses of Great Men," *Representative Men*, p. 615).

He preaches self-reliance because he thinks that all people already have self-reliant moments and could more successfully become self-reliant if they tried. Self-reliance is thus not a doctrine of superiority to average humanity. Rather it is a doctrine urging the elevation of democracy to its full height, free of the aristocratic, but also free of the demotic.

I wish also to indicate summarily other attitudes opposed to Emersonian self-reliance. As Emerson works out his ideas, we are able to see that the defense of self-reliance is an attack on the common tendency to act on the idea that the core of individualism is economic self-centeredness and that the true individual is acquisitive or possessive or consumerist. For Emerson, the exclusively materialistic life is not life, but a misdiagnosed dying. Relatedly, Emerson's self-reliance does not amount to a celebration of intimacy or of privacy. His elaborations in "Love" and "Friendship" are unhomelike. Finally, self-reliance is not thinking and acting on the belief that one is alone in the world, but that only oneself is real, that the world is what I say or think it is. Emerson is a qualified critic of subjectivity, as in chapter 7 ("Spirit") of *Nature* (1836). He denounces everyday egotism; he is skeptical of philosophical egoism. Indeed, so far is Emerson from praise of the ego that he sounds a remarkable note of existential indebtedness. He says:

> Indeed what is our own being but a reproduction, a representation of all the past? I remember the manifold cord— the thousand or the million stranded cord which my being and every man's being is,—that I am an aggregate of infinitesimal parts and that every minutest streamlet that has flowed to me is represented in that man which I am so that if every one should claim his part in me I should be instantaneously diffused through the creation and individually decease, then I say I am an alms of all and live but by the charity of others. What is a man but a congress of nations? (Notes to "Private Life," *Early Lectures, 3*, p. 251)

In sum, Emerson as a theorist of self-reliance is a theorist of democratic individuality, and he is therefore averse to all the sorts of individualism that I have just mentioned.

Positively, self-reliance is self-trust. "In self-trust all the virtues are comprehended" ("The American Scholar," p. 65). Napoleon commands our respect, says Emerson, "by his enormous self-trust" ("Greatness," *Letters*, p. 314). He goes on to define Napoleon's self-trust as "the habit of seeing with his own eyes." From such self-reliance or self-trust would flow a further daring: to experience honestly and act adventurously. The power which resides in every person is "new in nature" ("Self-Reliance," p. 259). Every individual is a new individual and can, with self-trust, do in the world something not yet done but worth doing. Creativity is always possible; creativity is actual when people trust themselves:

> There are creative manners, there are creative actions, and creative words; manners, actions, words, that is, indicative of no custom or authority, but springing spontaneous from the mind's own sense of good and fair. ("The American Scholar," p. 58)

Such creativity is released only when conformity gives way: "imitation is suicide" ("Self-Reliance," p. 259). "Whoso would be a man must be a nonconformist" (p. 261). With a rare vehemence, Emerson says in his essay, "Persian Poetry":

> We accept the religions and politics into which we fall; and it is only a few delicate spirits who are sufficient to see that the whole web of convention is the imbecility of those whom it entangles. (*Letters*, p. 248)

A nice uncertainty is in this sentence. It seems to suggest either that conventions are imbecile in substance; or that they are not imbecile, but the devout way in which they are accepted is imbecile. Emerson elsewhere defends both sentiments. In sum, "Custom is the defacer of beauty, and the concealer of truth" ("English Literature: Introductory," *Early Lectures, 1*, p. 226). "Decorum is the undress of virtue" ("The Present Age," *Early Lectures, 2*, 162).

Conformity rests on being ashamed. Shame converts virtues into penances and life into one long expiation. Conformity is the postponement of life, not life; it scatters one's force, blocks the work that one can do well, or especially or uniquely well; but "with the exercise of self-trust, new powers shall appear" ("Self-Reliance," p. 275). The only absolution is self-forgiveness. Only self-trust can induce self-forgiveness. Without self-forgiveness, people are "timid and apologetic" (p. 270). Indeed, so timid and apologetic, that they are no longer upright; they are "ashamed before the blade of grass or the blowing rose" (p. 270).

It is no revelation to say that Emerson's mission is to preach courage, inspire hope. He aims to carry out his mission radically. The amazing passion that drives Emerson's "Address" to the Harvard Divinity School (1838) is to proclaim the divinity of each person, as if to ground an absolute self-trust. In this address, he says:

> That which shows God out of me, makes me a wart and a wen.
> There is no longer a necessary reason for my being. (p. 81)

Each of us must be convinced that he or she has an indispensable existence: the world would be unthinkable without any one of us. To feel this way is to have the right kind of self-trust. But Emerson does not find it in the society he knows.

He looks around him and sees a people with immense energy, but the energy is misdirected, usually deriving from the desire to prove oneself; "raging riders, who drive their steeds so hard, in the violence of living to forget its illusion" ("New England Reformers," p. 603). Despair and self-doubt frantically impel. The animation is in the service of conformity, but adequacy to conformity seems an endless task. From all this waste Emerson tries to reclaim his hearers and readers. Like his greatest European heir, Nietzsche, he tries to seduce us to life. But Emerson makes the job sound less burdensome than Nietzsche does; he has much more trust in the people around him. He even may be said to love them.

From this poetical or Socratic love, Emerson produces images and examples in order to encourage more self-reliant being and acting. What Nietzsche playfully but meanly calls the will to power, Emerson considers common creativity or a common need for self-expression. Emerson's premise is stated on many occasions, but one statement is all the more compelling for being made in the essay "Experience," which is mostly devoted to presenting the best case for the *unlikelihood* of genuine expression. He says:

> I had fancied that the value of life lay in its inscrutable
> possibilities; in the fact that I never know, in addressing myself to
> a new individual, what may befall me. (p. 475)

The fact of human unpredictability must be insisted on. There is fearful resistance to it. In fact, people can act as if they did not believe it and thus provide mechanistic determinism a temporary vindication. People sleepwalk: that is how conformist obedience can strike the disappointed observer, and Emerson uses the trope. But Emerson is not resigned to disappointment. He hopes to coax self-reliance.

Self-reliance is a process, not a state in which one can rest. Self-reliance is too difficult to be possessed securely; on the other hand, life's unexpectedness (its "inscrutable possibilities") can and will unsettle even the most self-reliant individual. In the essay "The Transcendentalist" (1842), Emerson attributes to the young and disaffected idealists or transcendentalists (and eventually claims for himself) the occurrence of "a certain brief experience, which surprised me in the highway or in the market, in some place, at some time—whether in the body or out of the body." He continues:

> God knoweth—and made me aware that I had played the fool with fools all this time, but that law existed for me and for all; that to me belonged trust, a child's trust and obedience, and the worship of ideas, and I should never be fool more. Well, in the space of an hour probably, I was let down from this height; I was at my old tricks, the selfish member of a selfish society. My life is superficial, takes no root in the deep world; I ask, When shall I die and be relieved of the responsibility of seeing a Universe I do not use? I wish to exchange this flash-of-lightning faith for continuous daylight, this fever-glow for a benign climate. (p. 205)

Emerson refers to this condition of occasional illumination and habitual self-loss as "double consciousness." The "two lives" are disconnected or "parallel" for the most part ("Duty," *Early Lectures, 3*, p. 143). Yet he clings to the hope that "the moments will characterize the days" ("The Transcendentalist," pp. 205–206). "How slowly the highest raptures of the intellect break through the trivial forms of habit" ("Duty," p. 144). Perhaps not only slowly but forever incompletely: "all men do value the few hours of real life," as if even the purest vision left the self untransformed, and confined its effects to only a short time ("Address" [Harvard Divinity School], p. 89).

I read the passage from "The Transcendentalist" as an indication of the sense that, for Emerson, self-reliance as an intermittent process is more than a mood, but only with persistent struggle, something appreciably more than a mood. The point is to make self-reliance attractive. He knows how unattractive it can be. In an early lecture he speaks of how it feels to reach the age of one's majority: "The burdensome possession of himself he cannot dispose of ("The Present Age," *Early Lectures, 2*, p. 170). The temptation is to live on terms prescribed anonymously or by nameable others. American democracy, the opportunity of the New World, exists, however, for the sake of self-reliance, for the sake of weakening the grip of routine and subservience. Democracy may make it possible for people in society to stop being "puppets of routine" ("Reforms," *Early Lectures, 3*, p. 265). If poetical thinking is "departure from routine," then so is living in the spirit of independence ("The Poet," p. 462). To be free and equal is to be self-reliant: that is one short way of putting it. Yet ordinary persons hold back. They are often content to "slide into the vacant places of the last generation" ("Address on Education," *Early Lectures*, 2, p. 197). Emerson will, then, appeal to them. He imputes to all people, as I have said, a fundamental need (and capacity) for self-expression. He is insistent:

> all men live by truth and stand in need of expression. In love, in art, in avarice, in politics, in labor, in games, we study to utter our painful secret. The man is only half himself, the other half is his expression. ("The Poet," p. 448)

(Notice that he includes avarice.)

In an earlier version of "The Poet," he gives another articulation of the half-buried urge to express oneself. He says:

> Does happiness depend on "uninterrupted prosperity," as it is called? Oh no, but on Expression. Expression is prosperity. I must say what is burning here: I must do what I shall perish if I cannot do, I must appear again in my house, in my fortune, in my marriage, in my speech, or else I must disappear, and the brute form must crowd the soul out of nature. (*Early Lectures*, 3, p. 349)

Emerson proposes that as observers we should try to see almost all activity as expression, as self-expression, as exertion motivated as much by the urge to disclose oneself as by the wish to get a job done. The attempt to expose or discover one's secret, one's real talent, is often displaced or off-center, and thus a person's secret may remain a secret even to that person. It is very hard to find one's own way; one falls back on conventionally-defined opportunities. The greater the element of conformity, the greater the chance of avoiding one's deepest truth. Only independent conduct can be perceived as the truth of a person.

In "Self-Reliance," Emerson likens any attentive activity to prayer, the only genuine prayer:

> As soon as the man is at one with God, he will not beg. He will then see prayer in all action. The prayer of the farmer kneeling in his field to weed it, the prayer of the rower kneeling with the stroke of his oar, are true prayers heard throughout nature, though for cheap ends. (p. 276)

The complication is that activity may very well seem like prayer only to the contemplative observer. The inwardness of the worker may not be prayerful. To take inspiration from a kneeling farmer may be to play a trick on oneself. But Emerson's point is probably more generous to the worker.

Especially in his writings before *Essays: First Series*, but not only there, Emerson makes much of finding one's vocation as the key to being oneself. This frequent sense is that each person exists to do what only that person can do well or can do at all. Singularity or individuation is tied to one's active vocation. Self-reliance means yielding to one's real work, if one is released enough to insist on discovering it. One's active vocation is the expression and completion of one's being, but it is also the reason for being. Later on, I will discuss Emerson's idea of vocation at some length. I simply want to indicate its salience here.

Just as steady as Emerson's praise of vocation is his dismay at most occupations. We thus come up against a major obstacle in our efforts to see the essence of self-reliance as a principle of action or as an existential choice rather than as a method of intellect. He can go only so far in investing daily work, even when undertaken as prayer, with a dignity commensurate with the proper expectations for human individuals. The abrupt phrase "though for cheap ends" in a lyrically adorative passage on activity as prayer is indicative of Emerson's attitude. He does not instinctively love the expression he sees. In "The Poet," he can speak of how "hunters, farmers, grooms and butchers" express their love of nature by their very choice of life, "and not in their choice of words." They worship "nature the symbol ... body overflowed by life." Yet their active life, which is their worship, is constituted by "coarse, but sincere rites" (pp. 453–454). Emerson sees the coarseness, not only the sincerity. He is desperate to praise in order to encourage, so he says that the "aboriginal Self" in each, the unknowable inner power, "shoots a ray of beauty even into trivial and impure actions, if the least mark of independence appear" ("Self-Reliance," p. 268). He labors to love labor, and succeeds partly. However, he says in "The Poet":

> Notwithstanding this necessity to be published, adequate expression is rare. I know not how it is that we need an interpreter; but the great majority of men seem to be minors, who have not yet come into possession of their own, or mutes, who cannot report the conversation they have had with nature. (p. 448)

Emerson certainly exemplifies his theory that the poet's vocation is to interpret human beings to themselves. He is a poet because he could not endure the world if it were left uninterpreted: It would be "cheap," "coarse."

It is therefore not surprising that when Emerson gives in *Nature* examples of activities that rise above the usual condition wherein "man applies to nature but half his force," they make up an amazingly unnormalized sampling:

> the traditions of miracles in the earliest antiquity of all nations; the history of Jesus Christ; the achievements of a principle, as in religious and political revolutions, and in the abolition of the slave-trade; the miracles of enthusiasm, as those reported of Swedenborg, Hohenlohe, and the Shakers; many obscure and yet uncontested facts, now arranged under the name of Animal Magnetism; prayer; eloquence; self-healing; and the wisdom of children. (pp. 46–47)

For the most part, he reaches for the extraordinary or the unadult, as if only these are worth expressing. Though *Representative Men* is a kind of rebuttal to Carlyle's worship of heroes, still the very fact that five of the six representative men are thinkers (and the other is Napoleon) makes it hard for us to believe that Emerson appreciates the typical activities of ordinary persons in the world. As for the realm of the extraordinary, he says in a lecture:

> I like artists better than generals. Goethe and Swedenborg are far more formidable agitators than Napoleon or O'Connell.... These persons can never compete with the artist.... He takes his counters from heaven and plays his game by a skill not taught or quickened by his appetites. ("Literature" [Second lecture], *Early Lectures*, 3, p. 225)

I believe that Emerson gives us indications throughout his work that self-reliant existence or action and endeavor can only be marginal or eruptive; it is dependent on the chances the world gives to make a difference. If the idea of self-reliance is to be realized more self-sufficiently, less contingently—difficult as its realization must always be—it must find its location elsewhere than in worldly appearance or activity. Self-reliance must then refer primarily to the work of the inner life, to the life of the mind. But let me hold off this insistence of mine a bit longer.

Is there a completed picture of a truly self-reliant ordinary individual in Emerson's writing, of one who, leading an everyday life, projects the powers within and independently. makes his or her life expressive? Perhaps we find one in the sometimes harrowing essay on his aunt, Mary Moody

Emerson—an essay that also looks like a self-portrait. Perhaps his eulogy of Thoreau is a picture of self-reliance; but the reservations he inserts add up to a deep ambivalence, which Emerson voiced on other occasions. Indeed it is the very self-reliance of being and acting, common to his aunt and Thoreau, that elicits Emerson's ambivalence. It is as if the project of existential or active self-reliance verges on the inhuman. Its success may not be success. In any case, it is perhaps right that Emerson leaves all forms of self-reliance except mental self-reliance undefined or ill-defined. Persons have to find their own way. Whatever the reasons, the conceptualization is incomplete. What we have instead of a full portrait is an image of an ideal, an image of being oneself by realizing oneself, of being self-reliant rather than imitative (or conventional and hence unnatural). This image, however, signifies Emerson's inevitable failure to redeem the idea that the principal realization of self-reliance lies in independent being, doing, or acting.

After lamenting everyone's timidity and apology ("he dares not say 'I think,' 'I am,' but quotes some saint or sage"), Emerson says:

> These roses under my window make no reference to former roses or to better ones; they are for what they are; they exist with God today. There is no time to them. There is simply the rose; it is perfect in every moment of its existence.

He goes on:

> But man postpones or remembers; he does not live in the present.... He cannot be happy and strong until he too lives with nature in the present, above time. ("Self-Reliance," p. 270)

But the lovely image is not lovely. Human beings characteristically *postpone* too much; but we do not think unless we *remember*. Trying to live in the present is hopeless; so is assimilating living to being, living one's life to being oneself. In what I say I only repeat what Emerson usually says, rose or no rose. The fact is that Emerson insists with a characteristic insistence that we can assimilate our active experience only retrospectively and that this condition is not lamentable but productive of intense intellectuality. It may be easier to observe immediately than to experience immediately, but memory is needed even to make the best of one's immediate observations. To exist or live in the present is to live the past intellectually, not to live actively now, or be fully there. Though Emerson did not write a piece on memory until rather late in life (1857), memory in the form of active recollection is fundamental to his notion of mental life. This thought is crystallized in words from the earlier version of "Love" (1838), which tell of the impact of falling in love: "when we became all eye when one was present, and all memory when one was gone" (*Early Lectures, 3*, p. 57). The best of life, including love, is all eye and all memory.

I grant that there is a sense of living in the present which avoids some of the objections that can be made to the image of the rose. In a lecture given in 1836, Emerson advocates "The present moment against all time" ("Modern Aspects of Letters," *Early Lectures, 1*, p. 384). I read this formulation as an incitement to seize the day and to live or act in defiance of the knowledge that time without beginning precedes one's existence, and time without end will roll on after one's death. One strains to overcome the futility inherent in the comparison of eternity with the brief flash of one's existence. "Works and Days" in *Society and Solitude* develops this thought. There can be, in Emerson's striking phrase, "consent to be nothing for eternity" ("Natural History of Intellect," *Natural History*, p. 56). "The day is great and final. The night is for the day, but the day is not for the night" ("Success," *Society and Solitude*, p. 307). If, then, living in the present means not wasting one's life, though it is absurdly brief, then the thought is salutary. But the image of the rose does not best represent this thought. Human beings cannot be, as roses are. We may look like roses, now and then, to the friend or lover, or to the poet. But only now and then. And if we try to exist as roses exist, we will be foolish or insensitive or cruel or mad, or merely vulgar. The complaint of "double consciousness," to which I referred above, is impossible to assuage, except falsely. The most we can have are moments of activity in which we feel as if all our powers were under our control, in which we feel that the present moment is worthy of lasting forever, that we achieved or restored our identity. Emerson complains that:

> A man acts not from one motive, but from many shifting fears and short motives; it is as if he were ten or twenty less men than himself, acting at discord with one another, so that the result of most lives is zero. ("The Preacher," *Lectures and Sketches*, p. 224)

He outdoes Plato in rendering the wasteland of self-division. But is there reality in his prophecy? He says:

> When he shall act from one motive, and all his faculties play true, it is clear mathematically, is it not, that this will tell in the result, as if twenty men had cooperated. (pp. 224–225)

The distancing phrase "is it not" and the insertion of "mathematically" are meant to reveal, I think, Emerson's strain, his doubt that self-unity can ever be anything but hit and miss.

If, too, we are unpredictable, if our deeds often surprise ourselves as well as others, that can mean, in a good or bad sense, that we are beside ourselves, but not that, at last, we are all that we can be. Roses in any case are predictable. A rose is only a rose. It does not have the "infinitude" that Emerson is intent on attributing to human beings. Infinitude is a concept that precludes living in the present because the all-sufficient present precludes endless potentiality. Emerson says all that is needed to subvert the aspiration to a composed essence:

> Other creatures are generic but have no individuals. Every lion is like every other lion: all horses of the same breed will act alike in given situations: but every man is a new and incalculable power. (Introductory, *The Philosophy of History, Early Lectures*, 2, p. 9)

In several ways, then, Emerson undercuts the idea that the supreme realization of self-reliance should lie in being and acting. He encounters everywhere reasons to be dissatisfied with attempted expressiveness, despite his profound dislike of the unexpressiveness of conformity. His genius, in its power, and perhaps also in its temperamental limitations, inclines to the view that a contemplative mind can be more truly self-reliant than a person striving for self-reliance in the world. With an independent mind, one can see and know, observe and trace the intricacy and complexity of the world. This mental process more nearly reaches self-reliance than being and acting individualistically do. Evidence seems to compel Emerson's judgment.

There are impediments to active self-reliance that Emerson ponders and that I will explore in the next chapter. But even if these impediments were less strong, active self-reliance would still be, in his theory, inherently less worthy, less dignified, than mental self-reliance. I think there are two reasons for this. First, only mental self-reliance can be impersonal. Second, active self-reliance—even when and to the extent that it can be achieved— seems incomplete or inadequate unless one makes the effort to disclose it and make it signify, and such an effort of contemplation and interpretation is of course a mental one. I will take up the second reason in the context of discussing impediments to active self-reliance, but at this moment I wish to attend to the theme of impersonality.

Emerson frequently suggests that truly to be an individual one must become "public"; it means losing "personality" as well as losing the partiality or distinctiveness flowing from one's identification with a group. The attempt may make one resemble an impervious egoist, or a person without qualities; but the appearance would be deceptive. One tries to overcome obstacles to receptivity, to "impressionability" ("Success," *Society and Solitude*, p. 301). We go out of ourselves so that we may enter the world, rather than remaining imprisoned in ourselves. Emerson renders this going out of oneself as a kind of self-forgetting, where the self to be forgotten is the everyday self, a prisoner of habitual mental associations converting newness into a mere exoticism. He says:

> How tedious is the perpetual self preservation of the traveller. His whole road is a comparison of what he sees and does at home with what he sees and does now. Not a blessed moment does he forget himself and yielding to the new world of facts that environ him, utter without memory that which they say. Could he once abandon himself to the wonder of the landscape he would cease to find it strange. (*Journals*, 7, pp. 235–236)

Regularly going out of our selves prepares for the possibility of occasionally losing oneself—being beside oneself, lost in ecstatic contemplation. We ascend by abandonment—that is, by the deliberate struggle against being calculating, against becoming obsessively self-absorbed, self-furthering, even self-realizing. "We are not strong by our power to penetrate, but by our relatedness. The world is enlarged for us, not by new objects, but by finding more affinities and potencies in those we have" ("Success," *Society and Solitude*, p. 302). We abandon pride of personality. We mitigate what I have called "positive individuality" because it distorts self-reliant receptivity. There is a wonderful passage in a letter by Keats, which he wrote under the influence of Hazlitt's great reflections on Shakespeare in *Lectures on the English Poets* (1818) that makes almost the same point in an unusually spirited way, and thus throws light on Emerson's meaning:

> A poet is the most unpoetical of any thing in existence; because he has no Identity—he is continually in for—and filling some other Body—The Sun, the Moon, the Sea and Men and Women who are creatures of impulse are poetical and have about them an unchangeable attribute—the poet has none; no identity ... It is a wretched thing to confess; but is a very fact that not one word I utter can be taken for granted as an opinion growing out of my identical nature—how can it, when I have no nature? When I am in a room with People if I ever am free from speculating on creations of my own brain, then not myself goes home to myself:

but the identity of every one in the room begins ... to press upon me that, I am in a very little time annihilated. (To Richard Woodhouse, 27 October 1818, *Letters of John Keats*, pp. 157–158)

Emerson, unlike Keats, does not separate the poet from all other persons, but rather urges all of us to have moments when we lose our identities for the sake of poetical apprehension. He democratizes Keats's thought by trying to persuade us that impersonality is generally available. And he provides a basis for the capacity to become impersonal. Our impersonality is actually a refusal to shut out any aspect of oneself from the reach of cultivated self-awareness in order to position ourselves to use all our aspects—all our warring impulses and thoughts—as bridges to the kindred phenomena actualized in the world.

Nietzsche's rendering of the Dionysian condition in a passage later than *The Birth of Tragedy* also resembles Emersonian impersonality:

It is impossible for the Dionysian type not to understand any suggestion; he does not overlook any sign of an affect; he possesses the instinct of understanding and guessing in the highest degree, just as he commands the art of communication in the highest degree. He enters into any skin, into any affect: he constantly transforms himself. ("Skirmishes of an Untimely Man," *Twilight of the Idols* [W. Kaufman, Trans.], Sect. 10, pp. 519–520)

We are impersonal not only when we regard everything with as much sympathetic withholding as possible but also when we have sufficient self-acquaintance to know that all that has happened in the world has a source or echo in ourselves. The power to impersonate depends on impersonality. Impersonality registers an individual's universality or infinitude. Such an impersonal aspiration is a decisive indication that for Emerson, self-reliance is most itself when it is a method of intellect rather than a way of being or acting in the world. Let us, therefore, give a definition of self-reliance at its best: it is the steady effort of thinking one's thoughts and thinking them through. It is intellectual independence, reactive and responsive self-possession. Here, rather than in worldly appearance or enactment, we find the greater possibility of a more sustained independence.

Really, how could determinate being or specific doing and acting follow from the cultivation of a readiness to lend oneself to contrasting or even directly opposed ideas and values, practices and institutions? What

Emerson says of Plato can apply to Emerson himself: "his garment, though of purple, and almost sky-woven, is an academic robe, and hinders action with its voluminous robes" ("Swedenborg; or the Mystic," *Representative Men*, p. 677). Some of one's particular commitments and engagements must survive sympathetic understanding of forces antagonistic to oneself or a sense of their beauty or appropriateness or necessity. But in comparison to the universe in one's liberated mind, being merely oneself, as well as doing and acting as oneself, can feel like such a narrowing of possibility and such a forcing of choice as to look capricious or willful. Grace lies in impersonality.

Action has to be hindered if the mind is to be liberated and thus made adequate to the vastness of the world:

> Nature can only be conceived as existing to a universal and not to a particular end, to a universe of ends, and not to one,—a work of ecstasy, to be represented by a circular movement, as intention might be signified by a straight line of definite length. ("The Method of Nature," p. 120)

The work of ecstasy ("ecstasy is the law and cause of nature") deserves an ecstatic response ("The Method of Nature," p. 127). One's personal "intention" is little in comparison. Emerson says that all nature, "oppressed by one superincumbent tendency, obeys that redundancy or excess of life which in conscious beings we call ecstasy" (p. 121). The conscious ecstasy comes only when we witness the ecstasy endured unconsciously by all creatures, including ourselves most of the time. In a journal entry, Emerson says, "Live all you think, is a noble ethics which I cannot now forget" (*Journals*, 7, p. 342). But this ethics is not possible. Philosophical thinking in Emerson's sense always exceeds the possibilities of realization, whether public or private. No individual (or group) can sanely enact the whole range of indispensable contrasts and contradictions. Even the whole world at any given time omits and loses.

"Shakespeare taught us," Emerson says, "that the little world of the heart is vaster, deeper and richer than the spaces of astronomy" ("Shakespeare," *Miscellanies*, p. 448). The word, not the deed, makes the individual impersonal or infinite: isn't that Emerson's meaning? Still, it would be absurd for me to divorce self-reliance from being and acting or doing altogether. Emerson does not permit it. Rather, he makes active self-reliance lesser than mental self-reliance. In "Tendencies," a lecture of 1840 which supplied thoughts for some of *Essays: First Series*, Emerson gives a preliminary summary of his comparative estimation:

Yet a strong will is a feeble force. It is a surrender of a man to the
visible facts of his desire, the habit of proceeding directly to them
without any reckoning of other wills, of opposition or of favor. It
is a low species of self-reliance and inspires among the trustless
fear and respect. But it has no power over the good. It is strong
beside custom, imitation, and indulgence. It is weakness beside
the renunciation of will. Beside love and wisdom, the self-
abandonment of goodness and of truth, this which seeks merely
low and conventional gratifications, power and fame, self-
aggrandizement, is unholy and profane. (*Early Lectures*, 3, p. 312)

Later, he rephrases the idea:

in the scale of powers, it is not talent, but sensibility, which is
best: talent confines, but the central life puts us in relation to all
... Such a man feels himself in harmony, and conscious by his
receptivity of an infinite strength. ("Success," *Society and Solitude*,
p. 295)

In "Self-Reliance," the motive that Emerson often (though not
exclusively) appeals to is not the self-reliance of "self-aggrandizement," but
the wish to be oneself, to live as one thinks best, to take chances deviantly, to
pursue one's special vocation, to define oneself as different from others, to
follow the line of one's distinctiveness without deflection. By Emerson's
reckoning, this composite motive is better than many or even most social or
worldly motives, even though it retains a conformist (because comparative)
element. It is the project of practical democracy. Of course it can never and
should never be completely or continuously abandoned. Much should be said
in its defense. (In later chapters I will return to active self-reliance.) The
question is whether there is any self-reliant activity (or manner of presence)
in the world that follows naturally from, or is in perfect consonance with,
mental self-reliance, indefinite receptivity. Or does an aroused and energetic
contemplation leave one immobile, while relegating all one's activity and
presence, even self-reliant kinds, to a secondary status and a separate realm
of realization? I have already indicated my sense that mental self-reliance is
discontinuous with active self-reliance. But let us say a little more.

With effort, can the "biographical Ego," as he calls it, be reduced, and
another kind of self-reliant practical activity show itself ("Natural History of
Intellect," *Natural History*, p. 62)? It is not motivated by the wish to be
oneself and act as oneself, but rather by the determination to act, if at all
possible, at the behest of "the grand spiritual Ego," at the behest, that is, of

one's impersonal reception of the world. The positive individuality of the biographical Ego will result from independent practical thinking, but thinking that is not yet philosophical or poetical. What, on the other hand, may result from the grand spiritual Ego? It is very difficult, if at all possible, to specify the nature of activity that may flow from a philosophical or poetical reception of the world.

It may be tempting to think that Emerson has solved the difficulty in the following words:

> But in the face of our libraries it must still be affirmed that every subject of human thought down to most trivial crafts and chores ought to be located poetically,—religion, war, law, politics, money, housekeeping. It would be easy to show that they must all be handled poetically in action in order to any success. A judge and a banker must drive their craft poetically as well as a dancer or a scribe. That is, they must not suffer the facts to stand superior to them ... Then they are inventive; they detect the capabilities of their affair. ("Politics," *Early Lectures*, 3, p. 239)

But "poetical" in Emerson usually means something other than mastering or constraining facts for the sake of a practical advance. Poetry in action is better than caution or routine; it shows imagination. But the practical imagination serves the biographical Ego; it may enable that Ego to act rapaciously or sordidly; it is self-concerned, not open to the world. Why not just say that thinking, speaking, and writing are the activities that comprise the highest self-reliance, that verbal expression is the only philosophical or poetical activity, and that it is therefore the greatest activity, especially when words affirm life and liberate wonder? This view certainly finds abundant support in Emerson.

Is there more to say? Can one say that if one is filled with a sense of the world's beauty, one wants the world to go on and hence will feel an irresistible desire to do what one can to preserve the world? Consequently, practical activity resulting directly from self-reliant thinking that has achieved, if only some of the time, a philosophical or poetical relation to life's splendid contraries and antagonisms, would consist in doing what lay in one's power to keep the world going and spreading to others the feeling of attachment to it. The project would be the avoidance of human and natural extinction or reversion to a scarcely describable simplicity. Not only self-reliant words but innovative action amid unprecedented circumstances would comprise the activity. But Emerson does not formulate the idea of preservative politics; I elicit it. In any case, to act even out of the most philosophical or poetical purpose would require submission to the discipline of partisanship. The means seem inconsistent with the purpose.

Let us take another tack. Is conscientious action, especially conscientious political action, an expression of self-reliance in the highest sense? It certainly shows independent thinking. But is the thinking philosophical or poetical, or only moral and practical? That question is not easy to answer. Did Socrates's conscientious courage in the face of wicked commands come from his possible belief that there was no afterlife? Was it assisted by a receptive love of individuals and their thwarted potentiality? In regard to Emerson, nonviolent objection to war seems mandated by Emerson's statement that,

> If we believed in the existence of strict *individuals*, natures, that is, not radically identical but unknown, unmeasurable we should never dare to fight. ("The Heart," *Early Lectures*, 2, p. 285)

(He says in an earlier version of "Politics," "Let us treat all men as gods. Let us drop violence" [*Early Lectures*, 3, p. 245].) Because he is not satisfied to base his opposition to the waste of war on the preciousness of individual distinctiveness, Emerson returns in the same essay to the "radical identity" he had for the moment forsaken:

> Courage is grounded always on a belief in the identity of the nature of my enemy with my own; that he with whom you contend, is no more than you ... It will be found the mind is too much One to be any longer English or French, Indian or White; that for the same reason why a soldier can muster spirit now to attack a soldier he will then feel that the blow aimed at his brother's heart strikes his own. ("The Heart," pp. 285–286)

The insistence on the radical identity rather than the radical incommensurability of individuals is thus the deeper ground for nonviolence as both a tactic and a condition of life, because it recognizes the equal vastness of every heart. It sees each person as a universe of splendid antagonisms and contradictions. Just as the self-reliant mind may feel impelled to act so as to try to preserve the world for the sake of its scarcely conceivable variety, so such a mind may feel impelled not to take a single life, because every person's equal internal richness makes him or her sacred.

It is therefore possible that no-saying action, not only forbearance from action, comes from the inner voice; that nonviolent resistance well suits or is indeed necessitated by self-reliance in the highest sense; that it is philosophical politics. Though Emerson disapproved of Thoreau's civil disobedience in 1846, he concurred, after 1850, in the refusal to obey the Fugitive Slave Law, and spoke warmly of principled disobedience. (But he also idolized John Brown for his very violence.) It may be more sensible, however, to say that the no-saying deed is the best kind of action that is independent, but that its source is not clearly philosophical or poetical. It falls short of the latter qualities because it takes sides, even though the side it takes is the side that helps people gain or keep the preconditions of self-reliance. It judges harshly and dualistically, praiseworthy though it is. It is, however, the best kind of practical action because there is greater reality in resistance than initiative, in refusal than in the effort to shape the ungraspable and impenetrable world. (In the next chapter I will discuss Emerson's reasons for thinking the world so unamenable to an individual's constructive effort.) But I offer these views knowing them to be inconclusive.

In any event, no matter where we turn in Emerson's world we find the intellect elevated above the manual, the physical, the practical, the nonverbal or the mental that serves any of these. All these latter modes of expression can suit self-reliance, but it must be of a lower sort because these modes are not impersonal and hence not intrinsically poetical or philosophical. They can be made so only in the observation and contemplation of someone who does not engage in them. Is, then, self-reliant comprehension of the world the end itself? I think that Emerson's answer is yes, after all is said; but he says a lot to make that conclusion uneasy. It turns out, as I hope to suggest later, that though no worldly activity, in Emerson's account, manifests the highest self—reliance, two personal relationships—love and friendship—are intimately bound with it. These are not, of course, activities in the usual sense, but they are engagements with the world.

STANLEY CAVELL

Emerson's Constitutional Amending:
Reading "Fate"

W hat follows is the latest installment of a project, or experiment, of about a dozen years' standing, to reappropriate Emerson (I sometimes call this overcoming his repression) as a philosophical writer. I am aware of a number of reasons for my interest in such a project. Since Emerson is characteristically, almost obsessively, said—by his admirers as well as by his detractors—not to be a philosopher, my thought was that if I could understand this denial I would learn something not only about Emerson, and not only about American culture, but something about philosophy, about what makes it painful.

If the thought of Emerson's work as constituting philosophy—or, as I sometimes put it, as calling for philosophy—is considered, then something further could be considered. It is more or less obvious, and is given more or less significance by various philosophers, that Western philosophy has, roughly since the death of Kant, been split between two traditions, call them the German and the English traditions; and each of these has its internal splits. I take Wittgenstein to be the culmination of one line of English-speaking philosophy arising from the work of Frege and Russell; and I take Heidegger to be the culmination of one line of German-speaking philosophy arising from the work of Hegel and Husserl. I am not alone in regarding Wittgenstein and Heidegger as perhaps the two major voices of philosophy

From *Emerson's Transcendental Etudes*. © 2003 by the Board of Trustees of the Leland Stanford Junior University.

in the middle third of the twentieth century. Yet it seems to me that no one—however intelligent or cultivated—is equally at home, say equally creative, with the writing of both, so that the distance between them, in content and in procedure, remains to my mind unmeasured. I might say that to inherit philosophy now means to me to inherit it as split. Against this rough background, the figure of Emerson represents for me (along with Thoreau) a mode of thinking and writing I feel I am in a position to avail myself of, a mode which at the same time can be seen to underlie the thinking of both Wittgenstein and of Heidegger—so that Emerson may become a site from which to measure the difficulties within each and between both.

The lecture to follow is a continuation of the work of the first chapter of my *Conditions Handsome and Unhandsome*, concerning Emerson's concept of thinking, a concept I call "aversive thinking." That title alludes to a pair of sentences from "Self-Reliance": "Conformity is the virtue most in request. Self-reliance is its aversion." By "self-reliance" I take Emerson to mean the essay of that title, and by synecdoche his individual body of writing. So for him to say "self-reliance is the aversion of conformity" is to say that his writing and the dominantly desired virtue of his society incessantly recoil from, or turn away from one another; but since this is incessant, the picture is at the same time of each incessantly turning *toward* the other. But why call this writing *thinking*?

Emerson characterizes thinking as marked by transfiguration and by conversion. I will merely assert here that these predicates refer essentially to the action of words, under subjection to some kind of figuration, in causing understanding or illumination on a par with that of religion—the religion always under criticism (held in aversion)—in Emerson's thought. My claim is accordingly that the implied sentence "Self-reliance is the aversion of conformity" when itself subjected to the operation of transfiguration and conversion, means something like: To think is to turn around, or to turn back (Wittgenstein says lead back), the words of ordinary life (hence the present forms of our lives) that now repel thought, disgust it. (Repels him, Emerson, of course, but he is also part of that life, which is therefore disgusted with itself.)

The only way to become convinced of such a reading, and its possible significance, is of course to try it out in scores of instances. We will see some cases in what follows from the essay "Fate."

Before beginning on that, I should say why it is just now in my adventure with Emerson that I choose, or feel forced, to emphasize a political theme in his work. I specify a brief answer at the close of these remarks, but I might indicate at once the general stakes in play. I have over the years ever more closely linked Emerson and Heidegger through the intermediary of Nietzsche, who is intimately, pervasively involved in the thinking of each. In *Conditions Handsome and Unhandsome* I associate each of them in a view of the moral life I call Emersonian perfectionism—at a moment in which the revelations of Heidegger's lasting investments in Nazism were producing a new convulsion of response from at least half of the Western philosophical world. Does Heidegger's politics—by association, to say the least—taint Emerson's points of contact with it?

The essay "Fate" is perhaps Emerson's principal statement about the human condition of freedom, even about something Emerson calls the paradox that freedom is necessary; we might formulate this as the human fatedness to freedom. This comes to speaking of the human fatedness to thinking, since "Intellect annuls Fate. So far as a man thinks, he is free.... The revelation of Thought takes man out of servitude into freedom." Could it be that the founder of American thinking, writing this essay in 1850, just months after the passage of the Fugitive Slave Law, whose support by Daniel Webster we know Emerson to have been unforgettably, unforgivingly horrified by, was in this essay not thinking about the American institution of slavery? I think it cannot be. Then why throughout the distressed, difficult, dense stretches of metaphysical speculation of this essay does Emerson seem mostly, even essentially, to keep silent on the subject of slavery, make nothing special of it? It is a silence that must still encourage his critics, as not long ago his admirer Harold Bloom and his detractor John Updike, to imagine that Emerson gave up on the hope of democracy.[1] But since I am continuing to follow out the consequences of finding in Emerson the founding of American thinking—the consequence, for example, that his thought is repressed in the culture he founded—the irony of discovering that this repressed thinking has given up on the hope and demand for a nation of the self-governing would be, so I fear, harder than I could digest.

I was myself silent about this question of Emerson's silence when I wrote an essay in 1983 mostly on Emerson's "Fate" (I called it "Emerson, Coleridge, Kant"[2]), my first somewhat extended treatment of an Emersonian text. It was seeming to me so urgent then to see to the claim of Emerson to be a philosophical writer, in principle imaginable as founding philosophy for a nation still finding itself, that I suppose I recurrently hoped that Emerson had, for the moment of the essay "Fate," sufficiently excused or justified his silence in saying there, "Nothing is more disgusting than the crowing about liberty by slaves, as most men are." But no sooner would I see this as an excuse or justification for silence than it would seem empty to me, so that I could never appeal to it. Isn't the statement that most men are slaves merely a weak, metaphorical way of feeling and of speaking, one that blunts both the

fact of literal slavery and the facts of the particular ways in which we freely
sell ourselves out? How is this conventional use of words essentially different
from the sort of "[shameful capitulation] to badges and names, to large
societies and dead institutions" that had so chagrined Emerson in "Self-
Reliance":

> If malice and vanity wear the coat of philanthropy, shall that pass?
> If an angry bigot assumes this bountiful cause of Abolition, and
> comes to me with his last news from Barbadoes, why should I not
> say to him, "Go love thy infant; love thy woodchopper; be good-
> natured and modest; have that grace; and never varnish your
> hard, uncharitable ambition with this incredible tenderness for
> black folk a thousand miles off. Thy love afar is spite at home."

It is not news that high philosophy can be used to cover low practice; nor that
the love in philanthropy is tainted. Is Emerson so in doubt about the state of
his own malice and vanity and anger and bigotry and charity and love that he
has to clear them up before he can say clearly that he sides against slavery?

On March 7, 1854, Emerson delivered a lecture called "The Fugitive
Slave Law," marking the fourth anniversary of Webster's decisive speech in
favor of that legislation. Emerson's lecture goes this way:

> Nobody doubts that Daniel Webster could make a good speech.
> Nobody doubts that there were good and plausible things to be
> said on the part of the South. But this is not a question of
> ingenuity, not a question of syllogisms, but of sides. *How came he
> there?* ... There are always texts and thoughts and arguments....
> There was the same law in England for Jeffries and Talbot and
> Yorke to read slavery out of, and for Lord Mansfield to read
> freedom.... But the question which History will ask [of Webster]
> is broader. In the final hour when he was forced by the
> peremptory necessity of the closing armies to take a side,—did he
> take the part of great principles, the side of humanity and justice,
> or the side of abuse and oppression and chaos?

So Emerson names and would avoid both those at home who choose to
interpret the law so as to take the side on behalf of slavery nearby, as well as
those whom in "Self-Reliance" he had named angry bigots incredibly
varnishing their uncharitable ambition at home by taking the side against
slavery afar. Both may count as what Emerson describes as "crowing about
liberty by slaves," and his refusal of crowing (for or against) would perhaps

be what strikes one as his essential silence on the subject precisely in an essay on freedom paradoxically entitled "Fate."

The suggestion is that there is a way of taking sides that is not crowing, a different way of having a say in this founding matter of slavery. If Emerson is who I think he is, then how he finds his way to having his say, how he undertakes to think—whether, most particularly, he is serious (as opposed to what?—literary?) in his claim that "so far as a man thinks, he is free"—is as fateful for America's claim to its own culture of thinking as its success in ridding itself of the institution of slavery will be for establishing its claim to have discovered a new world, hence to exist.

We have to ask what kind of writing—philosophical? political? religious?—takes the form of the pent, prophetic prose of "Fate." Emerson speaks there also (as well as later in "The Fugitive Slave Law") of the taking of a side. His formulation in "Fate" is of the capacity, when a person finds himself a victim of his fate—for example, "ground to powder by the vice of his race"—to "take sides with the Deity who secures universal benefit by his pain." This may strike one as the formulation less of a course of action than of inaction. But take Emerson's reference in his phrase "the vice of his race" (by which a person finds himself victimized) to be specified in the description earlier in the essay of "expensive races,—race living at the expense of race." But *which* vice does "expensive" suggest? The literal context of that predicate takes the"races in question to be the human race living at the expense of the races of animals that serve us as food: "You have just dined, and however scrupulously the slaughter-house is concealed in the graceful distance of miles, there is complicity, expensive races." It happens that we can produce evidence that this passage about human carnivorousness, and its companion human gracefulness in keeping its conditions concealed from itself, is a parable about the cannibalism, as it were, in living gracefully off other *human* races. The evidence comes from an early paragraph in Emerson's address "On Emancipation in the British West Indies," delivered in 1844, the tenth anniversary of that emancipation legislation, the year of Emerson's breakthrough essay "Experience." In Emerson's West Indies address, he remarks that "From the earliest monuments it appears that one race was victim and served the other races" and that "the negro has been an article of luxury to the commercial nations." He goes on to say there, "Language must be raked, the secrets of the slaughter-houses and infamous holes that cannot front the day, must be ransacked, to tell what negro-slavery has been."

I propose to take "Fate" pervasively—beyond the reach of the sort of textual intersection I just adduced as evidence—to be something I might call a philosophical enactment of freedom, a parable of the struggle against slavery, not as a general metaphor for claiming human freedom, but as the absolute image of the necessary siding against fate toward freedom that is the condition of philosophical thinking; as if the aspiration to freedom is philosophy's breath.

Doesn't the sheer eloquence of the West Indies address—with its demand to rake language and ransack slaughter-houses to tell of negro slavery—compromise this proposal from the outset? And again, always again, the question returns whether Emerson in "Fate"—the same man who younger, in that earlier West Indies address, confessed himself heartsick to read the history of that slavery—isn't courting the danger of seeming to avoid the sickening facts of the slavery that continues not metaphysically afar but at home.

What is he thinking of—whom is he thinking of—when in "Fate" he says, "In the history of the individual is always an account of his condition, and he knows himself to be party to his present estate"? If the sentences of "Fate" are to be brought to the condition of slavery, are we to imagine this statement about the individual knowing himself to be party to his estate to be said to the individual who is in the condition of enslavement? What would prevent this announcement from constituting the obscene act of blaming the slave for his slavery? (My intermittent sense of this possibility, and of the fact that I had no satisfying answer to it, was brought home to me by a letter from Professor Barbara Packer, whose book *Emerson's Fall* is indispensable to readers of Emerson, following a brief conversation between us concerning Emerson's politics. She writes in her letter of her sense of what I called obscene announcement in "Fate" as something that she had yet to bring under control, and asked for my thoughts. That was in the autumn of 1989. The present version of this essay, meant to collect and incorporate those thoughts, was composed the following year.)

An implication of saying "you know yourself party to your estate"—if it is not pure blame—is that you are free to leave it. John Brown might say something of the sort, without obscenity, to a person in the condition of enslavement, given that he would be saying, if with a certain derangement, "I know the only way to exercise your freedom and leave your estate is to court death, and I'll court it with you." And Walt Whitman might say something related, as in the altogether remarkable "I Sing the Body Electric," in which he watches the man's body at auction and the woman's body at auction, and he declares his love for, his sameness with, the body— hence, he declares, with the soul—of the slave. What gives to the knowledge of American slavery the absoluteness of its pain is the knowledge that these human beings in that condition, in persisting to live, persist in taking part in every breath in interpreting and preserving what a human existence can bear. But do we imagine that Emerson, like John Brown and Walt Whitman, has a way to bear the knowledge of that pain—he who is habitually supposed to have turned aside from the philosophically tragic sense of life?

Then perhaps Emerson only means to say of us Northerners, neither slaves nor slave owners, that we are party to our estate—meaning perhaps that we make ourselves slaves to, let us say, the interests of Southern slave owners that never even paid for us. But that is not exactly news. Emerson reports in the West Indies address that when "three hundred thousand persons in Britain pledged themselves to abstain from all articles of island produce ... the planters were obliged to give way ... and the slave-trade was abolished." Such responses to slavery as economic boycott are evidently not Emerson's business in "Fate." Whom, then, in that mood, is he writing to? Who are we who read him then?

If "taking sides with the Deity" does not, for Emerson, (just) mean taking the right side in the crowing about slavery, the side Daniel Webster failed to take as the armies were closing on the issue, how might it be taken? Here is more context from "Fate": "A man must ride alternately on the horses of his private and his public nature.... Leaving the daemon who suffers, he is to take sides with the Deity who secures universal benefit by his pain." That the human being is the being who *can* take a representative—public—stance, knows the (moral, objective) imperative to the stance, is familiar and recurrent Emersonian—not to say Kantian—ground; nothing is a more founding fact for him. I read this Platonic image here about riding alternately the horses of human nature, so that taking sides with the Deity is a refusal to take sides in the human *crowing* over slavery. Emerson's turn to take sides with the Deity, like and unlike the political extremity of Locke's appeal to Heaven, is not exactly a call to revolution but a claim to prophecy.[3] "Leaving the daemon who suffers" means leaving one's private, limited passions on the subject of slavery, for or against.

What is the alternative horse, the public expression of a beneficial pain (given in the absence of a constituted public, since so much of the human voice, the slave's voice, is unrepresented in that public)? The alternative is, let us say, not venting your pain, but maintaining it; in the present case, writing every sentence in pain. (Freud comparably says: remembering rather than repeating something.) It contains the pain of refusing human sides, shunning argument, with every breath. The time of argument is over. Where is pain's benefit? Is philosophy over?

At the opening of "Fate," Emerson says: "We are incompetent to solve the times.... To me ... the question of the times resolved itself into a practical question of the conduct of life." I have in effect said that in "Fate" the "question of the times"—what Emerson calls in his opening "the huge orbits of the prevailing ideas" whose return and opposition we cannot "reconcile," and what he describes near his close by saying, "Certain ideas are in the air"—is the question of slavery; and certain ideas in the air, accordingly, are emancipation and secession, issues producing the compromise of 1850, which concerned, besides the Fugitive Slave Act, the slave trade and the admission of territories into the union with or without slaves. Setting out the terms for "the greatest debate in Congressional history," Henry Clay prefaces his resolutions of compromise by saying, "It being desirable, for the peace, concord and harmony of the Union of these States to settle and adjust amicably all existing questions of controversy between them, arising out of the institution of slavery, upon a fair, equitable and just basis; therefore"— and then follows with eight paragraphs each beginning with the word "Resolved" or the words "But, resolved."[4] Emerson in effect prefaces "Fate" by speaking, in his opening paragraph, as noted, of our incompetence to *solve* the times, and of resolving the question of the times; in the second paragraph he states that "The riddle of the age has for each a private *solution*"; and continuing in effect to reverse or recapture the word "Resolved" Emerson says in the middle of "Fate," "Thought *dissolves* the material universe by carrying the mind up into a sphere where all is plastic"; and in the closing paragraphs he speaks of a "solution to the mysteries of human condition" and of "the Blessed Unity which holds nature and souls in perfect solution." This is not Henry Clay's imagined union.

Of course Emerson is quite aware that compared with Henry Clay, and the Houses of Congress, his words about resolution and unity will sound, at best, or at first, private, not to say ethereal. But he seems some how also to know that he is speaking with necessity ("Our thought, though it were only an hour old, affirms an oldest necessity"), and speaking with universality (being thrown "on the party and interest of the Universe [i.e., taking sides with the Deity], against all and sundry; against ourselves as much as others"). Now necessity and universality are the marks, according to the Kantian philosophy, of the a priori, that is, of human objectivity; so if Emerson's claim is valid, it is the opposing party who is riding the horse of privacy, of what Emerson also calls selfishness, something he would have taken Henry Clay's use of the word "desirable" to have amounted to.

We of course must ask—since Emerson would also know, as well as what is called the next man, that anyone can *claim* to be speaking on the part and interest of the universe and on the side of the Deity—what the source is of his conviction in his own objectivity, his ability, as he puts it in the poem he composed as an epigraph for "Fate," to read omens traced in the air. I understand the source to be his conviction that his abilities are not exclusive, that he claims to know only what everyone knows.

Toward the close of the essay: "The truth is in the air, and the most impressionable brain will announce it first, but *all* will announce it a few minutes later." Emerson is not even saying that *he* is announcing it first, since the truth that is in the air is also, always already, philosophy; it contains not just the present cries for freedom and union and the arguments against them, but perennial cries and arguments. This is surely something the gesture means that Emerson so habitually enjoys making, of listing his predecessors and benefactors—that they are the benefactors of the race, part of our air, our breath. In the essay "Fate" he cites the names of Napoleon, Burke, Webster, Kossuth; Jenny Lind; Homer, Zoroaster, Menu; Fulton, Franklin, Watt; Copernicus, Newton, Laplace; Thales, Anaximenes, Empedocles, Pythagoras; Hafiz, Voltaire, Christopher Wren, Dante, Columbus, Goethe, Hegel, Metternich, Adams, Calhoun, Guizot, Peel, Rothschild, Astor, Herodotus, Plutarch. And he says: "The air is full of men." (Emerson puts those words in quotation marks without saying who or what he is quoting. *Bartlett's Quotations* contains the line "In the air men shall be seen" in a list of rhymed prophecies attributed to Mother Shipton, according to *Bartlett's* editors a witch and prophetess fabricated in the seventeenth century. I'll have a suggestion about why Emerson might have wanted in this essay to associate himself with such a figure.)

I associate the men in the air with—as in Emerson's epigraph poem— "Birds with auguries on their wings / [who] Chanted undeceiving things, / Him to beckon, him to warn." The "few minutes later" Emerson calculates between the first announcements of truth and, for example, his own impressionable announcings of it—which the world may measure as millennia but which are a few minutes of eternity—are equally no more than the few minutes between, for example, our reading Emerson's pages (his wings of augury, flapping as we turn them forth and back, before us, above our horizon) and our announcing or pronouncing, if just to ourselves, what is chanted from them (not crowed). I have noted elsewhere another of Emerson's master figures for a page of his writing—that of its representing a "standard," that is, a measure to aspire to, specified concretely as a flag, to which to rally oneself. This idea of a standard—by which "Self-Reliance" alludes at the same time to Kant's idea of humankind's two "standpoints"— takes pages one at a time; whereas "wings" pictures them as paired, bound symmetrically on the two sides of a spine.

As with his great reader Thoreau, Emerson loves playing with time, that is, making time vanish where truth is concerned: "'Tis only a question of time," he says casually a few minutes later in "Fate" than, and as a kind of answer to, the earlier, more portentous phrasing, "the question of the times." (In invoking the idea of the casual, as one characteristic tone he gives his prose, I am thinking of Emerson's characteristic association of that idea with the idea of casualty; as if he misses no opportunity for showing that we do not see our fate because we imagine that it is most extraordinary and not yet; rather than most ordinary and already, like our words.)

Emerson's philosophical sentence strikes the time of conversion and transfiguration that he calls thinking, the time—past crowing—of aversion (inversion, perversion, subversion, "unsettling all things," verses, reversals, tropes, turns, dancing, chanting ...).

Here are three successive sentences to this effect from "Fate." First, "If the Universe have these savage accidents, our atoms are as savage in resistance." That is, speaking philosophically, or universally, "accidents" are opposed to "necessities," and in thus implying that slavery is accidental, or arbitrary, and resistance to it necessary and natural, Emerson takes away its chief argument. Second, "We should be crushed by the atmosphere, but for the reaction of the air within the body." That is, the ideas that are in the air are our life's breath; they become our words; slavery is supported by some of them and might have crushed the rest of them; uncrushed, they live in opposition. Third, "if there be omnipotence in the stroke, there is omnipotence of recoil." That is, every word is a word spoken *again*, or against again; there would be no words otherwise. Since recoil and aversion have been expressed at any time only by breathers of words, mortals, their strokes may be given now, and may gather together now—in a recoiling—all the power of world-creating words. The sentence introducing the three just cited asserts: "Man also is part of [Fate], and can confront fate with fate." Emerson's way of confronting fate, his recoil of fate, I will now say, is his writing, in every word; for example, in every word of "Fate," each of which is to be a pen stroke, a common stroke of genius, because a counterstroke of fate. You make your breath words in order not to suffocate in the plenum of air. The power he claims for his words is precisely that they are not his, no more new than old; it is the power, I would like to say, of the powerlessness in being unexceptional, or say exemplary. ("We go to Herodotus and Plutarch for examples of Fate; but we are examples.") This unavoidable power of exemplification may be named impressionability, and seen to be responsibility construed as responsiveness, passiveness as receptiveness.

These are various ways of looking at the idea that the source of Emerson's conviction in what I called the objectivity (I might have called it the impersonality) of his prophesying, his wing-reading and omen-witnessing, lies in his writing, his philosophical authorship, a condition that each of his essays is bound to characterize and authenticate in its own terms.

A characteristic of this authorship is announced in the opening paragraph of the quite early "Self-Reliance": "In every work of genius we recognize our own rejected thoughts; they come back to us with a certain alienated majesty." Even from those who remember this sentence, there is, I have found, resistance to taking Emerson to be naming his own work as an instance of the work he is characterizing, resistance to taking that sentence about rejected thoughts as itself an instance of such a rejected thought coming back in familiar strangeness, so with the power of the uncanny. The mechanism of this rejection and return is, I suppose, that characterized by Freud as transference, a process in which another person is magnified by our attributing to him or to her powers present in our repressed desires and who, putting himself or herself aside for a moment, gives us usably what we have shown ourselves unusefully to know. It is an interpretation of Kant's mechanism of projection that he calls the sublime, reading our mind's powers in nature, in the air. Emerson's authorship enacts, I have gone on to claim in the most recent work I have been doing, a relationship with his reader of moral perfectionism in which the friend permits one to advance toward oneself, which may present itself, using another formulation of Emerson, as attaining our unattained self, a process which has always happened and which is always to happen.

The word *majesty* reappears in "Fate," again in a context in which the presence of a "thought and word of an intellectual man ... [rouses] our own mind ... to activity": "'Tis the majesty into which we have suddenly mounted, the impersonality, the scorn of egotisms, the sphere of laws, that engage us." A "sphere of laws" into which we have suddenly mounted, as if attaining a new standpoint, suggests Kant's realm of ends—call it the eventual human city—in which the reception of the moral law, the constraint, as Kant names the relation, by the moral imperative, expressed by an "ought," is replaced by the presence of another, like and unlike myself, who constrains me to another way, another standpoint, Kant says (Emerson says, transfiguring Kant, a new standard). This other of myself—returning my rejected, say repressed, thought—reminds me of something, as of where I am, as if I had become lost in thought, and stopped thinking. In "Experience," Emerson expresses finding the way, learning as he more or less puts it, to take steps, as to begin to walk philosophically, in the *absence* of another presence—more accurately, in allowing himself to present himself to the loss of presence, to the death of his young son.

His description of his authorship in that essay takes the form—I have given my evidence for this elsewhere[5]—of fantasizing his becoming pregnant and giving birth to the world, to his writing of the world, which he calls a new America and calls Being. In "Fate" he is giving the basis of his authorship in that passage about riding alternately on the horses of his private and his public nature. Those are descendants of the horses he

invokes, in his essay "The Poet," in naming the Poet as one whose relation
to language is such that "In every word he speaks he rides on them as the
horses of thought." The idea is that the words have a life of their own over
which our mastery is the other face of our obedience. Wittgenstein, in
Philosophical Investigations, affirms this sense of the independent life of words
in describing what he does as "leading words back from their metaphysical to
their everyday use,"[6] suggesting that their getting back, whatever that
achievement is, is something they must do under their own power if not
quite, or always, under their own direction. Alternating horses, as in a circus
ring, teach the two sides of thought, that objectivity is not a given but an
achievement; leading the thought, allowing it its own power, takes you to
new ground.

The achievement of objectivity cannot be claimed for oneself, that is,
for one's writing. As in "Self-Reliance": "I would write on the lintels of the
door-post, *Whim*. I hope it may be better than whim at last." But in the
necessity for words, "when [your] genius calls [you]," you can only air your
thoughts, not assess them, and you must.

In Emerson's as in Wittgenstein's way of thinking, ethics is not a
separate field of philosophical study, but every word that comes from us, the
address of each thought, is a moral act, a taking of sides, but not in argument.
In Emerson's terms, the sides may be called those of self-reliance and
conformity; in Wittgenstein's terms, those of the privacy and emptiness of
assertion he calls metaphysical, and the dispersal of this empty assertiveness
by what he calls leading words home, his image of thinking. It strikes me that
the feature of the intersection of Emersonian with Wittgensteinian thinking
that primarily causes offense among professional philosophers is less the
claim to know peculiar matters with a certainty that goes beyond reasonable
evidence (matters like the location of the Deity's side, or of the temptation to
insistent emptiness), and less the sheer, pervasive literary ambition of their
writing, than the sense that these locations, diagnoses, and ambitions are in
the service of a claim to philosophical authorship that can seem the antithesis
of what philosophical writing should be, a denial of rational or systematic
presentation apart from which philosophy might as well turn itself into, or
over to, literature, or perhaps worse.

The worse one may call esotericism, an effect it seems clear to me both
Emerson and Wittgenstein recognized in themselves. Wittgenstein
recognizes it in his continuous struggle against his interlocutors, whose role
sometimes seems less to make Wittgenstein's thoughts clearer than to allow
him to show that his thoughts are *not* clear, and not obviously to be *made*
clear. They must be *found* so. Emerson recognizes his esotericism in such a
remark from "Fate" as: "This insight [that] throws us on the party of the

Universe, against all and sundry ... distances those who share it from those who share it not." But what is the alternative? At the close of "Experience" Emerson suggests that the alternative to speaking esoterically is speaking polemically (taking sides in argument), which for him, as for Wittgenstein, gives up philosophy, can never lead to the peace philosophy seeks for itself.[7] (The philosopher I am reading who preceded Emerson in contrasting something like the esoteric with the polemical in considering the presentation of philosophy, as a matter internal to the present state of philosophy, is Hegel.) The dissonance between these thinkers and professional philosophers is less an intellectual disagreement than a moral variance in their conceptions of thinking, or perhaps I can say in their concepts of the role of moral judgment in the moral life, in the way each pictures "constraint."

If slavery is the negation of thought, then thinking cannot affirm itself without affirming the end of slavery. But for thinking to fail to affirm itself is to deny the existence of philosophy. It is accordingly no more or less certain that philosophy will continue than that human self-enslavement will end. Philosophy cannot abolish slavery, and it can only call for abolition to the extent, or in the way, that it can call for thinking, can provide (adopting Kant's term) the incentive to thinking. The incentive Emerson provides is just what I am calling his authorship, working to attract our knowledge that we are rejecting, repressing thinking, hence the knowledge that thinking must contain both pain and pleasure (if it were not painful it would not require repression; if it were not pleasurable it would not attract it).

The linking of philosophical thinking with pain is expressed in an Emersonian sentence that seems a transcription at once of Plato and of Kant: "I know that the world I converse with in the city and in the farms, is not the world I *think*." To think this other world, say the realm of ends, is pleasure; to bear witness to its difference from the actual world of cities and farms is pain. Here, perhaps, in this pleasure and pain, before the advent of an imperative judgment, and before the calculation of the desirable, is the incentive to thinking that Kant sought. The pain is a function of the insight that there is no reason the eventual world is not entered, not actual, hence that I must be rejecting it, rejecting the existence of others in it; and the others must be rejecting my existence there.

I note that it is from here that I would like to follow on with Emerson's understanding of the origination of philosophy as a feminine capacity, as following his claim, toward the end of "Fate," that I excerpted earlier: "The truth is in the air, and the most impressionable brain will announce it first, but all will announce it a few minutes later." He continues: "So women, as most susceptible, are the best index of the coming hour. So the great man, that is, the man *most* imbued with the spirit of the time, is the impressionable man"—which seems to divine that the great man is a woman. The idea that philosophical knowledge is receptive rather than assertive, that it is a matter of leaving a thing as it is rather than taking it as something else, is not new and is a point of affinity between Wittgenstein and Heidegger. Emerson's thought here is that this makes knowledge difficult in a particular way, not because it is hard to understand exactly, but because it is hard to bear; and his suggestion, accordingly, is that something prepares the woman for this relation to pain, whereas a man must be great to attain it. I grant that this may be said stupidly. It may be used—perhaps it most often is, in fact—to deny the actual injustice done to actual women. Must it be so appropriated? By philosophical necessity? But I associate Emerson's invocation of the feminine with a striking remark of Hélène Cixous, in which she declares her belief that, whereas men must rid themselves of pain by mourning their losses, women do not mourn, but bear their pain. The connection for me here is that the better world we think, and know not to exist, with no acceptable reason not to exist, is not a world that is *gone*, hence is not one to be mourned, but one to be borne, witnessed. The attempt to mourn it is the stuff of nostalgia. (In the closing paragraph of "Experience," I remember: "Patience, patience, we shall win at the last." I had not until now been able to understand this as the demand upon Emerson's writing, and his readers, to let the pain of his thoughts, theirs, collect itself.)

Is philosophy, as Emerson calls for it—we must keep reposing the question, without stopping it—an evasion of actual justice? It hasn't kept Emerson from sometimes writing polemically, as his West Indies and his Fugitive Slave Law addresses attest. His direct idea, to repeat, is that polemic is an evasion, or renunciation, of philosophy. How important a loss is the loss of philosophy?

I think sometimes of Emerson, in his isolation, throwing words into the air, as aligned with the moment at which Socrates in the *Republic* declares that the philosopher will participate only in the public affairs of the just city, even if this means that he can only participate in making—as he is now doing—a city of words. As if without the philosopher's constructions, the actual human city would not only lack justice in fact, but would lose the very concept, hence the imagination, of justice. Whether you think keeping that imagination alive is a valuable activity depends on how you think the reign of justice can come about.

I began, in effect, by saying that for Emerson the loss of philosophy is the loss of emancipation—of the imagination of the possibility of emancipation as such—from all forms of human confinement, say enslavement. I make explicit now, again, for a moment the thought about thinking that I claim is implicit throughout Emerson's writing (not solely in "Fate," however painfully there)—the thought that human freedom, as the opposition to fate, is not merely called for by philosophical writing but is instanced or enacted by that writing: the Emersonian sentence is philosophical in showing within itself its aversion to (turning away in turning toward) the standing conformation of its words, as though human thinking is not so much to be expressed by language as resurrected with it.

Let us accordingly transfigure once again: "In the history of the individual is always an account of his condition, and he knows himself to be party to his present estate." The days of the individual are told, counted out, in his condition by the words he suffers, and in his estate by the statements he utters: to know himself, as philosophy demands—or say to acknowledge his allegiances—is to take his part in each stating and in each silence.

In my encounter in 1983 with the essay "Fate," I did not speak of Emerson's philosophical authorship and esotericism, and I did not see the connection between Emerson's mode of thinking and his moral perfectionism, his constraint of his reader through his conviction in the magnified return of the reader's own rejected thoughts. It is as if in my desperateness to show Emerson capable of rigorous, systematic thinking, against the incessant denial of him as a philosopher, I felt I could not at the same time show his practice of thinking as one of transfiguring philosophy, in founding it, finding it, for America. I could not, as it were, *assume* his right to speak for philosophy. My primary focus in my earlier encounter with "Fate" is on Emerson's use of the term condition, and his relation of it to the term *terms* (meaning words and meaning stipulations) and the term *dictation*, which I claim shows Emerson turning the *Critique of Pure Reason* on itself, taking its fundamental term *condition* in its etymological significance as speaking *together*, so suggesting that the condition of the possibility of there being a world of objects for us is the condition of our speaking together; and that is not a matter of our sharing twelve categories of the understanding but of our sharing a language, hence the task of philosophy is not the deriving of privileged categories but of announcing the terms on the basis of which we use each term of the language. Any term may give rise to what Wittgenstein calls a grammatical investigation, but beyond *condition* and its relatives, my earlier essay got just to the idea of "character" as, as always in Emerson, meaning the fact of language as well as the formation of an individual. But even that distance allowed me to summarize the essay's word as saying that character is fate, that the human is fated to significance, to finding it and to revealing it, and—as if tragically—fated to thinking, or to repressing thinking. Emerson—the American who is repeatedly, famously, denied the title of philosopher and described as lacking the tragic sense—writes an essay on freedom entitled "Fate" and creates the mode of what we may perhaps call the tragic essay.

If I now add the use of the word *constitution* in the essay "Fate" to the terms whose terms I demand, Emerson's claim for his philosophical authorship becomes unpostponable. Along with *condition* and *character*, other philosophical terms Emerson allows the reader to find unobtrusive are *possibility* and *accident*, and *impression* and *idea*. *Constitution* appears in "Fate" only a few times, but its placement is telling, and the essay's array of political terms or projects magnifies its force: I cited earlier the term *resolved*; and we have heard of our being party to our estate; and then a not notably obtrusive sentence speaks of "this house of man, which is all consent, inosculation and balance of parts"—where "consent" works to associate "balance of parts," with "checks and balances," and "house" thus names each of the branches of Congress. Here is an example of what I called "placement":

> Jesus said, "when he looketh on her, he hath committed adultery." But he is an adulterer before he has yet looked on the woman, by the superfluity of animal and the defect of thought in his constitution. Who meets him, or who meets her, in the street, sees that they are ripe to be each other's victim.

In "Emerson, Coleridge, Kant," I read this as the claim that most of what we call marriage is adultery, not a thought original with Emerson. Now, according to my implied hypothesis that every metaphysical claim in "Fate" about freedom, and its deprivation, is to be read also in a social register, as applying also to the institution of slavery, I read the phrase "the defect of thought in his constitution" to refer to the famous defect in the Constitution of the United States concerning those persons who are, let's say, interminably unfree, a defect which adulterates our claim to have established a just and tranquil human society, corrupts it, makes it spurious. I'll come back in a moment to the passage I mean.

From at least as early as "Self-Reliance," Emerson identifies his writing, what I am calling his philosophical authorship, as the drafting of the nation's constitution; or, I have come to say, as amending our constitution. When he says there, "No law can be sacred to me but that of my nature," he is saying no more than Kant had said—that, in a phrase from "Fate," "We are as law-givers," namely, to the world of conditions and of objects, and to ourselves in the world of the unconditioned and of freedom. But the next sentence of "Self-Reliance" takes another step: "Good and bad are but names readily transferable to that or this; the only right is what is after my constitution; the only wrong what is against it." (The anticipation of

Nietzsche's genealogy of morals is no accident.) Such a remark seems uniformly to be understood by Emerson's readers so that "my constitution" refers to Emerson's personal, peculiar physiology and is taken to be the expression of his incessant promotion of the individual over the social. Such an understanding refuses the complexity of the Emersonian theme instanced in his saying that we are now "bugs, spawn," which means simultaneously that we exist neither as individual human beings nor in human nations.

The promise that we are capable of both is the fervent Emersonian theme to the effect that each of us is capable of speaking what is "true for all men." This capacity Emerson envisions in endless ways, often as speaking with necessity (a transfiguration of what philosophers, especially of what Kant, means by necessity). The theme is fervently announced in Emerson's various formulations of the vision that the innermost becomes the outermost: In "The American Scholar," "[The scholar] is one who raises himself from private considerations and breathes and lives on public and illustrious thoughts [as if they were air] "; in "Self-Reliance," "To believe your own thought, to believe that what is true for you in your private heart is true for all men—that is genius," specifically, it is that which in every work of genius comes back to us with the alienated majesty of our own rejected thoughts. Speaking what is "true for all men," what in "Fate" Emerson speaks of as "truth com[ing] to our mind," is the event of insight he describes as "throw[ing] us on the party and interest of the Universe ... against ourselves as much as others." "[Throwing us] on the party ... of the Universe,"—as if to say taking its part (as if taking sides with the Deity)— puts me in mind of what Kant calls "[speaking] with the universal voice," which is the essential feature in making an aesthetic judgment (going beyond a mere expression of individual taste), namely, that it demands or imputes or claims general validity, universal agreement; a claim made in the face of the knowledge that this agreement is in empirical fact apt not to be forthcoming. Moral judgment also speaks with—or, rather, listens to—what we might call the universal voice, in the form of the capacity to act under the constraint of the moral imperative, the imperative of the universal (of the universalizable). Emerson is, I am suggesting, appealing to something of the kind in simply claiming as a fact that we can, in thinking generally, judge the constitution of the world and of the lives complicitous with it from a standpoint "all and sundry" may be expected to find in themselves. The great difference from aesthetic and moral judgment is that the constitutional judgment demanding the amending of our lives (together) is to be found by each of us as a rejected thought returning to us. This mode of access to what I am calling "constitutional judgment" seems to me no less well characterized by Emerson than moral or aesthetic judgments are by philosophers generally. (If

Emerson's "representativeness," his universalizing, is not to go unexamined, neither should his habitually condemned "individualism." If he is to be taken as an instance of "humanism" [as if he doesn't really mean much definite by being "thrown" on "the interest of the Universe"], then he is at the same time to be taken as some form of antihumanist, working "against ourselves," against what we understand as human [under] standing.)

It is the appeal to what we have rejected, as it were forgotten, say displaced, that gives to Emerson's writing (and to Wittgenstein's) the feel of the esoteric, of work to whose understanding one is asked to convert. It is an obvious sign of danger for professional, university philosophy, and it should be. Emerson ought to have to make his way, to bear the pain of his arrogating his right to speak for philosophy in the absence of making himself curricular, institutionalizable, polemical. Which is another way of saying that it does not follow from his institutionalized silencing that he has failed to raise the call for philosophy and to identify its fate with the fate of freedom. The fact of his call's repression would be the sign that it has been heard. The apparent silence of "Fate" might become deafening.

The absoluteness of the American institution of slavery, among the forms human self-enslavement takes, hence the absoluteness of philosophy's call to react to it, recoil from it, is announced, as I have more or less said, in the sentence cited earlier from the West Indies address: "Language must be raked, the secrets of the slaughter-houses and infamous holes that cannot front the day, must be ransacked, to tell what negro-slavery has been." I take the idea of raking language to be another announcement, in a polemical context, of Emerson's philosophical authorship, of what cannot be undertaken polemically.

A surface of the idea of raking language is a kind of Emersonian joke, namely, that we are to respond to the fact, be responsible to it, that the largely unquestioned form or look of writing is of being raked on a page, that is, raked in parallel straight lines, and then to recognize that bringing what writing contains to light, letting these words return to us, as if to themselves, to mount suddenly to their majesty, to the scorn of egotisms, is to let the fact of them rouse our mind to activity, to turn it to the air. Perhaps we are to think that the fact of language is more telling than any fact uttered within it, as if every fact utters the fact of language: against this fatedness to language, to character, against, that is, what I earlier called our condemnation to significance, it figures that it is we who are raked. To think of language as raking and recoiling is to think of it, though it may look tranquil, as aimed and fired (at itself, at us) as if the human creature of conditions, fated to language, exists in the condition of threat, the prize of unmarked battles, where every horizon—where the air of words (of what might be said) gravitates to the earth of assertion (of what is actually said)—signifies a struggle between possession and dispossession, between speech and silence, between the unspeakable and the unsilenceable. (Here I am letting myself express a little, as earnest of wishing to describe better than I can, the anguish I sense in Emerson's language in "Fate.")

The particular direction in the raking of language I emphasize now is its office in *telling*, which is to say, in counting and recounting—"[telling] what negro-slavery has been" is how Emerson put it—hence in telling every enslavement. An origin of the word "raking" is precisely the idea of reckoning, of counting, as well as recking, paying attention. Of the endless interest there may be in thinking of language itself as a matter of counting, I confine attention momentarily here to the connection between counting or telling and the writing of the American Constitution.

When in the second paragraph of "Experience" Emerson asks, bleakly, "How many individuals can we count in society?" he is directing our attention back, wherever else, to the famous paragraph containing what I earlier quoted Emerson as calling "the defect of thought in [our] constitution." That famous paragraph is the fifth—it is also just the fifth sentence—of the Constitution of the United States: "Representatives and direct Taxes shall be apportioned among the several States which may be included within this Union, according to their respective Numbers, which shall be determined by adding to the whole number of free Persons, including those bound to service for a Term of Years, and excluding Indians not taxed, three fifths of all other Persons." The paragraph goes on to specify the calculation of democratic representation, and I find the comic invoking in "Fate" of the new science of statistics, in its attention to populations, to be another allusion to the "defect," the lack of philosophical necessity, in our constitutional counting. In the large we do not see how many we are; in the small we do not know, as Emerson puts it in "The American Scholar," whether we add up to what the "old fable" calls "One Man." As if we do not know whether any of us, all and each, count. We are living our skepticism.

So again, Emerson's simultaneous use of the idea of "my constitution"—his transfiguration of these words—so that we know they name at once his makeup and the makeup of the nation he prophesies, is a descendant of Plato's use of his *Republic*—his city of words—to form a structure at once of the soul and of its society. That is part of my cause in finding Emerson's philosophical prose, his authorship, to earn something like Plato's description (a city of words) for itself—as I find Thoreau's *Walden* to do—hence to imagine for itself the power to amend the actual city in the philosophical act of its silence, its power of what Emerson calls patience, which he seeks as the most active of intellectual conditions. (Even one who recognizes this possibility of his or her own constitution as entering into an imagination of the constitution of the just city may find no city even worth rebuking philosophically—through the proposal of a shared imagination—but purely polemically. This condition may sometimes be pictured as a form of exile rather than of Emerson's agonized membership. Yet it is not clear how different these forms are. I have elsewhere identified Emerson's idea of American membership, his philosophical stance toward America, as one of immigrancy.[8])

Nothing less than Emerson's peculiar claim to amendment would satisfy my craving for philosophy. But nothing so much creates my fears for it. I am aware that I have mentioned the name of Heidegger once or twice in these remarks, but cited no word of his. And yet in my present return to Emerson's "Fate" and my sense of its tortured, philosophical silence about the tyranny of the institution of slavery—in its effort, as I have more or less put the matter, to preserve philosophy in the face of conditions that negate philosophy—I am aware of a kind of preparation for some explicit coming to terms on my part with Heidegger's relation with the tyranny of Nazism, an explicitness I have, with growing discomfort, postponed over the years. Here is motivation for the present essay I cited at the outset. It is to pose for myself the following questions: Am I prepared to listen to an argument in Heidegger's defense that he was, after his public falling out of favor with the regime, attempting to preserve philosophy in the face of conditions that negate philosophy? If not, how am I prepared to understand, as in his 1936 lectures on Nietzsche and in his contemporaneous "Origin of the Work of Art," his call of a people to its historical destiny, and his announcement of a form of the appearance of truth as the founding of a political order? Such questions press me now not alone because of the oddly late and oddly stale recent accounts of Heidegger's extensive involvements with Nazism, and the inundation of responses to these revelations by so many of the major philosophical voices of Europe, but because of the pitch to which my sense of Nietzsche's absorption in Emerson's writing has come, and of Heidegger's absorption or appropriation, in turn, of Nietzsche.

Only some three years ago did I for the first time read all the way through Heidegger's sets of lectures on Nietzsche, delivered from 1936 to 1940, surely the most influential interpretation of Nietzsche to have appeared for serious philosophers in Europe. Emerson's presence in Nietzsche's thought as Heidegger receives it—in certain passages of Nietzsche that Heidegger leans on most heavily—is so strong at certain moments that one has to say that Nietzsche is using Emerson's words; which means that Heidegger in effect, over an unmeasured stretch of thought, is interpreting Emerson's words. Here are two instances: in volume 2 of the English translation of the Nietzsche lectures, Heidegger notes that Nietzsche's "early thought ... was later to become the essential center of his thinking." Heidegger mentions two school essays of Nietzsche. In a footnote the translator notes in passing that the essays exhibit the "influence" of Emerson and quotes two sentences from the longer of the essays, "Fate and History":

> Yet if it were possible for a strong will to overturn the world's entire past, we would join the ranks of self-sufficient gods, and world history would be no more to us than a dream-like enchantment of the self. The curtain falls, and man finds himself again, like a child playing with worlds, a child who wakes at daybreak and with a laugh wipes from his brow all frightful dreams.

Compare this with a sentence from the next to last paragraph of "Fate": "If we thought men were free in the sense that in a single exception one fantastical will could prevail over the law of things, it were all one as if a child's hand could pull down the sun." Nietzsche is not "influenced" by Emerson but is quite deliberately transfiguring Emerson, as for the instruction of the future. This happens early and late. In the section from book 3 of *Thus Spoke Zarathustra* called "The Convalescent," of which Heidegger's reading is among the high points of his opening set of Nietzsche lectures, Nietzsche says this: "To every soul belongs another world; for every soul, every other soul is an afterworld."[9] In Emerson's "Fate" we find: "The hero is to others as the world." The relation of transfiguration here is the clearer the more one goes into what Emerson means by the hero (who is in principle every soul) and into his view of how souls touch.[10]

So I am faced with the spectacle of Heidegger's in effect—unknowingly—facing certain of Emerson's words, guiding himself in these fateful years by signs from, of all places on earth, the waste of America. How do I guide myself? Do I guide myself by the thought that since Emerson is the philosopher of freedom I can, in his mediation through Nietzsche to Heidegger, in principle trust to our eventual success in showing Heidegger's descent into the allegiance with tyranny to be an aberration of his philosophical genius—hence redeemable? Or must I guide myself instead by the thought that, since Heidegger is so radically, unredeemably compromised, and since Emerson is mediated by philosophers of the powers of Nietzsche and of Heidegger, it is not even to be trusted that we will eventually succeed in showing Emerson's genius to be uncompromised by this mediation, so that the way of philosophy I care about most is as such compromised?

NOTES

1. See Chapter 8, above.
2. See Chapter 4, above.
3. See Locke, *Second Treatise*, chap. 4, §168, and, chap 19, §242.
4. See Commager, *Documents of American History*, p. 319.
5. See Chapter 6 above.
6. Wittgenstein, *Philosophical Investigations*, §116.
7. Ibid., §133.
8. See Chapter 2, pp. 30–1, above.
9. Nietzsche, *Thus Spake Zarathustra*, p. 217.
10. Exp 3.48.18.

HAROLD BLOOM

Afterthought:
Reflections in the Evening Land

Huey Long, known as "the Kingfish," dominated the state of Louisiana from 1928 until his assassination in 1935, at the age of 42. Simultaneously governor and a United States senator, the canny Kingfish uttered a prophecy that haunts me in this late summer of 2005, 70 years after his violent end: "Of course we will have fascism in America but we will call it democracy!"

I reflected on Huey Long (always mediated for me by his portrait as Willie Stark in Robert Penn Warren's novel *All the King's Men*) recently, when I listened to President George W. Bush addressing the Veterans of Foreign Wars in Salt Lake City, Utah. I was thus benefited by Rupert Murdoch's Fox TV channel, which is the voice of Bushian crusading democracy, very much of the Kingfish's variety. Even as Bush extolled his Iraq adventure, his regime daily fuses more tightly together elements of oligarchy, plutocracy, and theocracy.

At the age of 75, I wonder if the Democratic party ever again will hold the presidency or control the Congress in my lifetime. I am not sanguine, because our rulers have demonstrated their prowess in Florida (twice) and in Ohio at shaping voting procedures, and they control the Supreme Court. The economist-journalist Paul Krugman recently observed that the Republicans dare not allow themselves to lose either Congress or the White House, because subsequent investigations could disclose dark matters indeed. Krugman did not specify, but among the profiteers of our Iraq crusade are big oil (House of Bush/House of Saud), Halliburton (the vice-president), Bechtel (a nest of mighty Republicans), and so forth.

All of this is extraordinarily blatant, yet the American people seem benumbed, unable to read, think, or remember, and thus fit subjects for a president who shares their limitations. A grumpy old Democrat, I observe to my friends that our emperor is himself the best argument for intelligent design, the current theocratic substitute for what used to be called creationism. Sigmund Freud might be chagrined to discover that he is forgotten, while the satan of America is now Charles Darwin. President Bush, who says that Jesus is his "favorite philosopher," recently decreed in regard to intelligent design and evolution: "Both sides ought to be properly taught."

I am a teacher by profession, about to begin my 51st year at Yale, where frequently my subject is American writers. Without any particular competence in politics, I assert no special insight in regard to the American malaise. But I am a student of what I have learned to call the American Religion, which has little in common with European Christianity. There is now a parody of the American Jesus, a kind of Republican CEO who disapproves of taxes, and who has widened the needle's eye so that camels and the wealthy pass readily into the Kingdom of Heaven. We have also an American holy spirit, the comforter of our burgeoning poor, who don't bother to vote. The American trinity pragmatically is completed by an imperial warrior God, trampling with shock and awe.

These days I reread the writers who best define America: Emerson, Hawthorne, Whitman, Melville, Mark Twain, Faulkner, among others. Searching them, I seek to find what could suffice to explain what seems our national self-destructiveness. D.H. Lawrence, in his *Studies in Classic American Literature* (1923), wrote what seems to me still the most illuminating criticism of Walt Whitman and Herman Melville. Of the two, Melville provoked no ambivalence in Lawrence. But Whitman transformed Lawrence's poetry, and Lawrence himself, from at least 1917 on. Replacing Thomas Hardy as prime precursor, Whitman spoke directly to Lawrence's vitalism, immediacy, and barely evaded homoeroticism. On a much smaller scale, Whitman earlier had a similar impact on Gerard Manley Hopkins. Lawrence, frequently furious at Whitman, as one might be with an overwhelming father, a King Lear of poetry, accurately insisted that the Americans were not worthy of their Whitman. More than ever, they are not, since the Jacksonian democracy that both Whitman and Melville celebrated is dying in our Evening Land.

What defines America? "Democracy" is a ruined word, because of its misuse in the American political rhetoric of our moment. If Hamlet and Don

Quixote, between them, define the European self, then Captain Ahab and "Walt Whitman" (the persona, not the man) suggest a very different self from the European. Ahab is Shakespearean, Miltonic, even Byronic-Shelleyan, but his monomaniacal quest is his own, and reacts against the Emersonian self, just as Melville's beloved Hawthorne recoiled also. Whitman, a more positive Emersonian, affirms what the Sage of Concord called self-reliance, the authentic American religion rather than its Bushian parodies. Though he possesses a Yale BA and honorary doctorate, our president is semi-literate at best. He once boasted of never having read a book through, even at Yale. Henry James was affronted when he met President Theodore Roosevelt; what could he have made of George W. Bush?

Having just reread James's *The American Scene* (1907), I amuse myself, rather grimly, by imagining the master of the American novel touring the United States in 2005, exactly a century after his return visit to his homeland. Like T.S. Eliot in the next generation, James was far more at home in London than in America, yet both retained an idiom scarcely English. They each eventually became British subjects, graced by the Order of Merit, but Whitman went on haunting them, more covertly in Eliot's case. *The Waste Land* initially was an elegy for Jean Verdenal, who had been to Eliot what Rupert Brooke was to Henry James. Whitman's "Lilacs" elegy for Lincoln became James's favorite poem, and it deeply contaminates *The Waste Land*.

I am not suggesting that the American aesthetic self is necessarily homoerotic: Emerson, Hawthorne, Mark Twain, Faulkner, Robert Frost after all are as representative as are Melville, Whitman, and Henry James. Nor does any American fictive self challenge Hamlet as an ultimate abyss of inwardness. Yet Emerson bet the American house (as it were) on self-reliance, which is a doctrine of solitude. Whitman, as person and as poetic mask, like his lilacs, bloomed into a singularity that cared intensely both about the self and others, but Emersonian consciousness all too frequently can flower, Hamlet-like, into an individuality indifferent both to the self and to others. The United States since Emerson has been divided between what he called the "party of hope" and the "party of memory". Our intellectuals of the left and of the right both claim Emerson as ancestor.

In 2005, what is self-reliance? I can recognize three prime stigmata of the American religion: spiritual freedom is solitude, while the soul's encounter with the divine (Jesus, the Paraclete, the Father) is direct and personal, and, most crucially, what is best and oldest in the American religionist goes back to a time-before-time, and so is part or particle of God. Every second year, the Gallup pollsters survey religion in the United States, and report that 93% of us believe in God, while 89% are certain that God loves him or her on a personal basis. And 45% of us insist that Earth was created precisely as described in Genesis and is only about 9,000 or fewer years old. The actual figure is 4.5 billion years, and some dinosaur fossils are dated as 190 million years back. Perhaps the intelligent designers, led by George W. Bush, will yet give us a dinosaur Gospel, though I doubt it, as they, and he, dwell within a bubble that education cannot invade.

Contemporary America is too dangerous to be laughed away, and I turn to its most powerful writers in order to see if we remain coherent enough for imaginative comprehension. Lawrence was right; Whitman at his very best can sustain momentary comparison with Dante and Shakespeare. Most of what follows will be founded on Whitman, the most American of writers, but first I turn again to *Moby-Dick*, the national epic of self-destructiveness that almost rivals *Leaves of Grass*, which is too large and subtle to be judged in terms of self-preservation or apocalyptic destructiveness.

Some of my friends and students suggest that Iraq is President Bush's white whale, but our leader is absurdly far from Captain Ahab's aesthetic dignity. The valid analogue is the Pequod; as Lawrence says: "America! Then such a crew. Renegades, castaways, cannibals, Ishmael, Quakers," and South Sea Islanders, Native Americans, Africans, Parsees, Manxmen, what you will. One thinks of our tens of thousands of mercenaries in Iraq, called "security employees" or "contractors". They mix former American Special Forces, Gurkhas, Boers, Croatians, whoever is qualified and available. What they lack is Captain Ahab, who could give them a metaphysical dimension.

Ahab carries himself and all his crew (except Ishmael) to triumphant catastrophe, while Moby-Dick swims away, being as indestructible as the Book of Job's Leviathan. The obsessed captain's motive ostensibly is revenge, since earlier he was maimed by the white whale, but his truer desire is to strike through the universe's mask, in order to prove that while the visible world might seem to have been formed in love, the invisible spheres were made in fright. God's rhetorical question to Job: "Can'st thou draw out Leviathan with a hook?" is answered by Ahab's: "I'd strike the sun if it insulted me!" The driving force of the Bushian-Blairians is greed, but the undersong of their Iraq adventure is something closer to Iago's pyromania. Our leader, and yours, are firebugs.

One rightly expects Whitman to explain our Evening Land to us, because his imagination is America's. A Free-Soiler, he opposed the Mexican war, as Emerson did. Do not our two Iraq invasions increasingly resemble the Mexican and Spanish-American conflicts? Donald Rumsfeld speaks of permanent American bases in Iraq, presumably to protect oil wells. President Bush's approval rating was recently down to 38%, but I fear that this popular reaction has more to do with the high price of petrol than with any outrage at our Iraq crusade.

What has happened to the American imagination if we have become a parody of the Roman empire? I recall going to bed early on election night in November 2004, though friends kept phoning with the hopeful news that there appeared to be some three million additional voters. Turning the phone off, I gloomily prophesied that these were three million Evangelicals, which indeed was the case.

Our politics began to be contaminated by theocratic zealots with the Reagan revelation, when southern Baptists, Mormons, Pentecostals, and Adventists surged into the Republican party. The alliance between Wall Street and the Christian right is an old one, but has become explicit only in the past quarter century. What was called the counter-culture of the late 1960s and 70s provoked the reaction of the 80s, which is ongoing. This is all obvious enough, but becomes subtler in the context of the religiosity of the country, which truly divides us into two nations. Sometimes I find myself wondering if the south belatedly has won the civil war, more than a century after its supposed defeat. The leaders of the Republican party are southern; even the Bushes, despite their Yale and Connecticut tradition, were careful to become Texans and Floridians. Politics, in the United States, perhaps never again can be separated from religion. When so many vote against their own palpable economic interests, and choose "values" instead, then an American malaise has replaced the American dream.

Whitman, still undervalued as a poet, in relation to his astonishing aesthetic power, remains the permanent prophet of our party of hope. That seems ironic in many ways, since the crucial event of Whitman's life was our civil war, in which a total of 625,000 men were slain, counting both sides. In Britain, the "great war" is the first world war, because nearly an entire generation of young men died. The United States remains haunted by the civil war, the central event in the life of the nation since the Declaration of Independence. David S. Reynolds, the most informed of Whitman's biographers, usefully demonstrates that Whitman's poetry, from 1855-60, was designed to help hold the Union together. After the sunset glory of "When Lilacs Last in the Dooryard Bloom'd", the 1865 elegy overtly for Abraham Lincoln, and inwardly for Whitman's poetic self-identity, something burned out in the bard of *Leaves of Grass*. Day after day, for several years, he had exhausted himself, in the military hospitals of Washington DC, dressing wounds, reading to, and writing letters for, the ill and maimed, comforting the dying. The extraordinary vitalism and immediacy departed from his poetry. It is as though he had sacrificed his own imagination on the altar of those martyred, like Lincoln, in the fused cause of union and emancipation.

Whitman died in 1892, a time of American politics as corrupt as this, if a touch less blatant than the era of Bushian theocracy. But there was a curious split in the poet of *Leaves of Grass*, between what he called the soul, and his "real me" or "me myself", an entity distinct from his persona, "Walt Whitman, one of the roughs, an American":

> "I believe in you my soul, the other I am must not abase itself to you,
> And you must not be abased to the other."

The rough Walt is the "I" here, and has been created to mediate between his character or soul, and his real me or personality. I fear that this is permanently American, the abyss between character and personality. Doubtless, this can be a universal phenomenon: one thinks of Nietzsche and of W.B. Yeats. And yet mutual abasement between soul and self destroys any individual's coherence. My fellow citizens who vote for "values," against their own needs, manifest something of the same dilemma.

As the persona "Walt Whitman" melted away in the furnace of national affliction in the civil war, it was replaced by a less capable persona, "the Good Grey Poet". No moral rebirth kindled postwar America; instead Whitman witnessed the extraordinary corruption of President U.S. Grant's administration, which is the paradigm emulated by so many Republican presidencies, including what we suffer at this moment.

Whitman himself became less than coherent in his long decline, from 1866 to 1892. He did not ice over, like the later Wordsworth, but his prophetic stance ebbed away. Lost, he ceased to be an Emersonian, and rather weirdly attempted to become a Hegelian! In "The Evening Land", an extraordinary poem of early 1922, D.H. Lawrence anticipated his long-delayed sojourn in America, which began only in September of that year, when he reached Taos, New Mexico. He had hoped to visit the United States in February 1917, but England denied him a passport. Lawrence's poem is a kind of Whitmanian love-hymn to America, but is even more ambivalent than the chapter on Whitman in *Studies in Classic American Literature*.

"Are you the grave of our day?" Lawrence asks, and begs America to cajole his soul, even as he admits how much he fears the Evening Land:

> "Your more-than-European idealism,
> Like a be-aureoled bleached skeleton hovering
> Its cage-ribs in the social heaven, beneficent."

This rather ghastly vision is not inappropriate to our moment, nor is Lawrence's bitter conclusion:

> "'These States!' as Whitman said,
> Whatever he meant."

What Whitman meant (as Lawrence knew) was that the United States itself was to be the greatest of poems. But with that grand assertion, I find myself so overwhelmed by an uncomfortable sense of irony, that I cease these reflections. Shelley wore a ring, on which was inscribed the motto: "The good time will come." In September, the U.S. Secretary of State Condoleezza Rice was quoted as saying at Zion Church in Whistler, Alabama: "The Lord Jesus Christ is going to come on time if we just wait."

Chronology

1803	Born May 25 in Boston to William Emerson and Ruth Haskins Emerson
1811	May 12, Emerson's father, William, dies.
1812	Emerson enters Boston Public Latin School.
1817	Begins studies at Harvard College.
1820	Begins keeping his journal.
1821	Graduates from Harvard. Teaches at his brother William's school in Boston.
1822	Publishes his first article, "Thoughts on the Religion of the Middle Ages," in *The Christian Disciple*.
1825	Enters Harvard Divinity School.
1826–1827	Officially sanctioned to preach as a Unitarian minister. Sails to South Carolina and Florida in an effort to improve his health.
1828–1829	Becomes engaged to Ellen Louisa Tucker. Ordained at Second Church in Boston. Marries Ellen on September 10, 1829.
1831	Ellen dies of tuberculosis on February 8 at the age of nineteen.
1832	Resigns from post at Second Church. Travels in Europe.

1833	Meets Wordsworth, Coleridge, and Carlyle during travels abroad. Returns to Boston. Delivers his first public lecture, "The Uses of Natural History."
1834	Settles in Concord.
1835	Lectures on biography. Marries Lydia Jackson on September 14, whom he renames "Lidian."
1836	Meets Margaret Fuller; helps form Transcendental Club; publishes *Nature* anonymously. Birth of son Waldo.
1837	Delivers "The American Scholar" at Harvard before the Phi Beta Kappa Society. Writes "The Concord Hymn."
1838	Delivers "The Divinity School Address" at Harvard, which causes him to be banned from speaking at Harvard.
1839	Birth of daughter Ellen Tucker.
1841	Publication of first series of *Essays*. Thoreau comes to live with the Emersons. Birth of daughter Edith.
1842	Death of Waldo. Emerson Succeeds Margaret Fuller as editor of *The Dial*.
1844	Birth of son Edward. Delivers "Emancipation of the Negroes in the British West Indies." Publication of *Essays: Second Series*.
1845	Thoreau moves to Walden Pond. Delivers series of lectures on "Representative Men."
1846	Publication of *Poems*.
1847	Travels to Europe for most of the year.
1849	Publication of *Nature; Addresses, Lectures*.
1850	Publication of *Representative Men*. Margaret Fuller dies.
1851	Delivers series of lectures on "The Conduct of Life."
1853	Death of Emerson's mother.
1854	Lectures on poetry at Harvard Divinity School. Thoreau publishes *Walden*.
1855	Whitman publishes *Leaves of* Grass; Emerson writes letter to Whitman in praise of his accomplishment.
1856	Publication of *English Traits*.
1860	Publication of *The Conduct of Life*.
1862	Henry David Thoreau dies.
1865	Eulogizes President Lincoln.

1867	Publication of *May-Day and Other Pieces*. Named Overseer of Harvard College. Delivers "The Progress of Culture" address to the Phi Beta Kappa Society.
1870	Publication of *Society and Solitude*.
1871	Travels to California and meets naturalist John Muir.
1872	Travels to Europe and Mediterranean.
1875	Publishes *Letters and Social Aims*.
1882	Dies of pneumonia in Concord, Massachusetts.

Contributors

HAROLD BLOOM is Sterling Professor of the Humanities at Yale University. He is the author of 30 books, including *Shelley's Mythmaking* (1959), *The Visionary Company* (1961), *Blake's Apocalypse* (1963), *Yeats* (1970), *A Map of Misreading* (1975), *Kabbalah and Criticism* (1975), *Agon: Toward a Theory of Revisionism* (1982), *The American Religion* (1992), *The Western Canon* (1994), and *Omens of Millennium: The Gnosis of Angels, Dreams, and Resurrection* (1996). *The Anxiety of Influence* (1973) sets forth Professor Bloom's provocative theory of the literary relationships between the great writers and their predecessors. His most recent books include *Shakespeare: The Invention of the Human* (1998), a 1998 National Book Award finalist, *How to Read and Why* (2000), *Genius: A Mosaic of One Hundred Exemplary Creative Minds* (2002), *Hamlet: Poem Unlimited* (2003), *Where Shall Wisdom Be Found?* (2004), and *Jesus and Yahweh: The Names Divine* (2005). In 1999, Professor Bloom received the prestigious American Academy of Arts and Letters Gold Medal for Criticism. He has also received the International Prize of Catalonia, the Alfonso Reyes Prize of Mexico, and the Hans Christian Andersen Bicentennial Prize of Denmark.

The late STEPHEN E. WHICHER taught at Swarthmore College and Yale University. His study of Emerson's "inner life," *Freedom and Fate*, was his largest achievement in a lifetime devoted to the study of American literature.

BARBARA L. PACKER has taught at Yale and at the University of California, Los Angeles, where she is professor of English. She specializes in nineteenth century American literature and has written essays on Emily Dickinson and Ralph Waldo Emerson. Her book-length study of Emerson is entitled *Emerson's Fall: An Interpretation of the Major Essays*.

JULIE ELLISON is professor of English at the University of Michigan. Her publications include *Emerson's Romantic Style*; *Delicate Subjects: Romanticism, Gender and the Ethics of Understanding*; and *Cato's Tears*.

MARK EDMUNDSON is professor of English at the University of Virginia. He is the author of *Why Read?*; *Teacher: The One Who Made the Difference*; and *Nightmare on Mainstreet: Angels, Sado-Masochism, and the Culture of Gothic*.

DAVID BROMWICH is Housum Professor of English at Yale University. His books include *Hazlitt: The Mind of the Critic*; *Disowned by Memory: Wordsworth's Poetry of the 1790s*; *A Choice of Inheritance: Self and Community from Edmund Burke to Robert Frost*; and *Skeptical Music*.

SHARON CAMERON is William R. Kenan Jr. Professor of English at Johns Hopkins University. She is the author of *Lyric Time: Dickinson and the Limits of Genre*, *Thinking in Henry James*, and *Beautiful Work: A Meditation on Pain*.

GEORGE KATEB is emeritus professor of politics at Princeton University. His books include *Utopia and Its Enemies* and *The Inner Ocean: Individualism and Democratic Culture*.

STANLEY CAVELL is professor emeritus of philosophy at Harvard University. His recent books include *A Pitch for Philosophy: Autobiographical Exercises*, and *Philosophical Passages: Wittgenstein, Emerson, Austin, and Derrida*.

Bibliography

Allen, Gay Wilson. *Waldo Emerson: A Biography*. New York: Viking Press, 1981.

Anderson, Quentin. *The Imperial Self: An Essay in American Literary and Cultural History*. New York: Knopf, 1971.

Bercovitch, Sacvan. "Emerson, Individualism, and the Ambiguities of Dissent." *South Atlantic Quarterly* (Summer 1989): 623–662.

Bishop, Jonathan. *Emerson on the Soul*. Cambridge, MA: Harvard University Press, 1964.

Bloom, Harold. *The Ringers in the Tower*. Chicago: University of Chicago Press, 1971.

———. *A Map of Misreading*. New York: Oxford University Press, 1975.

———. *Figures of Capable Imagination*. New York: Seabury Press, 1976.

———. *Agon: Towards a Theory of Revisionism*. New York: Oxford University Press, 1981.

Buell, Lawrence. *Literary Transcendentalism*. Ithaca, NY: Cornell University Press, 1973.

———. *Emerson*. Cambridge, MA: Harvard University Press, 2003.

Bromwich, David. *A Choice of Inheritance: Self and Community from Edmund Burke to Robert Frost*. Cambridge, MA: Harvard University Press, 1989.

———. "The American Psychosis." *Raritan* 21 (Spring 2002): 33–63.

Burke, Kenneth. "I, Eye, Ay – Emerson's Early Essay 'Nature': Thoughts on the Machinery of Transcendence." In *Transcendentalism and Its Legacy*, eds. Myron Simon and Thornton H. Parsons. Ann Arbor, MI: University of Michigan Press, 1966.

Cadava, Eduardo. *Emerson and the Climates of History*. Stanford, CA: Stanford University Press, 1997.

Cameron, Sharon. "Representing Grief: Emerson's 'Experience.'" *Representations* 15 (Summer 1986): 15–41.

———. "The Way of Life by Abandonment: Emerson's Impersonal." *Critical Inquiry* 25 (Autumn,1998): 1–31.

Cavell, Stanley. *Emerson's Transcendental Etudes*, ed. David Justin Hodge. Stanford, CA: Stanford University Press, 2003.

Cheyfitz, Eric. *The Trans-Parent: Sexual Politics in the Language of Emerson*. Baltimore: Johns Hopkins University Press, 1981.

Cowan, Michael. *City of the West: Emerson, America, and the Urban Metaphor*. New Haven, CT: Yale University Press, 1967.

Dimock, Wai-Chee. "Scarcity, Subjectivity, and Emerson." *boundary 2* 17 (Spring 1990): 83–89.

Edmundson, Mark. "Emerson and the Work of Melancholia." *Raritan* 6 (Spring 1987): 120–136.

Ellison, Julie. *Emerson's Romantic Style*. Princeton, NJ: Princeton University Press, 1984.

Field, Susan L. *The Romance of Desire: Emerson's Commitment to Incompletion*. Madison, NJ: Fairleigh Dickinson University Press, 1997.

Firkins, O.W. *Ralph Waldo Emerson*. Boston: Houghton Mifflin and Co., 1915.

Garvey, T. Gregory, ed. *The Emerson Dilemma: Essays on Emerson and Social Reform*. Athens, GA: University of Georgia Press, 2001.

Gerber, John C. "Emerson and the Political Economists." *New England Quarterly* 22 (1949): 336–357.

Grusin, Richard A. "'Put God in Your Debt': Emerson's Economy of Expenditure." *PMLA* 103 (1988): 35–44.

Hopkins, Vivian. *Spires of Form: A Study of Emerson's Aesthetic Theory*. Cambridge, MA: Harvard University Press, 1951.

Hughes, Gertrude. *Emerson's Demanding Optimism*. Baton Rouge, LA: Louisiana State University Press, 1984.

Kateb, George. *The Inner Ocean: Individualism and Democratic Culture*. Ithaca, NY: Cornell University Press, 1992.

———. *Emerson and Self-Reliance*, new edition. New York: Rowman & Littlefield, Inc., 2002.

Konvitz, Milton R., ed. *The Recognition of Ralph Waldo Emerson: Selected Criticism Since 1837*. Ann Arbor, MI: University of Michigan Press, 1972.

Konvitz, Milton R., and Stephen E. Whicher, eds. *Emerson: A Collection of Critical Essays*. Englewood Cliffs, NJ: Prentice-Hall, Inc., 1962.

Larson, Kerry. "Individualism and the Place of Understanding in Emerson's Essays." *English Literary History* 68 (Winter 2001): 991–1021.

Leverenz, David. "The Politics of Emerson's Man-Making Words." *PMLA* 101 (1986): 38–56.

Levin, David, ed. *Emerson: Prophecy, Metamorphosis, and Influence*. New York: Columbia University Press, 1975.

Loving, Jerome. *Emerson, Whitman, and the American Muse*. Chapel Hill, NC: University of North Carolina Press, 1982.

Lowell, James Russell. "Emerson the Lecturer." In *The Literary Criticism of James Russell Lowell*, ed. Herbert F. Smith. Lincoln, NE: University of Nebraska Press, 1969.

Matthiessen, F.O. *American Renaissance: Art and Expression in the Age of Emerson and Whitman*. New York: Oxford University Press, 1941.

McAleer, John. *Ralph Waldo Emerson: Days of Encounter*. Boston: Little, Brown and Co., 1984.

Miller, Perry. *Errand into the Wilderness*. New York: Harper, 1964.

Morris, Saundra. "The Threshold Poem, Emerson, and 'The Sphynx.'" *American Literature* 31 (September 1997): 547–570.

Newfield, Christopher. *The Emerson Effect: Individualism and Submission in America*. Chicago: University of Chicago Press, 1996.

Packer, Barbara L. *Emerson's Fall*. New York: Continuum, 1982.

Paul, Sherman. *Emerson's Angle of Vision*. Cambridge, MA: Harvard University Press, 1952.

Poirier, Richard. *A World Elsewhere*. New York: Oxford University Press, 1966.

———. *Making a Difference: Emersonians and Modernists*. New York: Random House, 1985.

———. *The Renewal of Literature: Emersonian Reflections*. New York: Random House, 1987.

Porte, Joel. *Representative Man: Emerson in His Time*. New York: Oxford University Press, 1979.

———. *Emerson and Thoreau Reviewed*. New Haven, CT: Yale University Press, 2004.

Porter, David. *Emerson and Literary Change*. Cambridge, MA: Harvard University Press, 1978.

Richardson, Robert D. *Myth and Literature in the American Renaissance*. Bloomington, IN: Indiana University Press, 1978.

———. *Emerson: The Mind on Fire*. Berkeley, CA: University of California Press, 1995.

Rusk, Ralph L., ed. *The Letters of Ralph Waldo Emerson*. 6 vols. New York: Columbia University Press, 1964.

Schirmeister, Pamela. *Less Legible Meanings: Between Poetry and Philosophy in the Work of Emerson*. Stanford, CA: Stanford University Press, 1999.

Thomas, Joseph M. "Late Emerson: *Selected Poems* and the 'Emerson Factory.'" *English Literary History* 65 (1998): 971–994.

Waggoner, Hyatt H. *Emerson as Poet*. Princeton, NJ: Princeton University Press, 1974.

Whicher, Stephen E. *Freedom and Fate: An Inner Life of Ralph Waldo Emerson*. Philadelphia: University of Pennsylvania Press, 1953.

Wilson, Edmund, ed. "Emerson and Whitman: Documents on Their Relations (1855–1858)." In *The Shock of Recognition*. New York: Doubleday, Doran and Co., 1943.

Winters, Yvor. *In Defense of Reason*. Denver: Alan Swallow, 1943.

Wolosky, Shira. "Dickinson's Emerson: A Critique of American Identity." *Emily Dickinson Journal* 9 (2000): 134–141.

Yoder, R.A. *Emerson and the Orphic Poet in America*. Berkeley, CA: University of California Press, 1978.

Zwarg, Christina. *Feminist Conversations: Fuller, Emerson, and the Play of Reading*. Ithaca, NY: Cornell University Press, 1995.

Acknowledgments

"The Question of Means" by Stephen E. Whicher from *Freedom and Fate: An Inner Life of Ralph Waldo Emerson*: 72–93. © 1953 by the University of Pennsylvania Press. Reprinted by permission of the University of Pennsylvania Press.

"Emerson: The American Religion" by Harold Bloom from *Agon: Towards a Theory of Revisionism*: 145–178. © 1982 by Oxford University Press. Reprinted by permission.

"'The Curse of Kehama'" by Barbara L. Packer from *Emerson's Fall*: 148–179. © 1982 by Continuum Publishing Company. Reprinted by permission.

"Detachment and Transition" by Julie Ellison from *Emerson's Romantic Style*: 175–194. © 1984 by Princeton University Press. Reprinted by permission of Princeton University Press.

"Emerson and the Work of Melancholia" by Mark Edmundson from *Raritan* 6, no. 4 (Spring 1987): 120–136. © 1987 by *Raritan: A Quarterly Review*. Reprinted by permission.

"Emerson and the Ode to W. H. Channing" by David Bromwich. Reprinted by permission from *The Hudson Review*, Vol XXXIII, No. 2 (Summer 1980). Copyright © 1980 by David Bromwich.

Cameron, Sharon. "The Way of Life by Abandonment: Emerson's 'Impersonal.'" *Impersonality: Seven Essays*, pp 79–107. Copyright © 2006 The Univeristy of Chicago Press. Reprinted by permission.

"Self-Reliance and the Life of the Mind" by George Kateb from *Emerson and Self-Reliance*: 1–36. © 2002 by Rowman and Littlefield Publishers, Inc. Reprinted by permission.

"Emerson's Constitutional Amending: Reading "Fate" by Stanley Cavell from *Emerson's Transcendental Etudes*: 192–214. © 2003 by the Board of Trustees of the Leland Stanford Junior University. Reprinted by permission.

Every effort has been made to contact the owners of copyrighted material and secure copyright permission. Articles appearing in this volume generally appear much as they did in their original publication with few or no editorial changes. Those interested in locating the original source will find bibliographic information in the bibliography and acknowledgments sections of this volume.

Index